Welcome to the 2026 BBC Proms

Over 3,000 artists, more than 80 concerts, and eight weeks of world-class music-making. What a privilege it is to invite you to join us for the BBC Proms 2026 – and to share our plans for the summer ahead.

This year the Royal Albert Hall hosts a total of 72 concerts, while a further 13 take place in venues across the UK, from Bristol to Gateshead via Mold, Middlesbrough and Sunderland. Many of the world's most exciting soloists will be in the spotlight, with the festival bookended by two of the finest pianists on the planet: Yunchan Lim on the First Night and Yuja Wang on the Last Night.

For the first time in nearly a quarter of a century the Los Angeles Philharmonic returns to the Proms, conducted by its outgoing Music and Artistic Director Gustavo Dudamel. Performances from the likes of the Berlin Philharmonic, Spanish National Orchestra and The Met Orchestra further underline our commitment to showcasing the finest international orchestras. And, with nearly 20 world or UK premieres given this summer, the BBC's support for new music is abundantly clear.

British licence-fee payers fund not only the BBC's TV, radio and online content but also its five world-class orchestras and the only chamber choir of its kind in the world, the BBC Singers. I am therefore thrilled that our BBC ensembles once again provide the backbone to the Proms, performing in over 30 concerts this season, with highlights ranging from orchestral favourites by Mahler and Sibelius with the BBC Symphony Orchestra to a Late-Night Prom featuring the BBC Singers, and to Ryan Bancroft's final Proms season as Principal Conductor of the BBC National Orchestra of Wales.

Our youngest Prommers are in for a treat at the Horrible Science Prom; there's opera by Weber and Richard Strauss; and we mark a major centenary in jazz with a concert dedicated to the music of Miles Davis. Our wide-ranging offering also includes a concert from the Black Dyke Band, one of the oldest and best-known brass bands in the world, and an evening of prog rock from Robert Ames and the BBC Concert Orchestra.

As ever, every Prom is broadcast on BBC Radio 3 and available on BBC Sounds, while over 20 will be televised across BBC TV and iPlayer. What's more, if you'd like to join us in person, tickets are always priced from just £8 – no matter what the performance. On behalf of the entire team, thank you for your support of the BBC Proms. I hope you enjoy the festival just as much as we have enjoyed curating it for you.

Sam Jackson
Controller, BBC Radio 3 and BBC Proms

At a Glance

For Concert Listings, see pages 107–144
For Contents, including details of feature articles, see overleaf

The American Dream and Sunshine from Spain

We shine a torch on two countries to mark the 250th anniversary of American Independence and the centenary of the Spanish Civil War.

See pages 14–19, 64–67

For Your Ears Only

Suave, sharp, swift. And that's just the BBC Concert Orchestra's Edwin Outwater, who comes armed with a veritable dossier of music from the Bond movies.

25 AUGUST

From Enchanted Forest to Desert Island

Two operatic treats: Weber's Romantic masterpiece *Oberon* and Strauss's opera-within-an-opera *Ariadne auf Naxos*.

6 AUGUST, 19 AUGUST

A Life in the Balance

A series of works, sacred and secular, that dare to peer into the Beyond, reflecting on life, death and the hereafter.

See pages 86–89

At a Glance

VIP Visitors and …
A showcase for international talent, the Proms welcomes great conductors and orchestras from France, Germany, Italy, Norway, Spain, Sweden and the USA.

See Index of Artists

… Piano Powerhouses
From Yunchan Lim at the First Night to Yuja Wang at the Last, the range of pianists also includes Kirill Gerstein, Lucas and Arthur Jussen and Yeol Eum Son.

See Index of Artists

Private Benjamin
Though he lived away from the public glare, Benjamin Britten – born 100 years ago – produced a body of music that placed him at the heart of 20th-century music in England.

See pages 56–60

Disney Scores and Star Wars
The fantasy of Disney tracks in a tribute to composer Alan Menken, and the wonders of space as revealed by our friends at Horrible Science.

31 AUGUST, 25 JULY

Contents

1 Welcome
BBC Radio 3 and BBC Proms Controller Sam Jackson introduces the 2026 season

6 Music on the Front Line
BBC correspondents Clive Myrie, Lyse Doucet and Steve Rosenberg reflect on the healing power of music

12 Discover …
Bach's Mass in B minor

14 Music from the New World
As the Proms marks 250 years since US Independence, Paul Griffiths goes in search of the 'American' sound

20 I Made It to the Proms!
Proms faithful Nick Mohammed discusses what the festival – and classical music – means to him

24 Discover …
Berg's Violin Concerto

26 The Art of Prog
Ahead of the first ever Prog Rock Prom, Stuart Maconie charts the genre's chequered history

36 Secrets Beneath the Notes
Tom Service reveals – and revels in – some of classical music's greatest enigmas

40 Mood Music
Three of this year's commissioned composers preview their work in the form of musical 'mood boards'

46 Part of Our World
Dominic Broomfield-McHugh explains how Alan Menken redefined the sound of the Disney musical

50 Discover …
Edmund Thornton Jenkins's 'Dance Suite'

52 New Kids on the Block
Rebecca Franks introduces the bold, disabled-led National Open Youth Orchestra ahead of its Proms debut

56 Britten Today
Fifty years after Benjamin Britten's death, Lucy Walker considers the English composer's standing today

62 Discover …
Gabriela Ortiz's 'Revolución diamantina'

64
From the Azure Coast to the Golden Sierras
What is the essence of Spanish music? Carol A. Hess delves into the country's picture-postcard image

68
Early Music Comes of Age
Nicholas Kenyon examines the latest developments in early music performance

72
Discover …
Shostakovich's Symphony No. 11

74
Richard Strauss: Poet, Philosopher, Prankster
Stephen Johnson traces a line between masterworks by Germany's great musical mischief-maker

78
Northern Powerhouse
As the Black Dyke Band returns to the Proms, brass band expert Paul Hindmarsh charts its proud history

82
Hands That Do Magic
Flora Willson investigates the 19th-century fascination with musical virtuosity

86
Musical Afterlives
Emily MacGregor considers how composers have depicted the great Beyond in sound

90
A Composer's Life
Two leading Proms composers – Brett Dean and Betsy Jolas – offer an insight into their working lives

96
Discover …
Varèse's 'Amériques'

98
Miles Ahead
As the Proms celebrates Miles Davis's centenary year, Alyn Shipton profiles the great jazz pioneer

102
Discover …
Weber's 'Oberon'

106
The Proms on TV
Head of Arts and Classical Music TV Suzy Klein introduces this year's BBC TV and iPlayer offering

107
Concert Listings: RAH
Full details of all the 2026 Proms concerts at the Royal Albert Hall

140
Concert Listings: Across the UK
Full details of all the 2026 Proms concerts in Bristol, Gateshead Middlesbrough, Mold and Sunderland

Booking	145
Venues	148
Access at the Proms	151
Index of Artists	163
Index of Works	165

As political upheavals proliferate around the world, BBC correspondents **CLIVE MYRIE** *(main article)*, **LYSE DOUCET** and **STEVE ROSENBERG** reflect on the healing effect of music and the sounds that have accompanied them as they report from global conflict zones

Music on the Front Line

There seems to be an intensity to global events and news at the moment that we've all rarely experienced. The goings-on in the world touch us in a deeper, more visceral way than before. Prosaically, there's simply more news about, fed to us via the ubiquity of social media, and so even far-off events can end up disheartening us at times. It feels like so much more is happening than the human mind can absorb, and it's hard to avoid. But I think beyond the prosaic there's something else going on at the start of the second quarter of the 21st century. Even during the Cold War, or in the aftermath of 9/11, despite all the uncertainty, most of us seemed to know right from wrong. In the middle of controversies, we erred on the side of our common humanity and believed that ultimately light would lead us out of the darkness. The rock star Sting's plaintive cry, in his song 'Russians' from 1985, tried to capture the sense that, even though the armies of the West and the Soviet Union had enough nuclear bombs to destroy much of our world, 'what might save us, me and you, is if the Russians love their children too'.

But today the uncertainty feels all-encompassing and insurmountable, and it appears there are too few good people riding to the rescue. It's become easy for some to dehumanise their enemies, to not believe they may love their children too, whether it's because of their politics or skin colour, their ethnicity or religion. This fuels an anger and hard-heartedness in the world that's overwhelming, and we can feel impotent in the face of numerous crises. So, what's our escape?

Often it's the creative impulses that contain the seeds of salvation, where solace can be found, including in art, literature and, of course, music. It's no surprise that BBC Radio 3 and its new digital offshoot station, Radio 3 Unwind – focusing on calm and wellbeing – are so valued by listeners.

A particular piece of music can transport us away from the chaos of everyday life. That was partly the inspiration behind my Radio 3 series last year entitled *Music on the Front Line*, in which I chatted with some of the world's finest living journalists and chroniclers of our times about the music that helped them find peace while they were covering some of the most challenging of news stories. Lyse Doucet, Matt Frei, Janine di Giovanni, Christina Lamb, Sir Don McCullin, Steve Rosenberg and John Simpson were just some of my fellow reporters who shared details of their most painful moments on assignment and the music that helped them through the darkness.

From Syrian folk tunes to well-known classical pieces or more obscure orchestral works, the music was varied and touched each of my fellow journalists deeply. Their accompanying stories were often harrowing and disturbing, involving close encounters with death, as well as historic moments such as the fall of the Berlin Wall and the end of Soviet Communism, or the return of Ayatollah

◀ Instrument of war: an Iraqi Kurdish fighter plays the bağlama (long-necked lute) on the front line in northern Iraq in a break from defending the territory from Islamic State forces (August 2014)

Clive Myrie meeting Ukrainian President Volodymyr Zelensky for a BBC interview in April 2022, when the latest Russia–Ukraine conflict was only 50 days old; Myrie had reported from the country at the outbreak of Russia's full-scale invasion on 24 February that year and covered the early stages of the conflict

Khomeini to Iran, or the wars in Afghanistan and Iraq. Some of my interviewees ended up in tears.

Among their musical selections, from Stravinsky and Samuel Barber to Beethoven and Mozart, Dowland and Monteverdi, one composer's work featured the most, and that was J. S. Bach. Indeed, his compositions have been the soundtrack to so many episodes in my own working life, the score of my human dramas.

There's a seeming simplicity on the surface of works like the Cello Suites or Brandenburg Concertos or *The Well-Tempered Clavier* that belies a deep underlying complexity. It's that mix which, for me, sums up the human experience and the madness at times of trying to survive this world while simultaneously enjoying the simple pleasures of life. Much of Bach's music doesn't overtly demand anything of you. It's not necessarily asking you to be moved in some way, it's not manipulative. There's relatively little dissonance or anger, or any directed emotion. There's simply a comforting reassurance in the recurring motifs that allow your mind to drift, to alight on past occurrences or present feelings, whatever they may be. It's some of the most meditative music I've ever heard.

Exactly 30 years ago, I travelled to Afghanistan to report on the take-over of the country by a group of fighters who called themselves the Taliban, which in the Pashto language means 'students' or 'seekers of knowledge'. This was their very first incarnation as rulers. The West knew they were fundamentalists and that despite the name they very clearly didn't want to seek knowledge outside their own narrow interpretation of Islam. But Washington, London and Islamabad believed the stability the Taliban might bring to a country that had been at war for the best part of two decades would benefit everyone. Indeed, the militants were at first welcomed by the general population as liberators who would safeguard peace and security.

I flew to the Pakistani border town of Peshawar, from where the Red Cross was still making flights to the Afghan capital of Kabul. But as it turned out, my cameraman and I had too much equipment to load onto a plane already stuffed with far more important things, like food and aid for the Afghan people.

So, we had to drive the almost 300km journey, along the winding Khyber Pass, the path through the mountains of the Hindu Kush, along a section of the fabled trade route known as the Silk Road. Bach's *The Well-Tempered Clavier* accompanied me as I sat in the back seat of our car with my headphones on and Walkman whirring. András Schiff was at the piano.

By the time we reached our destination, it was clear the Taliban, who'd only been in power for three weeks, were pacifying the population through cruelty. Executions were public, lives snuffed out by gunshots in packed sports stadiums. The severing of limbs as a punishment for often minor infractions was also now made a public spectacle. Peace and stability, which is what the Afghan people had yearned for, was coming at a heavy price.

To an outsider, life felt joyless in the service of the Taliban's God, a notion Bach would have found impossible to understand, just as I did. Nearly three-quarters of the composer's compositions were written for use in worship. On acquiring a copy of Luther's three-volume translation of the Bible in his late forties, Bach pored over it, annotating its pages; and when he reached 2 Chronicles, chapter 5, verse 13, which mentions temple musicians praising God, he scribbled in the margin the words: 'At a reverent performance of music, God is always at hand with his

Sense out of Suffering

For Lyse Doucet, the BBC's Chief International Correspondent, music brings hope amid turmoil

I confess: my favourite instrument is the violin. It's not just its lustrous depth of emotion, it's also the lively foot-tapping fiddling of my Irish and Acadian ancestry (the latter group descended from 17th-century French settlers in Atlantic Canada).

But I was struck by the majesty of the piano thanks to the stirring courage of Aeham Ahmad, who dragged his instrument across rutted streets in the besieged Syrian suburb of Yarmouk. His uplifting songs, with children singing and dancing along, was a beautiful balm in terrible times when people couldn't even find bread to eat.

Then there was the power of Afghan teenager Arson Fahim pouring his pain into his piano, into his compositions honouring heroes killed in his country's never-ending strife. Arson's own life had changed forever when he heard Chopin's Nocturne in C sharp minor (Op. posth.) in the film *The Pianist*. It tells the true story of Jewish musician Władysław Szpilman, whose art helped him survive in Nazi-occupied Warsaw.

And I will never forget looking through my hotel window in Kyiv, on a cold winter's day in February 2022, while listening on my phone to my brilliant colleague Steve Rosenberg play his composition *Isolation* on his piano at home in Moscow. Russia had just invaded Ukraine.

It was the conductor and pianist Daniel Barenboim who first helped me to realise that music is a language, with which we can write our own story. It could be an escape from the world, or offer a different way to engage with our times – good and bad.

This belief led Barenboim and his friend the Palestinian philosopher Edward Said to establish in 1999 the West–Eastern Divan Orchestra, which brought Israeli and Arab musicians to perform together, and to eschew politics – at least in rehearsals and on the stage.

When I saw the orchestra perform in Ramallah in the occupied West Bank in 2005, during yet more trying times in beleaguered peace-making, there was not a dry eye in the hall, including mine.

At home in London, I often turn to contemporary composers like Max Richter whose soothing music lets our minds soar in reflection on issues which matter. Ludovico Einaudi's extraordinary *Elegy for the Arctic*, performed on a floating platform in the Arctic Ocean to the sound of ice tumbling from a glacier, is a stunning call to action. I've watched his video in awe too many times to count.

I also have to confess that in these days of forever wars I often find myself turning the dial on my radio, or moving my finger across the BBC Sounds app on my phone to BBC Radio 3, not to the more news-focused channels. It allows me to rise above the cacophony of the wars of words, the loss and the longing for peace in all too many places. But, as citizens, we still need to keep turning the dial back to know what's happening in our world – even as we embrace music to celebrate successes and make sense of the suffering.

gracious presence.' And yet the Taliban, in failing to seek knowledge beyond their closed world, decried music and enjoyment, and so by extension denied the Afghan people a simple and painless release from their woes.

Bach accompanied me to East Timor, and to Kosovo. He came along for the ride during the second Palestinian Intifada in Gaza. I listened to the Cello Suites while holed up in a hotel in Georgia, as that country waged war with Russia. In Baghdad on the night of Saddam Hussein's execution the Adagio from Bach's Sonata No. 1 in G minor for solo violin seemed appropriate. Yehudi Menuhin did the honours.

It's clear that music can be so much more than simply a distraction from the ills of our time. Yes, it can divert our attention, refocus the mind. But its power in a world of incessant news and cruelty is that it reminds us of the endless capacity of human beings to create, not simply to destroy. That knowledge is what, on a deeper level, consoles us and fires our spirits. Music can provide an affirmation of beauty and wonder, in representing the best of humanity, not the worst of it. It is flesh-and-bone creativity, not algorithmic and mechanical. It is organic and spiritual. It springs from the heart, from deep within us. Simple notes on a page, a distillation, in a world of inhumanity, of what it means to be human. ●

For nearly 40 years BBC News presenter Clive Myrie has served as BBC correspondent in Tokyo, Los Angeles, Paris and Asia. As well as hosting *Mastermind* and presenting the 15-part series *Clive Myrie's Caribbean Adventure*, he is the author of *Everything is Everything: A Memoir of Love, Hate & Hope* (Hodder & Stoughton 2023).

Duets with the President

BBC Russia Editor Steve Rosenberg finds solace – and an unusual musical partner – through the piano

'Why haven't we kicked the BBC and Steve Rosenberg out of Russia yet?' barked the Russian state TV anchor. 'He walks around looking like a defecating squirrel … he's an enemy of Russia!'

How do I deal with such remarks? I drive home from work, sit at the piano and play: pop, classic British TV themes, Russian folk melodies. Anything that transports me to a nicer place. My day job would be so much harder without music to support me.

Sometimes it actively aids my reporting. Following the Kremlin's full-scale invasion of Ukraine in 2022, repressive laws were adopted in Russia to silence dissent. Concerned for our safety, BBC bosses asked us to pause broadcasting while they assessed how the new legislation might impact our work. The BBC's Moscow office fell silent for three days.

During that time my piano provided not only solace, but also a means for breaking through the silence. If I couldn't use words and pictures to convey what was happening, there was still music. I wrote a piece called *Isolation* and posted it online.

The music reflected Russia's international isolation and the sense of a world turned upside down. Music has been a welcome accompaniment to my three decades in Russia.

In the 1990s Russian TV invited me onto a comedy show called *The White Parrot Club*: a special edition on British humour. I was asked not only to tell corny British jokes, but also to play the piano and perform 'a typical English song'. The first one that came to mind was 'Daisy, Daisy'. 'You'll look sweet upon the seat of a bicycle made for two,' I sang rather badly. But at that moment it felt as if Russia and Britain were on that 'bicycle made for two', such was the friendship, post-Communism, between East and West.

In 30 years we've gone from 'White Parrot' to 'defecating squirrel'. Quite a journey. Today pro-Kremlin commentators often accuse Western journalists of 'Russophobia', of working to undermine their country. They appear surprised when I tell them how much I love the music of Rachmaninov and Shostakovich.

My most memorable musical moments in Moscow were my encounters with former Soviet leader Mikhail Gorbachev, the man who helped end the Cold War. On two occasions, following interviews with him, I accompanied the former Soviet leader on his piano as he sang everything from 19th-century Russian romances to Ukrainian folk melodies. 'Raisa loved it when I sang,' he smiled, recalling his wife, who had died years earlier.

I learnt more about Mikhail Gorbachev in those few musical minutes than in a string of political interviews with him. The act of making music together seemed to help this often cautious politician bare his soul. He came across as a decent, warm-hearted man, who adored his family and loved music. On one occasion he listened to me playing one of his favourite tunes, then said: 'It's not for nothing that you're in Russia.'

BBC RADIO 3

ADVENTURES IN CLASSICAL

Listen on SOUNDS

Discover…

JOHANN SEBASTIAN BACH'S
Mass in B minor

LINDSAY KEMP maps the patchwork origins of Bach's vast statement of universal Christian faith

To say that Bach put the best of himself into the Mass in B minor is no exaggeration. This great piece was one of the very last things he worked on in the year before his death, and he meant for it to be something big. About faith, yes; although he was a lifelong servant of the Lutheran church, the Catholic Mass was a central text of Christianity, still used in Lutheran services. Earlier in his life Bach had composed music for the first two sections of the Mass – the Kyrie and the Gloria – on five occasions. For the B minor he took one of those 'short Masses' and added to it the remaining sections – the Credo, Sanctus/Benedictus and Agnus Dei – to make a complete one. To a tidy mind like his, it must have felt good to have got it all down.

But the work was never going to get used in a liturgical context, whether Protestant or Catholic. It was far too long, far too weighty, for that. And, sure enough, there is no sign that any performance of it was even planned during the composer's lifetime. So why did he do it? The answer appears to lie in the very process by which he constructed the piece, with nearly all of its nine arias and 18 choruses being reworkings and rewordings of movements from his huge back catalogue of German-language cantatas, written for use at weekly church services in Leipzig. Like many Baroque composers, Bach frequently re-used or adapted existing works to great effect – often we now know the later versions better than we do the originals, for instance the *Christmas Oratorio* and some of the harpsichord concertos. But he also had a penchant for collecting together groups of his own works – suites, sonatas, concertos, fugues – into ordered sets that demonstrated both the depth and the breadth of his skill in a particular genre. In the case of the Mass in B minor, by making choice selections from a body of church music originally destined to be heard on just one appointed day in the liturgical calendar, was he not doing the same for his choral-orchestral art: anthologising it for his own satisfaction – for posterity, even – in the shining new setting of a universal Christian statement?

The result is a mighty work indeed, by turns searching, jubilant, dancing, humble, loving, grief-stricken, optimistic, implacable, consoling. Recycled it may be, but the ear has no difficulty in accepting it as original and true, relishing the skill and care Bach poured into it, and recognising in it (as one of its most recent conductors has put it) 'the story of the whole of humanity in two hours of music'. •

Lindsay Kemp was for 30 years a producer for BBC Radio 3. He was the founding Artistic Director of the London Festival of Baroque Music and Baroque at the Edge, and is a regular contributor to *Gramophone*.

Bach Mass in B minor
THURSDAY 10 SEPTEMBER

IMPERIAL
SUMMER ACCOMMODATION

"So convenient for the Royal Albert Hall"

Guest, 2025 ★★★★★

Located a five-minute walk from the Royal Albert Hall, our affordable accommodation Prince's Gardens is open from July to September.

Book now

enquiries@imperial.ac.uk

(+44) 020 7594 3333

Imperial College London

imperial.ac.uk/visit/summer-accommodation

Music From the New World

As the Proms marks the 250th anniversary of the Declaration of Independence, **PAUL GRIFFITHS** dips into the melting pot of musical influences that have informed classical music culture in the USA, and asks whether there is such a thing as a distinctly 'American' sound

We probably all recognise the sound of America in classical music. It could be the clear, open consonance that Hollywood composers often use for panoramas of stillness and wide spaces. It could be the dash and brilliance of American orchestras. It could certainly be the energy of the popular musical traditions that have developed in the USA under the umbrella terms jazz, rock and soul.

For Jessie Montgomery, whose Cello Concerto *These Righteous Paths* is one of the first commissioned pieces to be heard this season, American classical music, in drawing on these other traditions, reflects the nature of the American population: 'The fact that the USA is a multicultural society plays into the sort of multifaceted influences that go into its music.' American music is therefore distinct: 'its own thing, its own unique voice, in relation to classical music' – that is, to European classical music. Montgomery evidently shares the general American sense that classical music is a European genre. Even before the Declaration of Independence in 1776 it was something brought in from across the ocean.

The largest city in the USA throughout the 18th century was also the place where the Declaration was signed: Philadelphia. Classical concerts and operas were going on there from the 1750s onwards, and

◀ The New York City skyline, its towering skyscrapers a symbol of the enterprising American spirit

the city was the natural destination for musicians arriving from overseas. Some of them were trained composers, such as Alexander Reinagle, of Scots-Hungarian ancestry, who arrived around 1790 and was responsible for the first keyboard sonatas composed on American soil. However, Philadelphia's population was then 30,000, comparable at the time with that of Portsmouth, England. The surprise is not that musical activity was modest in such an environment but that a theatre seating 2,000 was opened there in 1793, at the instigation of Reinagle and others, and had soon hosted the American premieres of Mozart's operas *Don Giovanni* and *The Marriage of Figaro*.

What might be called the Philadelphia model – of classical repertoire largely imported from Europe or at least provided by composers educated there – has persisted down to the present. The Los Angeles Philharmonic comes to the Proms this season, bringing two Beethoven symphonies, a piece by a British composer, Thomas Adès, and another by a Mexican composer trained in Paris and London, Gabriela Ortiz. For a long time European training was a requisite for American composers, from John Knowles Paine seeking teachers in Berlin in the 1850s to Aaron Copland, Roy Harris and others going to Nadia Boulanger in Paris in the 1920s to gain an edge of sophistication. To an extent, it's a pattern that continues: like several other US composers featured in recent Proms seasons, Julia Wolfe completed her studies in Amsterdam, only to learn

15

The Signing of the Declaration of Independence by American artist Sarah Paxton Ball Dodson (1847–1906); this season the Proms marks 250 years since the 56 delegates to the Second Continental Congress signed this foundational document in Philadelphia

that she was on alien territory: 'I felt very American. There's just a different sensibility, a different tie to history. You feel the weight of history more, I think, as a European.'

Hence the major alternative to the Eurocentric attitude: to ignore heritage and start over. Here again the prototypes can be found back in colonial times, with a scattering of composers across New England. They, much more than the gentlemen of Philadelphia, have come to be valued as the great ancestors of American classical music, even though they confined themselves to hymns for amateur singing societies. These New Englanders propounded a harmony that, breaking the rules, could be raw and robust, and the most productive of them was William Billings. Soon forgotten, Billings became a lodestar two centuries later for John Cage, a composer who took the break with Europe as far as it would go. Cage questioned everything the European classical tradition took for granted, including the necessity for there to be music at all. We could perfectly well listen in the absence of conventional music, he proposed in his 'silent' piece *4' 33"*.

Inevitably these two streams – of dependence on and independence from Europe – have often, and increasingly, come together, beginning in the music of Charles Ives (1874–1954). Though he had not studied in Europe, Ives could compose European-style music to compare with that of any of his contemporaries who had. This, however, did not satisfy him. He was interested in things European music left out, such as quarter-tones, or strands in different keys working simultaneously, or quotations – often multitudinous ones – from marches, dances, hymns and much else. Antonín Dvořák, who held a teaching position in New York in the 1890s and there composed his Cello Concerto, probably never met Ives and might well not have approved of music spilling with unassimilated quotations. In one sense, though, he was more adventurous. Where Ives's sources, so often reflecting his experience as a boy and young man in a small New England town, were almost invariably White, Dvořák created his Symphony No. 9, 'From the New World', to show how American classical music could reflect Black and Indigenous traditions.

This takes us back again to 1776 and soon after when, besides the New England hymn writers and the Philadelphia composers of chamber music and opera, there were other kinds of music in development. The culture of the Indigenous population was being destroyed except for a lingering trace. Black music, however, was evidently in strong growth. Spirituals were, in all probability, being sung for decades by Black people in congregations and at home before a Black student of Dvořák's, Harry Burleigh, sang some to him and so prompted the Bohemian to compose similar themes for the 'New World'. By the early 19th century other musical styles were starting to evolve in the large swathe of territory that had been purchased from France: the Cajun and Zydeco music of French-African and French people in what is now southern Louisiana and, originating at social celebrations among Black people in New Orleans, jazz.

Dvořák thought the future of classical music in the USA lay with spirituals, as he stated in a long contribution to the *New York Herald* in May 1893. 'There is no longer any reason,' he went on, 'why young Americans who have talent should go to Europe for their education,' since the materials existed at home. But though the sentiment was valid, it was not spirituals but jazz, popularised by recordings and the spread of musicians, that seemed to express the spirit of both the nation and the age from the time of the First World War onwards.

Sounds Wide Open

Gustavo Dudamel, Music & Artistic Director of the Los Angeles Philharmonic, shares his impressions of American orchestral culture

When people ask me what makes an orchestra sound 'American', I don't think first of a single accent or stylistic marker. I think of an openness that is sonic, physical and imaginative. The American orchestral sound, for me, is not fixed or inherited; it is constantly becoming, shaped by many journeys and voices meeting in the same vast landscape. That idea of space is deeply personal to me. I grew up in Venezuela surrounded by the plains, where the horizon seems endless and sound travels without obstruction. As my musical life expanded across the Americas, I encountered different geographies that encouraged long lines of thought, intensity of expression and an instinct for freedom. When I first came to the USA I recognised something familiar in a cultural openness that mirrors the physical one.

What struck me immediately about US orchestras was their curiosity. There is a willingness to engage deeply with tradition while also questioning it and sometimes joyfully breaking it open. It is a culture unafraid of influence; instead, it absorbs and refracts. The American sound is not about purity or preservation but possibility.

This sense of openness is something I feel powerfully with the Los Angeles Philharmonic. Our musicians come from all over the world yet they share an intensity of purpose and a generosity of spirit. There is a physicality and directness of expression to the playing that reflects the diversity of influences that shape musical life in the USA, from European symphonic traditions to Latin American rhythms to African American musical lineages, and so much more. That same expansiveness shapes the programmes we bring to the Proms this year. Beethoven sits at the centre, as he so often does, but even here the perspective feels distinctly American. These are works born in Europe, yet US orchestras approach them with a particular clarity and urgency, as if asking what they mean today, within a culture defined by plurality and reinvention.

We also bring Gabriela Ortiz's *Revolución diamantina* and Thomas Adès's *Inferno*. Together these works form a programme unified not by nationality but by openness. Ortiz, a composer deeply shaped by Latin American history and contemporary social movements, channels protest, identity and collective energy with an immediacy that feels inseparable from life in the Americas today. 'Inferno' reveals another side of the same landscape. While rooted in European literary tradition, it reflects an American context in which imagination is encouraged to be bold and uncompromising. Scale, risk and intensity are not curbed but embraced. In dialogue with Beethoven and Ortiz, this music reinforces the idea of the USA as a place where inherited forms collide with new energies and emerge transformed.

For me, this is the defining characteristic of American orchestral life. With committed players and adventurous audiences and institutions, the sound that emerges is not about national origin but openness. The American orchestra becomes a reflection of who is invited into the space and how fully every voice within it can resonate.

A young Louis Armstrong *(back row, second from left)* poses alongside the other members of King Oliver's Creole Jazz Band in 1923; Armstrong's hometown, New Orleans, is today recognised as the birthplace of jazz

Curiously, the jazz zest emerged first in the music of European composers, Debussy, Stravinsky and Ravel among them. But Americans soon caught on. Perhaps the first was John Alden Carpenter, in his 'jazz ballet' *Krazy Kat* (1921). Aaron Copland, returning to New York in 1925 having studied with Boulanger, came into contact with the photographer Alfred Stieglitz and took to heart his motto 'Affirm America'. This he did by having jazz patterns and syncopations energise, for example, the finale of the Piano Concerto he wrote the following year. Copland was also responsible, in such works as *Fanfare for the Common Man* and *Appalachian Spring*, for giving movie composers the tools for their 'prairie' style. It was, however, the validity and vitality of jazz in classical music that opened the door to a first generation of Black American classical composers, including Florence Price and William Grant Still. Price included in her First Symphony a Juba Dance, bringing to concert audiences a rhythm inherited from Central Africa.

Jazz gave classical music an edge of modernity, and the USA was now identified as the home of the modern – of the aeroplane, electricity, the affordable car. That was why Edgard Varèse moved to New York from his native France in 1915, determined to find a new music in the New World. With the recent memory of Stravinsky's *The Rite of Spring* in his head, he composed an orchestral work that was even more uncompromising. *Amériques* was explicitly designed to portray the impulse of discovery. Like other musical modernists in the USA between the wars, Varèse was promoted by Leopold Stokowski – who conducted the first performance of *Amériques* in 1926 – and was supported by wealthy patrons, in his case Gertrude Whitney.

Leaving Europe a little later, in 1918, Sergey Rachmaninov emigrated not to place himself in the modern world but to recreate Imperial Russia in a New York apartment. Nevertheless, the move revealed itself in the brilliant, American sound of his Third Symphony. Many more composers emigrated soon after the Nazi Party took power in Germany, in 1933, or when the Second World War broke out six years later. Among those forced out of Germany as Jews were Arnold Schoenberg and Kurt Weill, not to mention three who dominated film music in their new country: Erich Wolfgang Korngold (*The Adventures of Robin Hood*, 1938), Miklós Rózsa (*Ben-Hur*, 1959) and Franz Waxman (*Rebecca*, 1940). Later arrivals included Bartók and Stravinsky, whose *Symphony in Three Movements,* if in a different way from the Rachmaninov, accommodates itself to the American orchestral sound and the expectations of American audiences.

Those audiences come to classical music seeing it not so much as an aspect of (foreign) culture but as a medium of experience and expression in the here and now. Their expectations, that music should be emotionally open and responsive in some way to current situations and events (Stravinsky's was a war symphony), have not changed so much. Perhaps they add up to what makes American music so distinctive, even in all its present variety. Where the American Civil War left not a scratch on the nation's classical music, composers often feel bound now to take on national conflicts and upheavals, anxieties and hopes. This may be, at least in part, because classical music since the 1950s has become increasingly democratised, through the encouragement of wider participation in schools, the burgeoning of specialist radio stations, magazines and podcasts, and private philanthropy.

Steve Reich, beginning outside the classical circuit, used a recording of a Black preacher to make the tape composition that was his Op. 1, *It's Gonna Rain* (1965), implicitly transferring those stirring words from the story of Noah and the Ark to the Cold War threat of nuclear attack. Reich's continuing involvement with music of Black origin, whether American pop and rock or West African drumming, led within a decade or so to *Music for 18 Musicians*, which the classical record label Deutsche Grammophon declined to release because it sounded too much like popular music.

Since then, boundaries have developed holes, through which agile musicians can weave, backwards and forwards. Gabriel Kahane, who started out as a singer-songwriter, has gone on to compose classical pieces, including his new Clarinet Concerto. So has the jazz giant Wynton Marsalis, whose playful *Concerto for Orchestra* joins an output of four symphonies and more. The Proms has changed, too, to welcome this year the scores Alan Menken has written for Disney films. Some boundary-crossings, though, have become closed, with genre now seen as an expression of identity. If Reich were to compose *It's Gonna Rain* now he might well be accused of cultural appropriation. Perhaps only the openheartedness of John Adams's music has allowed him to touch on a wide range of American styles, including those from Black and Latino traditions.

Back to Jessie Montgomery. Her previous cello concerto, *Divided* (2022), responded to the helplessness that many feel in the face of racial injustice; her new one draws on poems written by her late mother about the African diaspora. She can speak for Black people and she can speak for women. And she can address us all. ●

Paul Griffiths is a former critic for *The Times* and *The New Yorker*. Among his books are studies of Boulez, Cage and Stravinsky, as well as *Modern Music and After* (OUP, 2011, 3rd edition) and *A Concise History of Western Music* (CUP, 2006). He is also a novelist.

John Adams Harmonium
SUNDAY 26 JULY

Barber Knoxville: Summer of 1915
SATURDAY 22 AUGUST

Symphony No. 1 in One Movement
THURSDAY 13 AUGUST

Copland Appalachian Spring – suite
MONDAY 24 AUGUST

Billy the Kid – suite
MONDAY 17 AUGUST

Fanfare for the Common Man
FRIDAY 17 JULY

Feldman Crippled Symmetry
FRIDAY 24 JULY • GATESHEAD

Gershwin An American in Paris
FRIDAY 17 JULY

Piano Concerto in F
THURSDAY 13 AUGUST

Porgy and Bess (arr. Davis) – excerpts
THURSDAY 20 AUGUST

Rhapsody in Blue (orch. Grofé)
MONDAY 24 AUGUST

Jessie Montgomery These Righteous Paths
MONDAY 20 JULY

Steve Reich Music for 18 Musicians
FRIDAY 7 AUGUST • BRISTOL

Tehillim
WEDNESDAY 2 SEPTEMBER

See Index of Works for other composers

I MADE IT TO THE PROMS!

As actor and comedian **NICK MOHAMMED** returns to the Proms presenting team, he traces the highs and lows of his musical journey – including violin screeching, overly brassy Beethoven … and an unexpected passion for Carl Nielsen

First off, it's safe to say that I never thought I'd feature in a BBC Proms Guide. Apart from maybe in one of those adverts at the back selling wine. Likely with my head cropped out, so just hands and a long-stemmed glass – you probably couldn't even tell it was me.

Either way, here I am, which either speaks to my utter adoration of classical music and the Proms in general, or to a rather significant error in the editorial planning. (Note to editor: please check my wording and correct accordingly.)

My journey into classical music began at the age of 9 at Horsforth Music Centre in Leeds which, at the time of writing, I'm delighted to hear is still going strong. I'm sure it's all handled online now but, back in the early 1990s, in order to book a place onto one of its music courses one had to queue for about two hours on the first Saturday of the academic year, before reaching the registration desk only to be told that the trumpet class was full and the only spaces left were in the beginner's violin class. Or, as I like to call it: fate!

One thing to say about learning the violin as a youngster – and it's probably best to get this out the way now – is that it has the potential to sound absolutely horrendous. Until you get to about Grade 5. On saying that, there's definitely been the odd occasion where I've given a Grade 7 piece a good battering, so please don't take that as a hard-and-fast rule. Indeed, when I auditioned to get into an orchestra as a student with Jules Massenet's Méditation from *Thaïs*, I subsequently overheard the auditioning committee refer to my efforts as 'more like a demolition', which was both character-building and – credit to Massenet – never how the piece was intended to be performed.

It was at Durham University, where I met my glorious wife, that my relationship with orchestral music deepened – which sounds very romantic until you realise that a good portion of that time involved disagreements about up-bows and down-bows. I was fortunate enough to play violin in both the Chamber and Symphony orchestras as part of DUOS (Durham University Orchestral Society), where I learnt that the difference between a chamber orchestra and a symphony orchestra is mostly the number of people who might bear witness to your mistakes.

Ah, yes – mistakes! What is it we're always told: you learn more from your mistakes than from your successes? Well …

During one particularly memorable performance of Nielsen's Symphony No. 2, 'The Four Temperaments' – for those who aren't aware, this is specifically about the Choleric, Phlegmatic, Melancholic and Sanguine (and why not?) – I got somewhat carried away towards the end of the slow movement. The third of the temperaments features a series of powerful *tutti* (full-orchestra) sections punctuated by rests. Preaching to the converted here, I know, but – purely as a polite reminder – rests are the silences, where you're not supposed to play. Simple enough idea, you'd have thought. I, however, was so swept up with the emotional intensity of Nielsen's writing that I charged through that first rest like it was an invitation rather than an instruction, filling the Fonteyn Ballroom of Durham Student Union (or 'Planet of Sound' if you're reading this on a Friday night) with a very confident E flat.

> We even did our own Last Night of the Proms-style concert. Nothing screams 'Rule, Britannia!' like belting out sea-shanties in a college hall that smells a bit like sick.

The rest of the orchestra stopped, as Nielsen intended – though, on reflection, it could easily have been out of shock. I, however, kept going! All the way to the next *tutti* section, where I proceeded to make *exactly the same mistake*. Same bar's rest. Same over-zealous violation of silence. At that point I considered several options: glaring at the person to my immediate left like they were the culprit, faking an asthma attack or living with the eternal shame in the hope that one day, decades later, I might seek some form of catharsis by retelling the tale in the Proms Guide. None seemed practical or realistic, so I just kept my eyes firmly glued to the music, hoping that the feeling might pass, while my desk partner tried very hard not to explode.

Yet, despite several protestations, I continued my musical journey undeterred!

Carl Nielsen caricatured on the conductor's podium; during a student performance of Nielsen's Symphony No. 2, Nick Mohammed gave himself an accidental – and rather regrettable – violin solo

During my final year at Durham I had the pleasure of taking on the role of conductor of the Hill Orchestra, Durham University's proudly non-auditioned ensemble. 'Music for All' was its motto and – much like the brilliance of the Proms – the Hill Orchestra's ethos was all about making music accessible to everyone, regardless of background.

Now that's not to say the Hill Orchestra didn't come with its own very specific challenges. I, for one, had to learn that conductors aren't just there to enjoy themselves (though I did enjoy the extra inches a podium lends to my somewhat vertically challenged stature!). But perhaps the biggest challenge of all was dealing with the hugely unbalanced make-up of instruments the orchestra attracted. Who doesn't appreciate Beethoven's Seventh with no cellos or double basses? Who doesn't enjoy Vaughan Williams's beautifully delicate *Fantasia on Greensleeves* when the harpist only knows one chord (and not the right one for the piece)? And who can't help but be swept away by the haunting theme from Tchaikovsky's *Swan Lake*, blasted out by 10 oboes? Dynamics were the Hill Orchestra's particular forte (pun well intended) in that, well, everything was *forte*. Even something marked *pianissimo* sounded *forte*. Or, if a night was especially well attended, *fortissimo* (everyone's favourite). We even did our very own Last Night of the Proms-style concert. Nothing screams 'Rule, Britannia!' quite like belting out sea-shanties in a college hall that smells a bit like sick.

And now, in 2026, I find myself in these pages and having the pleasure of hosting Proms this season on TV. What an absolute honour and privilege. The thing that I love about the Proms is that it manages to be both accessible and ambitious, simultaneously unpretentious and prestigious. And much like the Hill Orchestra, there's room for everyone: from first-timers to aficionados, from those who can read a score to those of us who just bash away at the piano until something resembling the theme to *The Traitors* emerges. Music brings people together, creates communities and can take us all on the most wonderful and unpredictable adventures. Gutted not to see any Nielsen in this year's programme, though …! •

Actor and comedian Nick Mohammed is best known for his roles in *Ted Lasso* and *Slow Horses* as well as for his appearances on *Taskmaster* and *The Celebrity Traitors*. This Proms season he returns to the BBC TV presenting team.

Nick's Pick of the Proms 2026

Mahler Symphony No. 6 (22 July)
In honour of my good friend Joe 'Marler'!

R. Strauss An Alpine Symphony (27 July)
Never has a piece painted a better picture.

Sibelius Symphony No. 2 (28 July)
For the most beautifully uplifting tug of war between D major and G major right at the very end – no spoilers as to who wins!

Prokofiev Romeo and Juliet – excerpts (29 August)
Just the most glorious and multifaceted music for the best story ever told.

Enchanted: Alan Menken's Music for Disney (31 August)
I mean, just try stopping me from joining in with this one!

Help Musicians

Music moves us all. Be there for those who make it happen.

Behind every Proms performance are musicians who dedicate their lives to music — often without the security or safety nets many of us rely on. When illness, injury or financial hardship strike, we're there, providing health, wellbeing and financial support.

Help Musicians is extremely grateful to the Promenaders' Musical Charities' long-standing support and commitment to our work, building a world where musicians thrive.

If you would like to help support the people who create the music that means so much to us all, we would love to hear from you.

Tommy Nguyen
Head of Philanthropy
tommy.nguyen@helpmusicians.org.uk
020 7239 9100

Love music? Donate today to support our work

Registered Charity No. 228089
Help Musicians is the working name of the Musicians' Benevolent Fund

Discover...

ALBAN BERG'S
Violin Concerto

JESSICA DUCHEN unwraps Berg's sumptuous blend of 12-tone serialism, folk song and late-Romantic pathos

Alban Berg's Violin Concerto bears one of the most poignant subtitles in the repertoire: 'To the Memory of an Angel'. This was Manon Gropius, the 18-year-old daughter of Walter Gropius and Alma Mahler-Werfel, who died of polio in 1935. Manon had been training as an actress and was due to appear as an angel in a Salzburg Festival production of a play by Hugo von Hofmannsthal. In tragic hindsight, however, the concerto also foreshadows Berg's own death later that year. It would be his last completed orchestral work, and he never heard it performed (the Nazi regime had by then banned his music in Germany).

The premiere took place in Barcelona in April 1936, given by the violinist Louis Krasner, who had talked the reluctant composer into writing it. Berg had been wary of the genre's virtuoso tradition. Krasner reminded him, however, that Beethoven and Brahms had written fine violin concertos and suggested that Berg could humanise the perception of the 12-note technique developed by his mentor, Arnold Schoenberg, in which all 12 notes of the chromatic scale are organised into a predetermined row from which the music is built. Berg's eventual agreement was spurred on by Manon's death – he and the family were close friends – and the wish to memorialise her. Created with, for him, unusual speed, the result is a seamless blend of modernity and Mahlerian anguish, blending 12-note technique with references to folk song and church chorales from Bach cantatas.

The work's two movements are each formed of two connected sections. The first opens with a prelude-like Andante, the solo violin drifting across its open strings over hushed orchestral colours, before a lilting Allegretto emerges, tinged with a Viennese lilt. Berg weaves in a Carinthian Ländler, 'Ein Vogel auf'm Zwetschgenbaum' (A Bird in the Plum Tree), which he associated with Manon's youthful manner.

The second movement begins as a ferocious, virtuosic Allegro – the soloist's closest moment to a cadenza – then gives way to an Adagio in which Berg introduces a chorale, 'Es ist genug' (It is enough), made famous in Bach's Cantata, BWV 60, 'O Ewigkeit, du Donnerwort' (O Eternity, thou Thunderous Word). On this he bases a series of luminously orchestrated variations. Ultimately the strings drop away, leaving only the soloist behind with the woodwind and brass. As the end approaches, the violin line rises heavenwards, closing the concerto in an atmosphere of tranquil acceptance. ●

Jessica Duchen's music journalism appears in *The Sunday Times*, *The i Paper* and *BBC Music Magazine*. She is the author of seven novels, three plays, biographies of Fauré, Myra Hess and Korngold and the librettos for two operas by Roxanna Panufnik.

Berg Violin Concerto
MONDAY 10 AUGUST

hyperion

SCHOLARSHIP · ARTISTRY · EXPLORATION

45 YEARS ON and still 'Britain's brightest record label', Hyperion continues to add to a catalogue famous for its excellence and featuring some of today's most important artists.

Whether choral, solo vocal, orchestral, chamber or instrumental, much of the repertoire is unique to Hyperion, with over 2,300 albums available on CD and vinyl, or to download and stream.

Start exploring

The Art of Prog

Ahead of the first ever Prog Rock Prom, DJ, author and broadcaster **STUART MACONIE** charts the genre's chequered history, introduces some of its best-known proponents and reveals its surprising kinship with classical music

For years, a fondness for 'progressive rock' was the love that dare not speak its name. As the rough, spittle-flecked beast that was punk slouched to the 100 Club to be born in the late 1970s, prog rock albums by Yes, Emerson, Lake & Palmer, Genesis and their grandiloquent, flamboyant peers went to the back of record collections. Sex Pistols frontman Johnny Rotten strolled London's King's Road in a customised T-shirt that read 'I Hate Pink Floyd'. Radio 1 DJ John Peel condemned ELP as a 'waste of electricity'. Very few people would risk a good word for 'prog', as it came to be known.

Fashionableness is a cruel metric for any art form, but prog was particularly vulnerable to shifts in taste because it had defined itself so loudly and so successfully in the early part of the 1970s. Punk's critique was not subtle but it was effective: prog was bloated, elitist, detached. Where prog prized virtuosity, punk valued immediacy. Where prog built cathedrals, punk preferred squats. It was a prejudice that proved tediously durable. As late as 1997, when it was put to Radiohead that its album *OK Computer* had distinctly Floydian shades of prog about it, frontman Thom Yorke instantly bristled: 'We hate progressive rock.'

But the 21st century brought a curious rehabilitation. As rock's cultural centrality waned, prog's sins seemed less urgent and culpable. Qualities once mocked –

◀ Pink Floyd, a leading proponent of prog rock, performing at the Merriweather Post Pavilion, Maryland, in July 1973

duration, difficulty, a willingness to risk boredom – began to look like resistance to the logic of the playlist. Younger musicians, raised on eclecticism rather than allegiance, approached prog without the baggage. Recently, when I was interviewing the band Black Country, New Road, singer Georgia Ellery – born in the same year as Radiohead recorded *OK Computer* – expressed affection for prog. A new cohort of bands such as her own, Field Music, Everything Everything, Lost Crowns and even Arctic Monkeys have embraced its principles: ambition, scope, complexity, unusual instrumentation and arrangements, sonic adventurism, even the courage to fail.

Canonically, King Crimson's 1969 debut *In the Court of the Crimson King* (the one with the angry purple face) is routinely cited as the first prog rock album. And with some justification, as it did distil many of the genre's essential elements: melodic and rhythmic expansiveness, and the dissonance and complexity of chamber and symphonic music. But I'd go back a couple of years for the real origin story. The Beatles' eighth studio album, *Sgt. Pepper's Lonely Hearts Club Band*, offered a template for prog as much in the permission it gave and the condition it aspired to as the actual sound. Albums could be unified statements; studios could be instruments; pop musicians could borrow from anywhere so long as they did it with confidence and aplomb. Prog was a giddy collision between British psychedelia, post-war art-school ambition and a sudden abundance of technology.

There was menace and beauty at the same time, and an admirable belief that listeners wanted to be challenged as well as entertained, that musical difficulty was a sign of respect rather than indifference. It shared, however unconsciously, the era's faith in cultural advancement. These were bands which seemed (and they may have only 'seemed') to care little for being 'Top of the Pops' or for chart success and yet, ironically, became colossally well liked, gallingly so for the unbelievers. For, lest we forget, even when it wasn't cool, prog was mindbogglingly popular. Jethro Tull has had 15 gold- or platinum-selling albums in the USA. Genesis has sold 150 million albums worldwide. Pink Floyd's *The Dark Side of the Moon* was the best-selling album of the 1970s and spent 966 weeks on the *Billboard* 200 chart. Bill Bruford, drummer and founding member of Yes, summed this up in a typically witty and urbane manner when he said, 'King Crimson was one of the only gigs for a rock drummer where you could play in 17/16 time and still stay in decent hotels.'

At its career-making debut concert in Hyde Park, opening for The Rolling Stones, King Crimson concluded its set with a savagely exciting rendition of 'Mars' from Holst's orchestral suite *The Planets*, an acknowledgment of our national musical heritage. This is key; there was and is something uniquely British about prog which, added to its classical associations, makes it a perfect fit for a BBC Proms concert. Genesis's album *Selling England by the Pound* took its title from a slogan in the Labour Party manifesto and muses

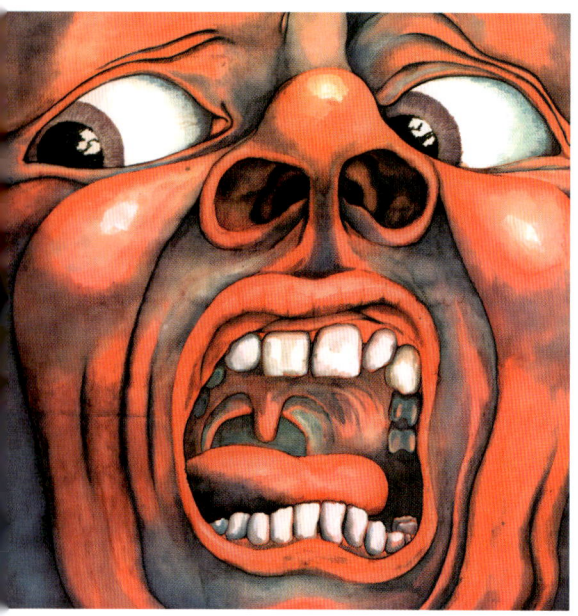

Artwork for King Crimson's 1969 debut *In the Court of the Crimson King*, routinely cited as the first prog rock album

Artwork for 1972's *Close to the Edge*, the fifth studio album by Yes and one of the band's most acclaimed releases

upon identity and the state of the nation. Pink Floyd wrote a song about Rupert Brooke's beloved Grantchester Meadows. Jethro Tull's *Songs from the Wood* is a delicious exploration of rural British folklore and tradition.

Alongside this, prog's classical kinship is well known. Rick Wakeman (of Yes) and Gentle Giant's Kerry Minnear were both graduates of the Royal College of Music. ELP released an album-length setting of Mussorgsky's *Pictures at an Exhibition* and had a global hit with its muscular reading of Aaron Copland's *Fanfare for the Common Man*. It also made an intense electronic arrangement of the fourth movement from Alberto Ginastera's First Piano Concerto – one which, according to the Argentine composer, 'perfectly captured the spirit of my music'. And there is a long-standing relationship with the Proms: in the summer of 1970, Soft Machine played selections from its brilliantly demanding album *Third* in a concert that also featured classical works by Tim Souster and Terry Riley.

The charge that progressive rock was somehow less 'real' and 'authentic' than the blues stylings of, say, The Rolling Stones has always been specious. If anything, for young musicians like ELP's Keith Emerson and King Crimson's Robert Fripp to develop ideas from within the European classical tradition was considerably more genuine and relatable than a grammar-school boy from Dartford (Mick Jagger) echoing the mannerisms and lived experiences of impoverished Black people in the Deep South.

But let's not argue. It's true that prog bred excesses and follies that can seem silly and vainglorious now. Rick Wakeman staging a concept piece about King Arthur on ice at Wembley, for example, or ELP's three individual lorry-loads of gear that included a Persian carpet (recently sold at auction for $34,375). In truth, I still haven't teased out exactly what Yes frontman Jon Anderson meant when he sang 'craving penetrations offer links with the self-instructor's sharp and tender love'. But in all of these cases, the artists themselves would probably permit themselves a wry smile and a self-deprecating eye roll. They were different, heady times. Times when a little of what Macbeth called 'vaulting ambition' was not seen as a flaw in one's musical make-up. The Beach Boys' 'Good Vibrations' is 'prog'. The Beatles' 'A Day in the Life' is 'prog'. Prog is simply great music released from the arid strictures of cool and from the sneers of gatekeepers.

It is hard to conceive of music that is more visceral and full-blooded than Yes's *Close to the Edge*, knottier than Gentle Giant, more dramatic and saturnine than ELP's *Brain Salad Surgery*, more beguilingly English than Genesis or Jethro Tull. You'll hear that diversity, playfulness and spirit of adventure at this summer's prog Prom. ●

Stuart Maconie is a writer, broadcaster and journalist whose books include *Cider with Roadies*, *Pies and Prejudice* and *Adventures on the High Teas*. He presents *Radcliffe and Maconie* and *The Freak Zone* on BBC Radio 6 Music.

Prog Rock: A Fanfare for the Common Man
SATURDAY 18 JULY

Concert Orchestra | National Orchestra & Chorus of Wales | Philharmonic Orchestra | Scottish Symphony Orchestra | Singers | Symphony Orchestra & Chorus

THE BBC ORCHESTRAS & CHOIRS

Music to keep you on the edge of your seat
Music to bring you to your feet
Music for everyone, everywhere, live and on air

bbc.co.uk/orchestras

iPLAYER SOUNDS

80TH ANNIVERSARY SEASON
September 2026 – May 2027

Royal Philharmonic Orchestra x Vasily Petrenko

Beethoven Triple Concerto *with Julia Fischer, Pablo Ferrández and Jan Lisiecki*

Wallen World premiere

Mozart 'Jupiter' Symphony *presented by Leah Broad*

Strauss Ein Heldenleben

Mahler 'Resurrection' Symphony *with Miah Persson, Beth Taylor and Philharmonia Chorus*

Stravinsky The Firebird: Suite

Grieg Piano Concerto *with Eric Lu*

Rachmaninoff Symphonic Dances

Ravel Daphnis et Chloé *with Philharmonia Chorus*

Strauss Also sprach Zarathustra

Performing at venues in London and around the UK. Visit rpo.co.uk for full details.

Book now at rpo.co.uk

Supported using public funding by
ARTS COUNCIL ENGLAND

WELLINGTON COLLEGE

With nearly 800 instrumental lessons each week from 60 specialist teachers, every student is given the opportunity to realise their musical potential.

To join our team of 80+ music award holders at 13+ and 16+ contact:
music@wellingtoncollege.org.uk

BRISTOL BEACON

SOUNDS BETTER WITH YOU

Never miss a moment at bristolbeacon.org

ARTS COUNCIL ENGLAND

SOUTHBANK CENTRE 75

CLASSICAL MUSIC

SPRING/SUMMER 2026

BOOK NOW FOR EXTRAORDINARY EXPERIENCES

LOTTERY FUNDED | Supported using public funding by ARTS COUNCIL ENGLAND

Where will your Love of Music take you?

Find out more

@rncmlive — Manchester, UK

RNCM — ROYAL NORTHERN COLLEGE of MUSIC

DULWICH COLLEGE
FOUNDED 1619

Scan to find out more

Music Scholarships

Dulwich College offers instrumental, organ and choral scholarships.

Mr Gareth Hemmings, our Director of Music, is always pleased to meet prospective candidates and their parents to advise and discuss musical life at the College.

Telephone: 020 8299 9258   Email: music@dulwich.org.uk   www.dulwich.org.uk

RHS Flower Shows 2026

Experience a floral symphony and compose memories together at an RHS Flower Show

RHS Chelsea Flower Show
TICKETS SELLING FAST
19 – 23 May

RHS Badminton Flower Show
8 – 12 July

RHS Sandringham Flower Show
22 – 26 July

BOOK NOW
rhs.org.uk/shows

Secrets Beneath the Notes

From musical monograms and number symbolism to hidden codes and never-to-be-solved enigmas, **TOM SERVICE** unlocks the messages and meanings that composers across the centuries have hidden in their scores

Listen very carefully, I shall say this only once. In fact I'll repeat the essential idea of this article a few times, unlike Michelle Dubois in the 1980s' sitcom *'Allo 'Allo!*. But the point is: this is a message that hopefully won't self-destruct after you've read it, but instead will lead you to think about the essential paradoxes of musical meaning, thanks to the lengths that composers go to when they hide – and simultaneously reveal – their deepest secrets through messages, codes and riddles buried within the notes they write in their instrumental and orchestral music.

And that's a good starting point for where the mysteries of musical ciphers really begin. Before we get to secret symbols that open up new dimensions in the music you thought you knew, once you've worked out how to use classical music's Rosetta stones – I'm looking at you, Robert and Clara Schumann, Alban Berg, Dmitry Shostakovich, and in particular you, Johann Sebastian Bach – we need to ask how it is that instrumental pieces like symphonies, sonatas, overtures and orchestral suites – with no words and no obvious dramatic narrative – can mean anything concrete at all?

It's not a new question. In 18th-century France, the philosopher Bernard de Fontenelle, perplexed by the rise of Baroque instrumental forms as opposed to the vocal music that had been France's most prestigious form of musical expression, asked the question: 'Sonate, que me veux-tu?' – 'Sonata,' – and by extension, all forms of purely instrumental music – 'what do you want of me?' Behind Fontenelle's frustration is the idea that instrumental music's abstract play of signs is radically incoherent compared to when music is doing its job illustrating drama in the theatre or accompanying the words of the liturgy. Music's role is to express *something* – an emotion, a character, a force of nature – not merely to create shapes in time that can't be clearly decoded.

Compared to the apparently obvious underscore and amplification of meaning that music makes when it's contributing to storytelling, from Figaro's wedding to Christ's Passion, what does a piece called 'Sonata No. 21' mean? 'Symphony No. 97'? 'Orchestral Suite No. 4 in D major'? Instead of human drama, these are mere sounds – sounds that are so abstract they can only be identified by their numbers.

In fact, the challenge of decoding instrumental music, to give it real and coherent meaning, was one that early 18th-century European musical culture was obsessed with. There was a codex of musical ideas that was thought to mimic and directly express the range of our feelings. At its broadest, deciding to write pieces in major keys or minor keys was a clue that you were composing at either end of the affective spectrum, so that by the late 18th century, pieces in minor keys are more intense and emotionally darker than pieces in major keys. The same goes for the associations of particular keys, so that a piece composed in voluptuous E major sets up a different sound-world of emotion than music in stentorian C major. And there were specific musical codes for extremes of feeling that European musical culture established at this time that are still going strong today: fast dotted rhythms in major keys that used to connote martial tones and marching bands and which now get your groove going on the dance floor or in the Royal Albert Hall Arena; or slow, gradual descents of harmony and melody to give us the feels and chills of lamenting and keening.

There are dozens more patterns and signs in the code-cracking semiotics of classical music. Yet, however closely composers clung to these ideas and modes of expression, composition was never as simple as joining them together in a display of neatly legible musical symbols – as if you could decode a fugue or a symphony as you might a Renaissance painting, with all those visual symbols expertly and logically explained. In manipulating these devices, composers inevitably invented new ways of combining them, and opened up zones of ambiguity in how instrumental music could be interpreted.

And it's in those places of uncertainty and expressive ambivalence that composers' imaginations could take flight. Instead of resisting the ambiguities of musical meaning, why not compose *with* them, so that instrumental and orchestral music could become endlessly interpretable, with meanings that are multiple and enigmatic …?

… And, indeed, *Enigma*-tic. Edward Elgar's set of variations, written in 1899,

The Three Boys in Mozart's masonic-themed opera *The Magic Flute* – in which numeric symbolism also extends to three opening chords, the Queen of the Night's three attendants, three temples and three trials of enlightenment (image from a 2011 production at the Théâtre des Champs-Élysées, Paris, directed by William Kentridge)

is the most notorious riddle in orchestral history, thanks to his challenge to posterity. He set musicological hares running that generations of musical cryptographers have tried to catch, attempting to find the real theme of these variations. That's not the one we actually hear at the start of the piece, but an unheard melody that Elgar said is the real secret of the piece, a meaning he never disclosed. 'It is so well known that it is extraordinary that no-one has spotted it,' he wrote in a programme note, and he went on, cryptically, to disclose that the tune we hear at the start of the piece conceals a 'dark saying [that] must be left unguessed', expressing a 'nothingness … the enigma I will not explain'. Elgar was true to his word until his death in 1934.

This is an enigma that has produced a whole library of Elgar-sleuthing books, articles and theories. The candidates for the identity of the unheard melody run an amazing gamut of diversity and ingenuity: people have said it's the slow movement of Mozart's 'Prague' Symphony (No. 38), or that it's 'Auld lang syne' – given that the *'Enigma' Variations* is a piece about friendship, with each variation a tribute to one of Elgar's closest friends, that's an appealing solution. 'Rule, Britannia!' is another of the runners and riders, along with Liszt's tone-poem *Les préludes*, Martin Luther's hymn tune 'Ein feste Burg ist unser Gott' – and the number Pi. The first four digits of Pi – 3.142 (rounded up), the ratio of a circle's circumference to its diameter – map onto the first four notes of the *Enigma* theme that we hear, if you interpret each number as the note of a major scale where 1 equals the 'home' note. Got it?

There is another mooted solution: that Elgar, a brilliant amateur cryptographer who once solved a supposedly insoluble cipher with six pages of hard-wrought mathematical workings, deliberately left this trail of musicological breadcrumbs knowing that he'd set an enigma that could never be solved: Elgar's ultimate riddle at our expense.

If that's true – and it might be (you read it here first!) – then Elgar's enigma is an outlier next to the codes that we know composers have devised to communicate with one another or to disclose their deepest secrets. In the mid-19th century, the circle around Robert and Clara Schumann loved nothing better than to come up with ways of imprinting their initials and aphorisms into their music: Robert's piano piece *Carnaval* is full of transliterations of names into musical notes, with monikers alluding to Ernestine, his fiancée at the time, and to Clara too; there's even a collaboratively composed violin sonata by Schumann, Brahms, Albert Dietrich and Joseph Joachim that's based on Joachim's personal motto, 'Frei aber Einsam' ('Free but lonely'), with each movement based on the notes F–A–E. In the 20th century, Dmitry Shostakovich's musical signature, interpreted via German nomenclature as D–S–C–H (S=E flat, 'Es' in German, and H=B natural), stalks many of his later compositions, the sound of the individual being obliterated by gigantic musical forces, screaming in protest, or finding vindication and liberty.

There are many more musical coders out there in musical history: the Freemason Mozart turned the masonic obsession with the number three into the guiding principle of instrumental pieces, cantatas and his opera *The Magic Flute*, and Alban Berg used the numbers he assigned for his own identity and that of his lover, 23 and 10, as generating principles for his later music.

But no composer has come close to the symbologist, numerologist and musical code-maker Johann Sebastian Bach. His musical signature, B-A-C-H, a snake-trail of semitones, is there in the final music he wrote, the unfinished Contrapunctus XIV of *The Art of Fugue*. And according to musicologists like Wilfrid Mellers, you can approach Bach's entire *oeuvre* like a gigantic series of numerological puzzles, if you interpret the number of notes in a fugue subject according to the Christian symbolism of numbers such as 3 or 7, or analyse the fact that Bach composes entire pieces to schemes based on adding up the numerical value of the initials of his name, after their place in the alphabet.

And yet: even if we could get to the bottom of, say, the *Enigma* mystery, or the secrets of why Bach's fugues have exactly the number of notes in them that they do, the ultimate meaning of all of these pieces would still elude us. The frustrating truth about music – for a cryptographer at least – is that its significance cannot be reduced to a line of code or a single tune, a theory of number or a set of initials. If that were the case then all music could be expressed as an equation, like: Elgar's *Enigma* = 'Auld lang syne'; Brahms's Third Symphony = F–A–E; Bach's '48' Preludes and Fugues = 4x12. That last one's at least mathematically correct, but none of them gets close to the meanings of these pieces of music.

Meanings, plural. The astounding fact is that these pieces have an absolute quality, particular properties of melody and harmony and orchestration that are shared in every performance we hear, but our interpretations of them are multiple, ever-changing, and irreducible to any secret formula. That's the fundamental riddle – and miracle – of how orchestral music moves us. There's no end to the games we can play in how we interpret its signs and messages, even while we feel its power to be definitive and indelible in every performance at the Proms.

So, problem solved? Hardly: in fact, another set of imponderables now present themselves, about what those multiple meanings actually – mean …

PS: Burn after reading. Actually – don't. Just keep listening to the endless labyrinths and enigmas of orchestral music: that's the invitation of this whole Proms season. Well, that, and the fact that if you add up the numerical position in the alphabet of every second letter of the surname of every third soloist throughout the season, and divide that total by the number of notes in the 'Nimrod' movement of Elgar's *'Enigma' Variations*, you may, just may, end up with the ultimate answer to the ultimate question – orchestral music's equivalent of Douglas Adams's 42 in *The Hitchhiker's Guide to the Galaxy*. Answers on an inflammable postcard. Good luck … •

Tom Service presents *Saturday Morning* and other programmes for BBC Radio 3, and has presented on BBC TV. A regular writer for *The Guardian* since 1999, he is the author of books including *Music as Alchemy* and *Thomas Adès: Full of Noises* (both Faber, 2012) and *A History of the World in 50 Pieces* (Penguin, 2025).

Improvisation on B–A–C–H
SUNDAY 26 JULY

Berg Violin Concerto
MONDAY 10 AUGUST

Elgar 'Enigma' Variations
WEDNESDAY 2 SEPTEMBER

MOOD MUSIC

Ahead of the 2026 Proms season, three BBC-commissioned composers put their creative process under the microscope, arranging the themes and inspirations behind their new compositions into a series of musical 'mood boards'

Dani Howard

Concerto for Brass, 'SIGNAL'
BBC co-commission: world premiere
SATURDAY 2 AUGUST

Following the world premiere of her work *Three, Four AND …* at the 2024 Proms, British composer Dani Howard returns with a new BBC co-commission inspired by brass instruments and their historic role in delivering signals and messages. The Concerto for Brass, 'SIGNAL', premiered by the BBC Symphony Orchestra under Paavo Järvi, puts the loudest, proudest section of the orchestra under the spotlight as horns, trombones, trumpets and tubas pass on musical messages to one another in a glistening musical mêlée.

'Classical' Music
The Roman god Mercury is often depicted holding a trumpet, symbolising his role as a divine messenger; Howard's new concerto explores the historic role that brass instruments have played in delivering messages.

Touch Paper
As with all her works, Howard began developing her new concerto with the humblest of compositional tools: pencil and paper.

Sound Patterns
Howard is a synaesthete: she associates sounds with specific shapes, and these connections form an important part of her compositional process, informing the way she approaches structural, textural and melodic patterns.

Dots and Dashes
Howard's concerto sees the various members of the brass section pass on and develop motifs, or musical 'messages', creating a rhythmic display reminiscent of the dots and dashes heard in Morse code signals.

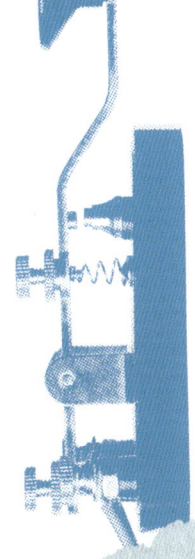

Sea Fever
Howard says that the sea is 'always my greatest source of inspiration' and, typically for her music, the Concerto for Brass reflects its 'shape, movement, depth and vastness'.

Composing with Texture
'It's all about texture,' says Howard. Like all of her music, the Concerto for Brass revels in a momentum borne of textural – rather than melodic – variation and repetition.

Jessie Montgomery

These Righteous Paths *BBC co-commission: UK premiere*
MONDAY 20 JULY

Jessie Montgomery's first BBC Proms co-commission is one of a series of works inspired by the poems and plays of her late mother Robbie McCauley – a leading figure in American Black theatre, which began to earn national recognition in the 1960s and 1970s. Taking the form of a concerto, it was written especially for the South African cellist Abel Selaocoe, whose unique musical palette – mixing Baroque continuo with Afro-centric rhythms and melodies, virtuoso classical performance and improvisation – is reflected in the work's many stylistic shifts. At its heart, though, sit McCauley's writings, and the way her work reflects inheritances from the African diaspora. 'It is from these ancestral traces that I shape a living soundscape,' says Montgomery, 'one that honours what has been passed down while allowing the music to conjure new hopes and memories.'

Sankofa
This Ghanaian concept conveys how we must look back in order to go forward – symbolised by a bird tilting its head, 'as if calling to the past for confirmation to take flight'. Sankofa has been a great source of inspiration for Montgomery, who in her concerto includes passages that reflect 'the cascade and cadence of birds in flight'.

Brotherhood of Sleeping Car Porters
Train porters were the first African American workers to form an officially recognised union; the same porters feature in Robbie McCauley's 'Another Train Poem', which inspired the central movement of Montgomery's new cello concerto.

> Robbie McCauley
> All the ancestors and I
> For Rhea Lore Greta & Zake
>
> I don't believe
> in heaven and hell
> I do accept beliefs
> Of whoever holds them
> I do stay in touch
> With family and friends
> no longer alive on earth
> I imagine them all
> in heaven.

Ancestral Connections
In this poem Montgomery's mother expresses the deep connection she feels to her ancestors; by taking its title from the same poem, the first movement of *These Righteous Paths* reflects Montgomery's own sense of connection to her mother, and the grief she still feels following her death in 2021.

Mommy Cool
Montgomery was born and raised by artist parents in New York City during the 1980s. Decades later her mother's poems and plays would inspire her to compose a series of pieces, including *These Righteous Paths*.

'Back when going South on the train'
In her new concerto, Montgomery paints in music her mother's written account of segregated steam trains carrying Black children South 'from New York Philadelphia Delaware Baltimore and DC'.

Georgia's Plains and Marshes
In 'Another Train Poem' McCauley riffs on the disconnect between the 'slow' American South, with its long-held segregation laws and humid landscapes, and the country as a whole, which 'believes so much in speed'.

Mark-Anthony Turnage

Festen Suite *BBC co-commission: UK premiere*
TUESDAY 28 JULY

Last year Mark-Anthony Turnage made the critics purr with his latest opera, *Festen* ('The Celebration'), an adaptation of the cult Danish film of the same name in which shocking family secrets are revealed during the 60th-birthday celebrations of the patriarch Helge. This Proms season sees the UK premiere of the orchestral *Festen Suite*, which threads together scenes and interludes from the opera. Turnage's music has been a regular feature at the Proms since 1990, when his Francis Bacon-inspired *Three Screaming Popes* was given its London premiere. Over 35 years later, this latest piece offers yet another example of his extraordinary gift for generating powerful, appealing music from the most challenging of sources.

The Artist
Turnage has several Francis Bacon prints in his home, and something of their grim, darkly comedic spirit has seeped into the composer's musical palette, informing works such as *Festen*.

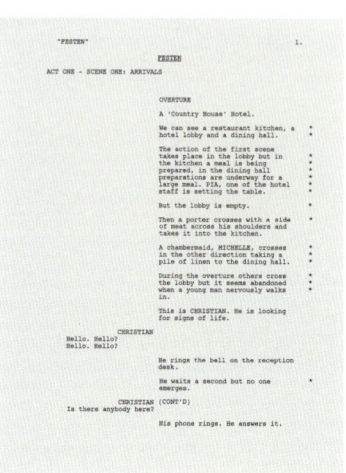

The Text
Playwright Lee Hall wrote *Festen*'s libretto, filling it with repetition, rhythm and a counterpoint of voices. Music 'seems to leap from the printed page', which, says Turnage, 'is really not always the case with a libretto – believe me!'

The Sets
Covent Garden's production of *Festen* featured set designs by Miriam Buether, whose sterile hotel spaces and clean, minimalist approach contrasted with the dark, emotional truth of the drama.

The Inspiration
Festen is an adaptation of a 1998 film by Danish director Thomas Vinterberg. 'It's got everything,' says Turnage. 'Big speeches that can be turned into arias, set pieces involving 10 or 12 people, and most of it happens in one room.'

The Partnership
Turnage's desire to collaborate with Lee Hall – librettist for *Billy Elliot the Musical* – was influenced by the latter's keen understanding of music: 'Lee knows which words sound good when they're sung.'

The Recognition
Festen was named Best New Opera Production at the 2025 Olivier Awards; Turnage and Hall accepted the trophy alongside soprano Natalya Romaniw, who sang the role of Helena.

Part of our World

As the Proms prepares to celebrate Alan Menken, the composer behind Disney's late-1980s 'Renaissance', **DOMINIC BROOMFIELD-McHUGH** speaks to Menken's friends and colleagues about his extraordinary contribution to contemporary musical storytelling and his place in the hearts of a generation of young music-lovers

For nearly four decades Alan Menken has been synonymous with the Disney musical, bringing his talent for storytelling and melodic invention to some of the world's favourite fairy tales. *The Little Mermaid* (1989), *Beauty and the Beast* (1991) and *Aladdin* (1992) are just three of the many Disney blockbusters Menken has scored, helping to revitalise the studio after its period in the doldrums – and earning him eight Academy Awards along the way. He has also made a major contribution to theatre music, not only in stage adaptations of Disney hits but also in originals such as *Little Shop of Horrors* (1982), *Sister Act* (2009) and *A Bronx Tale* (2016).

In recent years the Proms has regularly included programmes focused on figures from the 20th-century Broadway canon – composers such as George Gershwin or Richard Rodgers. This season's focus on a more contemporary figure such as Menken feels like a natural next step. Sir Tim Rice, who has worked with Menken on various projects for stage and screen, regards him as 'worthy to rank with the musical theatre greats' and 'the number one American theatrical composer of his generation'.

Born in New York City in 1949, Menken started composing as a child and, after abandoning thoughts of following his father into dentistry, eventually completed a degree in Music. He subsequently worked as a ballet pianist and jingle writer but dreamt of emulating the likes of Bob Dylan – a multifaceted background that is reflected in the impressive stylistic range of his compositional career. After attending Lehman Engel's famous BMI Musical Theatre Workshop, in 1979 he joined forces with the prodigious young lyricist Howard Ashman on the modestly successful off-Broadway musical *God Bless You, Mr. Rosewater*. *Little Shop of Horrors* followed. A black comedy that satirised sci-fi B-movies, it was an unexpected hit, moving to a bigger theatre and running for five years to become one of the highest-grossing off-Broadway productions of all time.

Lyricist Lynn Ahrens, perhaps best known for writing *Ragtime* (1996), agrees that Menken has a special facility for theatre composition. 'Alan and I wrote a version of *A Christmas Carol*, a holiday extravaganza that ran for 10 seasons at Madison Square Garden,' she explains. 'So I witnessed first-hand how he can sit down at the piano, put his fingers on the keys and create a beautiful new melody on the spot – one that is not only catchy and seemingly effortless but that also works dramatically for the musical. For a lyricist, this is a dream to work with.'

Success wasn't instant, though. For two years in the early 1980s Menken worked with Tom Eyen (*Dreamgirls*) on a musical about a group of dancers at the Roxy Theatre called *Kicks: The Showgirl Musical*, which went through several workshops but was never professionally staged. *The Apprenticeship of Duddy Kravitz* (1987), featuring lyrics by David Spencer, played in Philadelphia but failed to reach New York. Various other ideas were short-lived or abandoned altogether. But a reunion of the creative partnership of Menken and Ashman, instigated by the latter, led to a remarkable period in which they contributed the songs for three hit animations in a row. In 1988 they started work on an adaptation of Hans Christian Andersen's *The Little Mermaid*. Menken was rewarded with Academy Awards for both Best Score and Best Song ('Under the Sea'). The movie was an unexpected success and turned around Disney Studios' fortunes after years of critical failure and financial instability, leading to what is often called the 'Disney Renaissance'. What the score showcased was Menken's ability to create long melodic lines supported by a rich orchestral texture, epitomised by Ariel's song of yearning, 'Part of Your World'. It introduced many young people to the sound of a symphony orchestra and laid the ground for a string of great Disney ballads to come.

Menken and Ashman's second Disney release was an adaptation of the French fairy tale *Beauty and the Beast*. The transformation of a prince's servants into enchanted household objects formed the basis of some of Disney's most enduring characters, including the teapot Mrs Potts, memorably voiced by Angela Lansbury. The movie's wistful title-song, poignantly

◀ Ariel, Sebastian and Flounder *(left to right)* in Disney's 1989 film *The Little Mermaid*, which featured songs and an underscore by Menken

Alan Menken pictured in 2022, four decades after his first big success in the off-Broadway musical *Little Shop of Horrors*

delivered by Lansbury, won an Academy Award that year. Menken's score also revels in Broadway pastiche, as in 'Be Our Guest', which is combined with Busby Berkeley-esque visuals to create perhaps the greatest showstopper since Jerry Herman's (*Hello, Dolly!*) 1960s heyday.

Seemingly on the brink of long-term success as half of a team in the Rodgers and Hammerstein mould, Menken was devastated when Ashman died in 1991 of AIDS-related illnesses. It was just eight months before *Beauty and the Beast* was released: Ashman never saw his work realised on the big screen. Tim Rice stepped in to help complete work on *Aladdin*, including the Oscar-winning duet 'A Whole New World', and contributed new lyrics for the stage adaptation of *Beauty and the Beast*, which ran for 13 years. He believes that Menken and Ashman 'deserve unstinted praise' for the Disney animation revival. 'Alan has had numerous successes on Broadway and in theatres around the world but, perhaps ironically, his work in movies has made an even greater global impact, thanks to his ability to create theatrical emotion and drama to perfection for the screen.'

Menken's continued association with Disney led to another significant partnership, with Stephen Schwartz, best known as the composer-lyricist of *Wicked* (2003). Schwartz provided lyrics for another two Disney adaptations: *Pocahontas* (1995) and *The Hunchback of Notre Dame*, the 1996 version of Victor Hugo's beloved novel. *Hunchback* was a particular triumph, grossing over $325m worldwide. 'Alan is so talented that his skill can be mistaken for being facile,' Schwartz says. 'But he carefully and consciously limits what he calls his "musical palette" for each score so that it has its own distinct identity, perfect for the story's time, place and genre. His music for *Aladdin* could never be interchanged with that of *Pocahontas*, *Sister Act* or any of his many other scores.' Here, Schwartz points to Menken's use of an idea familiar from the mature operas of Verdi: the creation of a sound-world or set of musical colours (*tinta*) that gives each work its own identity. Returning to musical theatre after his stint at Disney, Menken has enjoyed success with multiple productions, but audiences have particularly embraced his disco-infused score for *Sister Act*, which opened in the West End in 2009. Another late adaptation was 2011's *Newsies*, which earned him his first Tony Award.

From soaring melodies to complex harmonies, and from clever pastiches to sincere lyrical ballads, Menken helped redefine the sound of the Disney musical. This summer's Menken Prom provides an opportunity to showcase a figure as culturally significant as those American Songbook composers – a writer of music with cross-generational appeal, loved by audiences around the world. ●

Dominic Broomfield-McHugh is Professor in Musicology at the University of Sheffield and co-editor of *The Oxford Handbook of the Disney Musical* (OUP, 2025).

Enchanted: Alan Menken's Music for Disney
MONDAY 31 AUGUST

Discover …

EDMUND THORNTON JENKINS'S
Dance Suite

TUFFUS ZIMBABWE introduces his reconstruction of an incomplete score by his pioneering great-uncle, one of the first composers to draw on African American music

The music of Edmund Thornton Jenkins (1894–1926) is heard for the first time this year at the Proms – a fitting centenary memorial – and yet the composer remains a deeply under-recognised figure. He was one of the first to incorporate jazz, blues and other African American traditions, such as folk and spiritual, into orchestral music, and he led jazz bands in London and Paris. A prolific composer and multi-instrumentalist, he died tragically young.

Born in Charleston in 1894, he studied in Charleston and Atlanta before entering London's Royal Academy of Music, where he won awards for clarinet and piano. He performed at numerous London venues, including the Wigmore Hall and Queen's Hall (at that time home to the Proms), and held a regular spot playing alto saxophone with Jack Hylton's band. Edmund would soon move to Paris to continue his career, starting his own band, the International 7, which performed across Europe. Around the same time he composed orchestral works and in 1925 he landed a performance of his American folk rhapsody *Charlestonia* with the Kursaal Orchestra in Ostend, Belgium. His career seemed to be making strides, until he was admitted in 1926 to a Paris hospital with appendicitis. He died there aged only 32.

Central to Jenkins's early training was the experience of playing in the band of the Jenkins Orphanage, founded in 1891 by his parents, Rev. Daniel Joseph Jenkins and Lena James. The band's purpose was to help fund the orphanage as it grew and at one point there were multiple Jenkins bands performing nationally. Among the prominent alumni were Cat Anderson, Jabbo Smith and Freddie Green, who would eventually work with Duke Ellington and Count Basie. The band played at the inaugural parades for presidents Theodore Roosevelt and Taft, as well as for King George VI. Edmund and his family were early pioneers of the new dance the Charleston and promoted it widely.

Edmund Thornton Jenkins conceived his *Ballet* (1918) in three movements – 'Processional', 'Pas seul' and 'Danse générale' – but some of the instrumental parts are missing. The *Dance Suite* is a concert suite I have reconstructed and it demonstrates Jenkins's masterful way with lyrical melodies, lush harmonies and intricate rhythms. On hearing the music, one can imagine scenes from nature – storms and forests, animals waking from hibernation and the celebration of spring. It is alive with echoing exchanges, birds singing, butterflies fluttering, fairy-tale characters, all woven together with spellbinding instrumental mastery. ●

Pianist and composer Tuffus Zimbabwe is a great-nephew of Edmund Thornton Jenkins and has restored and edited Jenkins's music. He has also recorded two of Edmund Jenkins's scores with the Prague Radio Symphony Orchestra under Julius P. Williams.

Edmund Thornton Jenkins, reconstr. & arr. Tuffus Zimbabwe Dance Suite
SATURDAY 22 AUGUST

The PARKHOUSE AWARD
Nurturing excellence in chamber music

19th International Chamber Music Competition for Piano Trio

- Auditions – Spring 2027 in London
- Finals Concert at Wigmore Hall

Application deadline 30 November 2026
Details: parkhouseaward.com

2025 winners
Davidoff Trio
perform piano trios by
Haydn, Murphy and Dvořák

Wigmore Hall, London
23 October 2026 at 1pm

Patron Lady Judith Swire
Registered charity 1014284   Supported by The Tertis Foundation   The Adrian Swire Charitable Trust

---

ROYAL CENTRAL
SCHOOL OF SPEECH & DRAMA
UNIVERSITY OF LONDON

Find your voice with Central for Business at the Royal Central School of Speech and Drama.

Our training, inspired by world-renowned performance education, transforms how professionals influence, communicate and lead. Book your bespoke workshop or leadership coaching to take place at your offices or our historic Swiss Cottage campus now, and start making your impact.

Find out more
cssd.ac.uk/business

CENTRAL FOR BUSINESS

arcola theatre

Grimeborn Opera Festival

15 July - 5 September

PROGRAMME INCLUDES:

Mozart: Così fan tutte & The Magic Flute

Handel: Rinaldo & Giulio Cesare

Tuluğ Tırpan: Lowest of the Low
Based on Günter Wallraff's Ganz Unten

Schoenberg: Erwartung

ARTS COUNCIL ENGLAND   Bloomberg Philanthropies

This summer the National Open Youth Orchestra, the world's first disabled-led national youth ensemble, makes its Proms debut at the Bristol Beacon. REBECCA FRANKS introduces the group and reveals the remarkable work it has done in bringing new audiences to classical music

Members of the National Open Youth Orchestra, pictured last year ahead of its UK concert tour

NEW KIDS ON THE BLOCK

When the National Open Youth Orchestra takes to the stage this summer for its Proms debut, it will be a landmark moment for the pioneering ensemble. 'Ten years ago the idea of NOYO was considered so radical that funders didn't believe it was possible,' explains Barry Farrimond-Chuong, the orchestra's CEO. 'Perceptions were still stuck on the model of disabled people taking part – but never leading. Now here we are on the biggest stage in classical music with the world's first majority-disabled national youth ensemble, showing what it can do with such exciting music.'

At the heart of the programme will be a new commission, *The Orchestra: A Young Person's Guide.* Written by the British composer Charlotte Harding, this 12-minute work is a 21st-century response to Britten's famous *The Young Person's Guide to the Orchestra* of 1945. 'My piece has a dual narrative in that it introduces young people to an orchestra in the way that Britten did but it's also a real opportunity to let young people introduce *their* orchestra to audiences of all generations,' explains Harding. 'It's a celebration of what the orchestra has been, what it is now and, importantly, where it's going in the future. Young people are really at the heart of that.'

This philosophy reflects the inclusive approach of NOYO, which was set up in 2018 by Open Up Music, a charity co-founded by Farrimond-Chuong to make music more accessible to young disabled musicians. After discovering there was no orchestral provision in the UK for special schools, Open Up Music founded the country's first three special-school orchestras. Now its Open Orchestras programme features 47 ensembles across the country. 'When we set up those up, we recognised there wasn't an obvious and clear progression route for many of the young people we were working with,' says Farrimond-Chuong. 'It was always the aspiration that we would create the National Open Youth Orchestra to plug that gap and give many of the young people we were working with the opportunity to progress.'

Young players aged 11 to 25 can now apply to play in one of the five regional NOYO ensembles around the UK and audition annually for the touring national ensemble (participation is free). The 20-player-strong NOYO meets for residencies and to give concerts at major venues, often in collaboration with major orchestras. An impressive list of partner organisations includes the BBC National Orchestra of Wales, whose players appear alongside NOYO at the BBC Proms this summer, and the Bristol Beacon, which hosts the concert. Indeed, the Prom is part of a partnership between the Proms, Open Up Music and the Bristol Beacon which draws on their collective expertise to champion representation of young disabled musicians as well as to model inclusive practice to both audiences and the music industry.

'Inclusion is often framed as a one-way street: an orchestra playing to a more diverse audience. Of course, that's true, but it's actually a two-way street,' says Farrimond-Chuong. 'The more diverse the players in an orchestra, the stronger the orchestral model becomes, the more diverse the music will be – and the more attractive to a broader range of audiences.' And, crucially, when the team asked NOYO's players who they most wanted their music-making to reach, top of the list were other young disabled people. They wanted 'to let them know that music and orchestras could be for them'.

Historically that hasn't been the case. So NOYO has rethought what an orchestra might look like and how it might function. Its work is framed by the social model of disability, which recognises that how society is organised can be disabling

Clarion player Alessandro Vazzana performing with NOYO in a concert at the Lighthouse, Poole, in 2022; Vazzana controls the Clarion's output by using a movement-detecting head mouse

for many. Farrimond-Chuong gives the example of a wheelchair user who might not be disabled until they want to get to the second floor and there's no lift. When it comes to music, seen through this lens, orchestras can disable people in a number of ways. 'Most instruments are designed to be played with two hands. If you can't use your hands, that becomes a barrier,' says Farrimond-Chuong who, helpfully, also happens to be an inventor of instruments. 'NOYO admits a broad range of instruments, which is creatively exciting, and it's brilliant for audiences to hear and experience them.'

One game-changing invention which Farrimond-Chuong helped develop is the Clarion, a digital instrument that can be played with any part of the body, including the eyes. 'What's unique about the Clarion is that you can arrange the instrument in whatever way is necessary for you as a musician. If you're using head movement, you can map notes to shapes on the screen,' he says. 'It's an expressive instrument, so you have full dynamic control and articulation.' The Clarion has generated new possibilities for performers and composers alike, in other words. And it's been a great success, even becoming the first digital instrument to be assessed by the Associated Board of the Royal Schools of Music.

'I'd never written for the Clarion before, but all the notes are associated with colours, which offers a whole other way of exploring musical materials,' says Harding. 'NOYO is really asking very different questions of composers about how and what we write. The Clarion uses an acoustic-electronic language and it's really exciting to explore that in an orchestral context. These kinds of instruments open up all these sonic colours and possibilities, and you don't get many ensembles where you can do that.' The repertoire for the instrument is growing. NOYO's Prom includes the world's first Clarion Concerto, written by Michael Betteridge and premiered by the orchestra in 2024, as well as Oliver Cross's *Barriers*, which features the Clarion and the LinnStrument, an expressive MIDI controller that senses nuanced finger movements.

> ❝ It's a two-way street. The more diverse the players in an orchestra, the stronger the orchestral model becomes, the more diverse the music will be – and the more attractive to a broader range of audiences. ❞

Commissioning new music for this bespoke ensemble is a key part of NOYO's work and has been ever since it gave its first concerts. These performances had initially been planned for 2020 but had to be put on hold until the Covid-19 lockdowns had been lifted. When that happened, 26 NOYO musicians were filmed performing a new piece, *What Fear We Then?*, written for them by Alexander Campkin. 'It was a real highlight. The video looked effortless, and I know the mountain of work that existed to make it all happen,' says Farrimond-Chuong. 'It was such an exciting way to come out of what was a desperately lonely and unhappy period for so many people.' Other composers to have written for the group include Liam Taylor-West and Alexandra Hamilton-Ayres, and collaboration is an important part of the creative process. 'It sounds a bit cheesy, but the number of smiles you see in the rehearsal room is a wonderful thing. The level of ownership that young people have over the orchestra and its creative direction is clear. It always feels like a hugely positive experience to be in the room,' says Farrimond-Chuong.

And NOYO's future is full of optimism. It's 10 years since Open Up Music was founded, and the organisation has big ambitions for the next decade. Building progression routes for NOYO players to move out into the wider industry is top of the list. 'A lot of orchestras want to make themselves more open and accessible to a more diverse range of people. There's lots of work to do to make sure that becomes the reality,' says Farrimond-Chuong. 'We take our responsibility seriously. We have young musicians on stage who are showing that if they're given equitable access to opportunity, then the music they make can be absolutely spectacular.' ●

Rebecca Franks is a classical music critic for *The Times* and works as an arts journalist, writer and editor.

National Open Youth Orchestra
SUNDAY 9 AUGUST • BRISTOL

Player's Perspective
NOYO violist Cass Alabaster reveals what makes the ensemble so groundbreaking

During my time with the National Open Youth Orchestra I've gone from using crutches to becoming a full-time wheelchair user. Having such significant changes in my needs while being a member of the orchestra has been a fascinating experience. The ease with which NOYO navigates accessibility shines a stark light on the rest of the world, which seems yet to discover that having a lift, a defined schedule or even just a description of where to go makes life easier for everyone. NOYO is living, breathing, playing proof that accessibility isn't difficult – as long as you don't build your foundation on inaccessibility. You wouldn't put a height limit on a maths competition, so why should musicians be limited by their ability to climb stairs or manage bright lights? To me, NOYO is exactly what an orchestra should be about: sharing and creating music without arbitrary barriers that have zero bearing on the quality of music.

Playing alongside members of the BBC National Orchestra of Wales, as we will be at the Proms this year, is as much a source of joy as it is an act of defiance. Sharing the stage with professionals is so important because it proves that physical, sensory or cognitive barriers are not the be-all and end-all: if a member of BBC NOW can perform alongside a Clarion player, it proves that this instrument is just as 'official' as a double bass or cor anglais. And if they can share a music stand with someone who's never been able to access mainstream education, it proves that societal barriers can be overcome – not just by a few select people but by massive organisations too.

The best part of the music we perform is the way it represents a declaration. In an age of media adaptations, why should music remain static? Our *Young Person's Guide* isn't written for the youth of Britten's era, but for the youth of today. It is written for those who play not just traditional instruments but electric, adapted and alternative instruments too, as well as for those who want to listen to those instruments being performed. Our *Guide* spotlights those people who have historically been left behind or forgotten, as well as the instruments they now use to demand a place at the table. We aren't pretending to be the musicians of the past, and we certainly won't let anyone try to make us act that way. NOYO is a community of people who are intrinsically present- and future-oriented, and who understand that the best thing for the arts is social progress. We play works such as Oliver Cross's *Barriers* – written specifically with systemic barriers for disabled people in mind – not to evoke pity but to incite defiance in the face of inequity, and to demonstrate that we have always been here.

The experience of seeing and hearing NOYO perform is not just that of a traditional concert. It is also a celebration of equity, inclusion and joy. It is the product of a group of people affected by systemic barriers who fight for each other, for ourselves and for everyone else who has been left behind by financial, social or physical inaccessibility.

Britten Today

An outsider in English music on several levels, Benjamin Britten forged his individual path in the sanctuary of Suffolk, steeped in the community in which he became a local hero. **LUCY WALKER** considers his profile now, 50 years after his death

In the opening moments of the first episode of the comedy series *Detectorists*, Lance and Andy are sitting under a tree in the middle of the countryside. They are discussing whether they got any questions right on the previous night's *University Challenge*: 'Nearly got Benjamin Britten,' comments Lance. Aside from the programme's many charms – it dramatises (if that's the right word) the gentle lives of two metal detectorists – it is gratifying to hear the name of a classical composer making a cameo in a piece of primetime television. Decades ago, in the revue *Beyond the Fringe*, comedian and musician Dudley Moore could create a witty musical spoof of both Britten's folk-song-arrangement style and Peter Pears's distinctive way of singing it in full confidence that his audience would get the joke. In the 21st century, this would be more unlikely. So how did Britten's name find itself in a contemporary comedy show? Does he, even today, command the name-recognition strong enough to transcend cultural boundaries?

Could Lance conceivably have dropped in another composer's name instead? Walton, Tippett, Vaughan Williams? Berlioz, Stockhausen, Lutosławski? Probably not, and there may be various reasons for this. Firstly, Britten was perhaps chosen because of the show's East Anglian setting. The tree Lance and Andy were sitting beneath is not far from Britten's great legacy, Snape Maltings, and much of *Detectorists* was filmed in Suffolk, his county of birth; other than for a brief residency in the USA in 1939–42, he lived in Suffolk for his entire life. Secondly, this episode was first broadcast in 2014, only a year after the extensive celebrations of Britten's centenary in 2013, when his name became attached not only to numerous performances but also to a 50p coin, and a new beer ('Native Britten') developed by Suffolk brewery Adnam's.

'Britten's Suffolk' might not have quite the same cultural currency as nearby 'Constable Country' but he is perhaps the British composer most indelibly tied to a physical location – maybe even more than Elgar and the Malverns. Britten's former home, The Red House, is a visitor attraction in Aldeburgh, situated a few miles from Snape Maltings, the performance venue and artist development centre which continues to expand and evolve to this day. The annual Aldeburgh Festival, which Britten co-founded in 1948, is still going strong. Britten's birthplace in Lowestoft has been recently adorned with a statue entitled 'Britten as a Boy' *(see opposite)*. And Year 7 schoolchildren from the Benjamin Britten Academy in the same town have an annual trip to The Red House baked into their schedule.

During his own lifetime Britten was considered somewhat eccentric in carving out a creative life so far from a metropolitan centre. Yet due partly to his ferocious work ethic and partly to his ability to cultivate a group of people prepared to advocate on his behalf, Britten succeeded in making a considerable name for himself further afield. There is a substantial 'machine' associated with Britten, which is surely unique among British composers. On his death in 1976 he left provision for a Foundation to preserve his papers and legacy more generally, and to administer the rights to his music. His papers are housed in a composer archive unparalleled in its comprehensiveness, ranging as it does from draft manuscripts of operas to reams of correspondence to receipts from shops on Aldeburgh's High Street.

> **Britten is perhaps the British composer most indelibly tied to a physical location – maybe even more than Elgar and the Malverns.**

In terms of his music, the 'machine' – initially fuelled by Britten's publisher Donald Mitchell, who founded Faber Music – has vigorously promoted performances of the composer's works, both nationally and internationally. Royalties from these performances helped fund the Britten–Pears Foundation (set up in 1986) and continue to provide support for Britten Pears Arts (created in 2020 following a merger with Snape Maltings). This infrastructure has in part driven the comfortable establishment of Britten's music as a staple in concert

◀ Aloft in Lowestoft: *Britten as a Boy*, the statue by Ian Rank-Broadley unveiled last year in the composer's Suffolk hometown, facing the sea

Ian Rank-Broadley/Britten as a Boy Statue Committee

A scene from Wes Anderson's 2012 *Moonrise Kingdom* in which Suzy Bishop and her three brothers listen to a record of Britten's *The Young Person's Guide to the Orchestra*; the film features Britten's music throughout, with a staging of the composer's children's opera *Noye's Fludde* forming part of the plot

repertoire as well as, remarkably for a 20th-century composer, the regular rotation in opera houses of his 15 stage works. One online resource detailing forthcoming international classical performances lists (at the time of writing) some 150 Britten performances between January and July 2026; only performances of Elgar can compete. Those of Britten's contemporaries, such as Tippett and Walton, number fewer than 30.

In Britten's own time such dominance of the performing scene caused a certain amount of irritation: a suspicion that the continuous flow of operatic commissions, for example, or Britten's profitable recording contracts, suggested he had unfair advantages over his musical colleagues. Even The Beatles noticed. In the 2021 documentary series about the band, *The Beatles: Get Back* (its extensive footage filmed in 1969), George Harrison grumbled that while The Beatles couldn't get an eight-track recorder sent to them by EMI, Benjamin Britten would have no such problem.

Supporters of Britten's contemporaries today might feel similarly irked by his consistent exposure. Yet there would hardly be so much Britten performed if – basically – there was not so much of it, and if his catalogue did not comprise so much engaging, often brilliantly written music spread across many genres. Even his relatively small orchestral output includes one of his most popular works, *The Young Person's Guide to the Orchestra*, in which he created a dazzling showpiece from a fundamentally didactic starting point. (It is currently one of his most-streamed works on Spotify, with over six million plays at the time of writing.) The muscular, jagged-edged Cello Symphony inhabits a more adventurous harmonic universe; yet the *Variations on a Theme of Frank Bridge* is so charming it is a perfect 'gateway' for those who think they don't 'get' Britten.

Further up the accessibility scale are the pieces Britten composed for children, which also feature prominently in the list of Britten's music used in film and television soundtracks. Wes Anderson's *Moonrise Kingdom*, released in 2012, is set in 1965 and centres around a school production of *Noye's Fludde* ('Noah's Flood'), Britten's 1958 opera for children and adults. Anderson's portrayal of the opera (in which he himself performed as a child, *see opposite*) is glowingly affectionate, as is his use of other children's pieces by Britten, including a magnificent montage set to the *The Young Person's Guide*.

Turning to a more broadly historical context, Britten is becoming increasingly noteworthy as a figure in LGBTQ+ history. His relationship of nearly 40 years with Peter Pears, mostly conducted at a time when homosexuality was illegal, intrigues those visiting The Red House, particularly younger visitors who often react with amazement to the couple's 'criminal' status for much of their lives together. While Britten was hardly an activist in this regard – he said nothing on the record in relation to the 1967 Sexual

Offences Act, for example – his status as one half of a prominent, historical gay couple has resonated strongly with subsequent generations. Several of his compositions written for Pears are held up as examples of overt gay eroticism, such as the *Seven Sonnets of Michelangelo*, or Canticle I: 'My Beloved is mine and I am his'. *Les illuminations*, a setting of the flamboyant poetry of Rimbaud – the rambunctious teenage lover of Verlaine – was completed during the early days of Britten and Pears's romance, and contains a number entitled 'Being Beauteous' dedicated to Pears.

At the same time, Britten was – in later life at least – an Establishment creature. His 1962 arrangement of the British National Anthem is frequently performed at the Proms, and he had a warm relationship with both the late Queen and the Queen Mother. Given all this, and as Britten's music is now reasonably popular for a classical composer, is he approaching 'national treasure' status? Perhaps not quite. In some quarters there lingers an uneasiness about certain aspects of his life, notably his apparent attraction towards adolescents. This has been written about at some length by John Bridcut in his book *Britten's Children* which, overall, found that while Britten wrestled with his attractions, he did not act on them.

Nonetheless, the subject matter of his operas *The Turn of the Screw* and *Death in Venice* – both of which concern the idealisation, or the potential abuse, of boys – has become more unsettling over

Britten in the Movies

Director Wes Anderson recalls how he turned to Britten's works in his film *Moonrise Kingdom*

Wes Anderson *(left)* with furry friend in 1979, dressed as members of the animal kingdom in a production of Britten's *Noye's Fludde*; Wes could hardly have known then that the otter would become *auteur*

I first learned about Benjamin Britten as a child in Texas when I played an otter in his children's opera *Noye's Fludde*. My older brother was an elk or some kind of animal with antlers, anyway. I loved being a part of that production. Britten wrote it to be performed by church groups with casts of all aged. It's a great concoction for a little company to get together and put on a show. It includes hymns for the audience to join in, too.

I loved the music, and it always stuck in my mind. When I decided to use Britten for my film *Moonrise Kingdom*, I bought all the Britten recordings on the London label (which also, by the way, have wonderful cover photographs). In the movie, our 12-year-old heroine, Suzy (who later runs away with Sam) is a raven. Britten and *Noye's Fludde* became a major part of the story. While I was writing the script, I also thought of another Britten piece: *The Young Person's Guide to the Orchestra*.

I knew Leonard Bernstein's presentation of it in his Young People's Concerts, which are narrated by a little boy. At the beginning of the film, Suzy's little brothers are listening to a record of it. We also included Bernstein's own voice, some of his original spoken introductions, and the 'Playful Pizzicato' from the *Simple Symphony*, too.

I found other Britten pieces I wanted to use, including the overture from his opera *A Midsummer Night's Dream* and some songs (including 'Cuckoo' and 'Old Abram Brown') from the collection for schoolchildren called *Friday Afternoons*.

I don't know if I would know how to direct an opera, but I'd like to try it. Britten's *Billy Budd* might be the one. Early this year I saw Ralph Fiennes's production of Tchaikovsky's *Eugene Onegin* in Paris, which was dazzling. I was also thrilled to sit in on a number of rehearsals to see Ralph work with the cast. I would say that definitely lit a spark!

> **"** Finding one's place in society as a composer is not a straightforward job. It is not helped by the attitude towards the composer in some societies. My own, for instance … has for years treated the musician as a curiosity to be barely tolerated. At a tennis party in my youth I was asked what I was going to do when I grew up. 'I am going to be a composer,' I said. 'Yes, but what else?' was the answer. The average Briton thought, and still thinks, of the Arts as suspect and expensive luxuries.

Benjamin Britten in his address on receiving the first Aspen Award in Aspen, Colorado (1964), designed to honour 'the individual anywhere in the world judged to have made the greatest contribution to the advancement of the humanities'

time and is often reframed in modern productions. The character of *Death in Venice*'s Tadzio for example, intended to be in his teens, is now usually portrayed by dancers in their twenties. *The Turn of the Screw* is more commonly told as a psychodrama on the part of the Governess, rather than a supernatural molestation of the boy Miles. Increasingly, little if any potential anxiety seems to affect Britten's programmability on the operatic stage, even in these highly sensitive times. The sometimes disquieting quality of Britten's music has also been effectively deployed in the recent BBC TV adaptation of *Lord of the Flies*: excerpts of the Four Sea Interludes from *Peter Grimes* underscore scenes of the boys discovering their new environment; while a slightly sinister rendition of the *Missa brevis* appears to foretell the later brutal divisions between them.

Britten's survival in the contemporary world of classical music as well as his occasional cut-throughs to non-classical environments, and his increasing standing as an eminent gay figure, make a strong case for him remaining a significant, even 'great' person. Yet his music still largely exists in the increasingly fragile world of classical music, which has its own vulnerabilities – lack of funding, perennial charges of elitism, disappearing presence in the school curriculum – and inhabits a listening environment Britten would hardly have recognised, and probably have disapproved of. However, we would be unwise to write off the next generation of classical music enthusiasts, or their ever-evolving listening habits. A recent TikTok trend among Gen Z contributors finds them using classical music to study to, or to play poker to – they are even irresistibly drawn to get up and groove to Vivaldi's *The Four Seasons*, or twerk to Offenbach. Britten's music does not (yet) appear in these videos. But while *Detectorists*' Lance 'nearly got Benjamin Britten' back in 2014, there are signs that more and more people *are* getting him now, and in a number of ways. At the time of writing, his music is drawing some 800,000 monthly streams on Spotify. And against any claims that 'Britten doesn't sell' comes the counter-claim, in a 2019 review of *Death in Venice* by Mark Pullinger: 'Just try and get tickets.' ●

Lucy Walker is a musicologist and public speaker. She has written and spoken frequently about Britten, and is Public Engagement Associate for Britten Pears Arts throughout 2026.

Cello Symphony
TUESDAY 28 JULY

Simple Symphony
SUNDAY 23 AUGUST

Violin Concerto
FRIDAY 4 SEPTEMBER

Les illuminations; Variations on a Theme of Frank Bridge
SUNDAY 6 SEPTEMBER

The Young Person's Guide to the Orchestra
SUNDAY 6 SEPTEMBER

Discover...

GABRIELA ORTIZ'S
Revolución diamantina

GABRIELA ORTIZ reveals the feminist ideas and collective ambitions that underpin her triple-Grammy-winning 'ballet for eight voices and orchestra'

Revolución diamantina ('Glitter Revolution') is named after a feminist protest movement that began in Mexico in 2019. During street demonstrations pink glitter was thrown at Mexico City's Chief of Police – a denunciation of the lack of reprisals following the alleged rape of a teenage girl by local officers. Using this – along with two other recent events in South and Central America – as a starting point, I asked the writer Cristina Rivera Garza to devise a ballet narrative that addressed different forms of violence against women. The result explores, across six acts, various scenarios and ideas related to feminism. These include sexual harassment, street protests, the confusion between the language of romantic love and practices of manipulation and control, and the conviction that only by walking together will we be able to find a way out.

It was up to me to imagine the music. This I did not only by using aesthetic languages already known to me but by taking risks, learning and experimenting with new tools. My orchestral writing is conceived as a ritual in motion. One of the main challenges was translating events that originated in the street into the concert hall, avoiding literal or illustrative gestures and instead moving towards a more abstract, emotional and profound musical language. As the ballet explores different forms of violence against women, so the music moves between tension and vulnerability, raw collective energy and fragile intimacy.

Ultimately, however, *Revolución diamantina* attempts to convey in music the idea that a way forward can only be found collectively – that responsibility and transformation belong to all of us. My hope is that audiences experience it not as a distant narrative, but as an invitation to listen, reflect and feel together.

Following an intense and deeply collaborative process, the work was premiered in 2023 by the Los Angeles Philharmonic under Gustavo Dudamel. The support and friendship of Gustavo have been profoundly meaningful to me, both artistically and personally. After many years of collaboration, he understands my aesthetic language with remarkable depth, which creates a rare level of trust and musical clarity. I was extremely moved when, last year, the work received three Grammy Awards. Beyond the personal impact, I believe it sets an important precedent for Latin American – and particularly Mexican – music, affirming that contemporary works from our region can resonate globally. It also reinforces the idea that music of our time can engage fully with urgent social issues, with artistic commitment and depth, without falling into stereotypes. In that sense, the response did not change my view of the work, but it strengthened my conviction about the path it represents. ●

Gabriela Ortiz Revolución diamantina
WEDNESDAY 12 AUGUST

ROYAL BALLET & OPERA

On Stage

In Cinemas

Stream on demand

Images, top to bottom: ©2016 ROH. Photographed by Sim Canetty-Clarke; ©2019 ROH. Photographed by Tristram Kenton; ©2018 ROH. Photographed by Bill Cooper.

Find out more at RBO.ORG.UK

For people, not profit
Making world-class ballet and opera for everyone

Supported using public funding by ARTS COUNCIL ENGLAND

FROM THE AZURE COAST TO THE GOLDEN SIERRAS

CAROL A. HESS draws out the essence of Spain as stamped into the country's music, reliving its picture-postcard heyday, its exotic allure to the French and the impact of its political upheavals

What does the term 'Spanish music' mean to lovers of classical music? Two British critics writing between the wars believed they had the answer. Constant Lambert in 1934 dismissed Spanish scores as 'glorified and tasteful picture-postcards of the come-to-sunny-Spain order'. Cecil Gray was even more direct. Bluntly comparing Manuel de Falla, Isaac Albéniz and Enrique Granados to Russia's composers, he concluded that 'Spanish national music has so far produced no Borodin or Mussorgsky, but only three Rimsky-Korsakovs – which is three too many.' Evidently musical tourism and mimicry were responsible for Spanish music's supposed defects.

Of course, the truth is far more complicated – and the music is far more compelling than anything Lambert and Gray would have us believe. For one thing, we can leave aside any notion of 'sunny Spain': just ask residents of Burgos, where below-freezing winter nights are not uncommon, or Cantabria, with its fogs and mist. The appealing travel commercial that has taken hold in the international musical imagination applies largely to Andalusia, the hub of flamenco. This gut-wrenching style of guitar-accompanied vocal music features the so-called Andalusian scale, with its initial half-step and prominent augmented second. Musical *andalucismo*, recognisable worldwide as 'Spanish' despite its regional origins, has inspired many Spanish composers along with their counterparts in France and Russia.

As for mimicry, that was precisely the issue Spanish composers themselves grappled with throughout the 20th century. It arose in 1898, with the Spanish-American War, when the remains of the mighty Spanish empire collapsed within a matter of weeks. This ignominious defeat was felt keenly throughout Spanish society – not for nothing did Spaniards refer to its impact as 'El desastre'. The war stirred intense debate. Why had the country lost its moorings? What moral or psychological or policy failure had prompted 'disaster'? One contingent believed that Spain was too isolated, too indifferent to the fruits of the Enlightenment that other European nations had long embraced. Another insisted that those very influences had corrupted 'the Spanish soul', or what we might nowadays call 'identity'. This conflict, often politicised, played out in any number of arenas over the 20th century, including in music.

As composers in greater Europe debated a plethora of aesthetic approaches (–isms), Spanish composers tested a variety of strategies. Those who looked beyond Spain might be charged with mimicry. When Enrique Granados's opera *María del Carmen* premiered in the final weeks of 1898, he was accused of trying to sound like Wagner. Another proponent of Wagner's leitmotifs (the technique of allotting specific themes to represent individual characters or ideas), chromatic harmony and formal fluidity was the Catalan composer Felipe Pedrell, whose vast opera *Los Pirineos* ('The Pyrenees', 1890–1) was only marginally successful. Other composers rejected foreign influences, dedicating themselves to *zarzuela* or Spanish-language operetta. Most *zarzuela*s are set in Spain and incorporate local customs and character types, with scores rooted in easily digested tonal harmony that nonetheless express Spanish identity through occasional excursions into *andalucismo* or folk dances from other regions of Spain. *Zarzuela* appealed to audiences uninterested in the grandiosity of Wagner while standing as a bulwark against sweeping modernisation.

This was the landscape the young composer-pianist Manuel de Falla confronted when he arrived in Madrid in the mid-1890s to make his career. Obliged to support his family, he experimented with *zarzuela*. None of his efforts in the genre yielded financial or aesthetic reward. (Our one 'souvenir' of this period is the single number Falla reworked almost 20 years later as the mincing, foppish Dance of the Corregidor in the ballet *El sombrero de tres picos* ('The Three-Cornered Hat'). Meanwhile, as the 20th century dawned, Falla began his opera *La vida breve* ('Life is Short'), which combines Wagnerian harmonies, *andalucismo* and other influences.

What most appealed to Falla was the music of France, not that well known

◀ *Sagunto*, one of the vibrant landscapes by Polish-French painter Moïse Kisling (1891–1953), produced in the ancient Spanish town near Valencia where he went to convalesce after being wounded at the Battle of the Somme

Édouard Manet's *Lola de Valence* (1862), one of the French Impressionist's many Spanish subjects, reflecting the appetite for Spanishry in French art and music of the late 19th and early 20th centuries

in turn-of-the-century Spain. In 1907 he took the bold step of performing his own piano transcription of the solo harp part from Claude Debussy's *Danse sacrée et danse profane*, and months later he moved to Paris. There he formed part of a 'Spanish colony', which included Albéniz, Joaquín Turina and the pianist Ricardo Viñes. Compositions such as *Trois mélodies* and *Noches en los jardines de España* ('Nights in the Gardens of Spain') show the extent to which Falla absorbed French Impressionism while integrating it with his own voice. He would have been happy to remain permanently in Paris but the outbreak of the First World War, in 1914, forced him to return to home and family.

Spain remained neutral during the war. Cultural life was energised, however, thanks to the sudden presence in Madrid and Barcelona of international artists and musicians unable to find bookings in war-torn Europe. Among them were the impresario Sergey Diaghilev with his celebrated troupe the Ballets Russes, and the composers Igor Stravinsky, Vincent d'Indy and Florent Schmitt. French music now gained an enthusiastic following. Even the Spanish-themed works of Debussy and Ravel won kudos in the musical press. Another visitor to neutral Spain was the Polish pianist Artur Rubinstein, who so enjoyed Falla's flamenco-inflected theatre work *El amor brujo* ('Love, the Magician') that he arranged one of its numbers, the Ritual Fire Dance, for piano solo. It became Rubinstein's most popular encore and was later arranged for various jazz and pop combinations, besides figuring in Hollywood films. Rubinstein also commissioned from Falla the *Fantasia baetica*, a large-scale piano work, rich in flamenco influences. ('Baetica' was the Roman descriptor for Andalusia.)

With all these outsiders in Spain, the question of foreign influence arose, just as it had at the turn of the century. While it was all well and good for French composers to 'sound French', Spanish composers adapted foreign styles at no small risk. The question remained: what is Spanish musical identity? When Falla's *El amor brujo* was given its premiere, one critic considered it a 'vigorous expression' of Spanish identity whereas another carped, 'clearly, it is impossible to write Spanish music while thinking of Debussy and Ravel'. Even more vehement attacks greeted Falla's *The Three-Cornered Hat*, the fruit of one of Diaghilev's wartime visits to Spain. With sets and costumes by Picasso and choreography by Leonid Massine complementing Falla's humorous score, the ballet was wildly applauded as the quintessence of Spanish character in London (1919) and Paris (1920). Not so with the Madrid premiere, in 1921. Controversy broke down along political lines: critics writing for left-wing papers defended the ballet as a true expression of 'the Spanish soul' whereas critics employed by the papers on the right condemned it as 'futuristic claptrap' and 'a chapter out of the Black Legend' (referring to the notion of the Spanish as a cruel and intolerant people).

Modernists in Spanish musical circles won out, however. Again, they looked toward greater Europe, where neo-Classicism was taking hold in the 1920s. Led by Stravinsky with his 1920 ballet *Pulcinella*, this movement enabled composers to be both modern and traditional: they incorporated bold new harmonies and arresting timbres into 18th-century formats (counterpoint, sonata, theme-and-variation form). Neo-Classicism was premised on ideals of 'purity' and 'universalism' rather than expressions of national or regional identity.

Falla's own brand of neo-Classicism was different. Instead of turning to 18th-century models from greater Europe, he drew on Spanish Renaissance and medieval musical forms. In enhancing these with the dissonant harmonies of modernism, he marked a suggestive new path while subtly asserting Spanish identity. Two of Falla's neo-Classical works, *El retablo de Maese Pedro* ('Master Peter's Puppet Show'), based on an episode from Cervantes's *Don Quixote*, and his Harpsichord Concerto, served as models for younger composers including, to an extent, Joaquín Rodrigo. At the same time, the Catalan composer Roberto Gerhard embraced serialism, the method of using the 12 semitones of the Western scale in a predetermined sequence, devised by the Austrian composer Arnold Schoenberg.

In 1936 the Spanish Civil War broke out. Its effects on music ran deep. As earlier, Falla was an object of both praise and attack, having initially supported the liberal government Franco overthrew but later, as a devout Catholic, half-heartedly backing the Church-allied Franco regime. In 1939, when the war ended, Rodrigo completed his *Concierto de Aranjuez* for guitar and orchestra, with its flamenco-inflected cadenza and mournful cor anglais solo in its second movement. With a 'picture-postcard' title evoking the palace of two Spanish kings, the work conjured up a safely distant past and a common heritage. Many took it up as emblematic of the new *franquista* (Francoist) Spain.

In contrast to its traditionalist social policies, the Franco government promoted avant-garde music. Thanks to Franco's cosiness with the Axis, Spain was a pariah state when the Second World War ended. But as America came to consider Franco an ally in the crusade against communism, cultural diplomacy channels gradually opened and the regime began sponsoring the sort of music favoured in the West: abstract, objective and anti-folkloric, all in contrast to the 'music of the people' favoured by the Soviet Union.

Several regime-funded festivals championed the avant-garde in Spain. At one such event, in 1964, a Spanish critic rejoiced that his compatriots had 'overcome' 'folkloric formulas' and 'picturesque curiosities'. In 1968, Spanish avant-garde music took centre stage at a festival in Washington DC. Titles such as *Objetos sonoros* ('Sonorous Objects') and *Geometrías* ('Geometries') eliminated any hint of the 'come-to-sunny-Spain order' that Constant Lambert had decried decades earlier.

Much the same way, extended techniques (woodwind players breathing through their mouthpieces or string players bowing behind the bridge) in these works prompted one critic to observe that 'avant-garde music sounds very much the same whether it originates in Madrid, Los Angeles, Cologne or Buenos Aires'.

Spanish composers in the past half-century or so have enjoyed great aesthetic freedom. One finds aleatory (chance) techniques and microtonality, Surrealist approaches comparable to those of the painter Salvador Dalí and even allusions back to flamenco. By contrast, the 'picture-postcard' offered by 20th-century Spanish music was a particular mix of identity-consciousness, political power and – the most important element of all – sheer artistry. ●

Carol A. Hess is a Distinguished Professor of Music at the University of California, Davis. She has received numerous awards for her research on music and politics in the Spanish- and Portuguese-speaking world. Her most recent book, *Manuel de Falla's 'El amor brujo'*, was published last year (OUP).

Rodrigo, arr. K. Bolton Concierto de Aranjuez – Adagio
SUNDAY 19 JULY

Ravel Alborada del gracioso; Boléro
Falla, orch. F. Coll Fantasia baetica
Rodrigo Concierto de Aranjuez
Falla The Three-Cornered Hat – Suites Nos. 1 & 2
SUNDAY 19 JULY

Miles Davis Sketches of Spain – excerpts
THURSDAY 20 AUGUST

Early Music Comes of Age

In recent decades, performances of Baroque and Classical music on period instruments have proved revelatory. **NICHOLAS KENYON** highlights a number of ensembles at the Proms pushing that musical exploration into the 19th and 20th centuries and unearthing a new haul of forgotten sounds

Early Music Comes of Age

In the beginning, early music was *very* early music. David Munrow thrilled audiences with his Early Music Consort in the medieval repertoire, and then the focus shifted forward in time to the Baroque: landmarks such as Handel's *Messiah* at the Proms in 1979 under Christopher Hogwood established period-instrument performance in the popular mind. Then, as players' skills became more sophisticated and the thirst of the record companies became intense, first Mozart, then Beethoven symphonies arrived. Soon the music of the 19th century beckoned. Experiments with Brahms symphonies, Wagner overtures and even Verdi's *Requiem* followed.

A generation later, experiment continues, but the mood has changed radically from the early years of the revival: there is a freer attitude now to the idea of trying to replicate the past. We cannot recreate history but, as the conductors of the large-scale masterpieces in this Proms season agree, there is so much to be learnt from the instruments and sonorities of the time.

Instrument technology was moving on by leaps and bounds at the start of the 19th century: larger concert halls, the need for greater chromatic flexibility in wind and brass instruments and the sheer imagination of composers propelled music forward. Carl Maria von Weber in his final opera *Oberon* of 1825–6 imagined a whole range of new sounds. The opening horn notes of the overture, and then the distinctive textures of the oboe, bassoon and clarinet, are all individually created, reflecting the development of the instruments. And as conductor Sir Mark Elder explains, this creates a tendency away from the homogeneous blend we later came to expect from orchestras: 'The flute is more fluty, the bassoon more bassoony!' That gives every item in the opera its own special character: 'It's like moving from room to room in a house, turning the lights on and finding a whole new sound in every space.' Every dramatic situation is freshly imagined – Weber's biographer John Warrack singles out high clarinet and bassoon framed by horn, and the swirling flutes and clarinets as Oberon appears in his boat drawn by swans.

> **The flute is more fluty, the bassoon more bassoony! It's like moving from room to room in a house, turning the lights on and finding a whole new sound in every space.**

As Elder notes, 'With an original-instrument orchestra, you can make all this come up really fresh and surprising and never, ever heavy and thick. Everybody has to be athletic, mercurial and full of verve. Weber's music has such natural brilliance, a sense of occasion, and thrives on the contrast which you need in the theatre. You have to be able to immediately change the atmosphere.'

The composer who formulated much of the new approach to instrumentation was Hector Berlioz: his famous treatise of 1843 praises Weber's originality and mentions the remarkable use in the overture to *Oberon* of high cellos sounding *above* low clarinets. Other commentators have registered Weber's vivid imagination: Donald Tovey was swept away by the symbolism of Oberon's horn, which is 'capable of real poetic power … its immense remoteness is that of our own inmost soul'. Berlioz himself expanded the scope of the Romantic orchestra from the *Symphonie fantastique* of 1830 onwards, and in his 'dramatic legend' *The Damnation of Faust* of 1845–6 a thrilling range of orchestral effects is brought to bear on the infernal story, with copious wind, brass (including an ophicleide, part of the tuba family), harps and percussion, added to which there's a chorus in seven parts, and a children's choir: Berlioz never stinted on his resources.

Jakob Lehmann, who makes his Proms debut this summer with the period instruments of Les Siècles, has recently been working with the Orchestre Révolutionnaire et Romantique (which Elder conducts in *Oberon*) on a major Rossini project. Turning to Berlioz is a welcome challenge for him. As he emphasises: 'A master orchestrator like Berlioz uses all the colours and textures of the orchestra to maximum effect. To perform on exactly the instruments he had in mind and knew, and employing playing

◀ A 19th-century performance of a Bach Passion; the composer's bust may appear on stage but he would have imagined radically different forces and instruments

Front cover by Georges Fraipont (1873–1912) for the score of Berlioz's 'dramatic legend' *The Damnation of Faust*, whose scintillating original orchestral colours are restored at the Proms by Les Siècles in a rare performance of the work on period instruments

techniques that were in use in the 19th century, is not only incredibly instructive but heightens the expressivity and impact of the music.' Lehmann is very alert to the differences of sound that Berlioz extracts: 'The lush colours of the French wind instruments, the transparency and lucidity of the gut strings and the earthy, dark, almost animalistic sounds of the brass give this multifaceted work an almost 3D-like intensity.'

The transformation of the orchestra in the first half of the 19th century was rapid, and strongly influenced composers from Wagner onwards. The use of period-style resources helps to open up textures that have been criticised in the past: Schumann's orchestration has often borne the brunt of superficial criticism. But as Sir Simon Rattle, who with typical adventurousness is bringing the Freiburg Baroque Orchestra to the Proms for an all-Schumann programme, points out, there is another perspective here: 'It's easy to forget that Schumann, among his multifarious talents, was also deeply knowledgeable about early music: he also passed this passion on to Brahms. Although he is the arch-Romantic composer/poet, his music benefits from its performers knowing how deeply rooted it is in the music of much earlier centuries.'

In this sense the early music revival comes full circle: both Schumann and Brahms looked back as well as forward (Brahms revived music going back more than 200 years to Gabrieli and Schütz in his choral concerts), and just as today's performers are looking back to the past, so did the composers of earlier times. Here Rattle has an asset in players steeped in music of the Baroque and before. 'The speaking warmth and clarity of the Freiburg Baroque Orchestra, their ability to change mood and texture instantaneously, should be a wonderful match with Schumann's quicksilver, febrile, almost impatient music. I look forward to it enormously!'

Now, the early music approach marches even into the 20th century: one of the most thorough current explorations of period practice is that of the Mahler Academy Orchestra, which brings Mahler's Ninth Symphony to the Proms. In its *Originalklang* ('Original Sound') project the orchestra has been exploring this masterpiece with conductor Philipp von Steinaecker. As he explains, 'Mahler was for 10 years the director of the Vienna Court Opera and he renewed all the wind, brass and percussion instruments in that time. We wanted to create their sound, so we looked for these instruments in auctions, on eBay, in attics, wherever. We bought them (some were very cheap, some were very expensive!), we restored them and we learnt to play them.' The Academy works on playing style with British scholar Clive Brown; half of them are young players who audition and half are experienced players from around Europe's great orchestras 'who want to come together to rediscover this music'. As Steinaecker puts it: 'They are wonderfully open … they agree to do the project because they're cool and they're game, and they want to try something new.'

CCI/Bridgeman Images

With all this thirst for taking an early music approach into the 19th and now the 20th century, what has become of the historical performance movement's enthusiasm for the Baroque? It has surely grown and deepened, and has become much less tied to the notion of faithfulness to an imagined past. A masterpiece like Bach's Mass in B minor, which Jonathan Cohen and Arcangelo perform at the Proms, can take endlessly varied forms depending on the circumstances of the performance and the space in which it is given. Gone are the days when modern Baroque trumpets were played, as one commentator put it, 'with a sense of impending apoplexy'. And receding into the background are the purist arguments which have swirled round Bach performance for decades now as to whether Bach expected his ensembles to consist of one voice to a part. Now, directors make their own choices in accordance with a continual interplay between information and instinct.

Cohen reflects that, 'In the Royal Albert Hall there are other considerations and challenges: we will double oboes and flutes in the 19th-century manner to adapt to the space for our performance.' But Cohen feels that so much works there: 'The transparency of the gut strings blends with the voices in the chorus, the bassoon which is lighter in sound keeps the bass line buoyant. And the trumpets sound lyrical and beautifully balanced with the orchestra.'

The flexibility with which musicians, whether or not on period instruments, can now converse with the music of the past is well demonstrated in this Proms season. In the Swedish Chamber Orchestra's concert with Martin Fröst as clarinettist and conductor, Baroque hits by Rameau, Handel and Bach are woven together into a continuous sequence with specially composed transitions for clarinet and orchestra by Hans Ek. And in a bold reworking of three of Vivaldi's *The Four Seasons* for the National Open Youth Orchestra, combining acoustic and electronic instruments, we will hear the response across 300 years of a new generation of young musicians to this endlessly reinterpreted masterpiece.

> To perform on exactly the instruments Berlioz had in mind is not only incredibly instructive: it also heightens the expressivity and impact of the music.

When the revival of early music started in our time, it was as a challenge and sometimes a reproach to the staid character of too much conventional music-making. It shook up our musical organisations, and for a while there was a dramatic stand-off between old and new, period- and modern-style performance. But with the rapid interaction of directors, conductors and players between the different worlds, the early music principles became increasingly integrated into mainstream practice. Now we have a dizzying diversity of approaches; nothing could more vividly demonstrate the inexhaustibly changing creative dialogue between past and present on which the most exciting music-making depends. ●

Nicholas Kenyon was Director of the BBC Proms (1996–2007) and Managing Director of the Barbican (2007–21). He is now Chief Opera Critic of *The Telegraph* and a Distinguished Affiliate Scholar of Pembroke College, Cambridge.

Weber Oberon
Orchestre Révolutionnaire et Romantique/ Sir Mark Elder
THURSDAY 6 AUGUST

Vivaldi, arr. R. Davies The Four Seasons – excerpts
National Open Youth Orchestra/Alice Farnham
SUNDAY 9 AUGUST • BRISTOL

Works by Rameau, Handel and Bach
Swedish Chamber Orchestra/Martin Fröst
SUNDAY 16 AUGUST

Berlioz The Damnation of Faust
Les Siècles/Jakob Lehmann
SUNDAY 30 AUGUST

Schumann Genoveva – overture; Violin Concerto; Symphony No. 2
Freiburg Baroque Orchestra/Sir Simon Rattle
MONDAY 7 SEPTEMBER

Bach Mass in B minor
Arcangelo/Jonathan Cohen
THURSDAY 10 SEPTEMBER

Mahler Symphony No. 9
Mahler Academy Orchestra/Philipp von Steinaecker
FRIDAY 11 SEPTEMBER

See also Jupiter Ensemble (21 July) and Orchestra of the Age of Enlightenment (9 August)

Discover...

DMITRY SHOSTAKOVICH'S
Symphony No. 11

MARINA FROLOVA-WALKER outlines the events of the 'Bloody Sunday' massacre of 1905, the Soviet-approved historical backdrop to a rousing cinematic symphony

Shostakovich tells us that '1905' is the subject of his 11th Symphony – specifically, the wave of strikes, protests and uprisings in Russia that we call the '1905 Revolution'. The music is like a film score without the film. The first movement gives us the deserted streets of St Petersburg early on a winter's morning, the stillness broken only by distant trumpet calls. Faint timpani strokes create an atmosphere of foreboding. The second movement's title reveals that the day is 9 January, when workers marched in columns towards St Petersburg's Winter Palace to present demands for better conditions. Some of Tsar Nicholas II's troops joined the march, but others charged, sabres drawn, leaving several hundred protesters dead. In the music, a surge of discontent rises in a huge moan and descends into nothing, and the snare drum leads to the music of the massacre.

A requiem follows, the slow tread of plucked strings accompanies phrases from a song heard at the funerals of many of the victims. At the centre of this movement there is a desperate orchestral cry of pain and indignation. Shostakovich had previously written a chorus on 1905, and here he quotes the music he wrote for the line 'Bare your heads!' appears. The stormy finale hovers between outrage and hope, ending with the deafening strike of the tocsin (an alarm bell) – a call to action. The symphony seems a good fit for Soviet art that commemorated revolutionary events and it was written shortly after the 50th anniversary of the 1905 Revolution. Only the emphasis given to slow and mournful moods seems a little out of keeping.

We can also interpret Shostakovich's 11th Symphony as a kind of scrapbook of the composer's early childhood. He was born only a year after the Revolution, but his life was deeply marked by the events. His own father was a survivor of the march. The symphony is full of revolutionary songs of the time, which its first audience would have recognised. So the symphony allowed Shostakovich to look back to his father's stories, and to the music he heard in those years. Among his earliest compositions was a funeral march for victims of the upheavals of 1917, so this too is part of the work's backdrop.

But there is a hidden side to the symphony. From his secret diaries, we now know of Shostakovich's private distress at the crushing of the 1956 Hungarian uprising by Soviet tank regiments. The Soviet regime, although it saw 1905 as its revolutionary heritage, had behaved much like the St Petersburg troops. We have not lived through these events as Shostakovich did, but this extraordinary score helps us see them through his eyes. ●

Marina Frolova-Walker is Professor of Music History at the University of Cambridge and Fellow of Clare College, Cambridge. She is the author of *Russian Music and Nationalism from Glinka to Stalin* (Yale UP, 2007) and *Stalin's Music Prize: Soviet Culture and Politics* (Yale UP, 2016).

Shostakovich Symphony No. 11
MONDAY 3 AUGUST

Richard Strauss: poet, philosopher, prankster

As the Proms presents a series of works by the great German composer, including his 'opera-within-an-opera' *Ariadne auf Naxos* and the bloodstained climax to his biblical 'music drama' *Salome*, **STEPHEN JOHNSON** uncovers the mischievous spirit that lies just beneath the music

There was always an element of Till Eulenspiegel about Richard Strauss. The German folk hero (his surname literally means 'owl-mirror') is one of the great gleeful subversives of world literature, and Strauss revels in depicting his adventures in the vivid orchestral tone-poem *Till Eulenspiegel's Merry Pranks* (1894–5): his hero mocking the pious, tripping up the self-important, always eluding the law – until slow-footed justice eventually catches up with him.

However controversial or scandalous his work, Strauss seemed to delight in the fuss he caused. Goading on timorous horn-players in a rehearsal for his youthful breakthrough masterpiece *Don Juan* (1888–9), he told them to imagine they were young men eagerly anticipating their wedding nights: 'Then you'll know how to play it!' *Don Juan's* tumultuous escapades, lovingly embodied in music, horrified the conservatives – including Strauss's own father, Franz, a brilliant horn-player who had created Siegfried's horn calls in Wagner's *Ring* cycle, while leaving the arch-modernist composer in no doubt that he detested his 'anti-music'. But the self-styled progressives weren't happy with Strauss (Jr) either. Wagner's widow, Cosima, despised *Don Juan* for its refusal to embrace her late husband's high seriousness. Strauss's Juan, she rightly suspected, was really another Till.

◀ Nadja Michael in the title-role of *Salome*, cradling the severed head of John the Baptist at the gory climax of Strauss's controversial third opera

Far from grumbling under the weight of such criticism, Strauss knew that all publicity was good publicity. The controversy surrounding his 1903–5 opera *Salome* was the kind of which composers today can barely dream. Here was a stunningly over-the-top depiction of perverse eroticism – *female* perverse eroticism! – based on a play by one Oscar Wilde, recently imprisoned for acts unmentionable in decent company. The whole thing stank of Freudianism and, worst of all, its composer seemed to have taken a demonic glee in unleashing it on the world. It was, of course, a huge success. Within two years *Salome* had been performed in opera houses around the world. Audiences and critics threw up their hands in horror – and fought for tickets. '*Salome* has done you a lot of damage,' Kaiser Wilhelm II informed Strauss. 'So much damage,' he replied, 'that with the proceeds I've been able to build my villa at Garmisch.'

Even when Strauss was a very young man, the prankster within was champing at the bit. His First Horn Concerto (1882–3) may superficially defer to Franz Strauss's Brahmsian neo-Classical values, but its exuberant solo writing bounces very close to the cheeky horn motif that would launch *Till Eulenspiegel* years later. Soon Strauss (to the horror of Franz) would be embracing the storytelling, scene-painting *élan* of progressives such as Liszt and Wagner in dazzling tone-poems, but – as we've seen – with an element of ironic mockery that seems almost designed to fend off potential modernist allies. So *Don Juan's* successor, *Death and Transfiguration* (1888–9), attempts nothing less than to depict the experience of struggling with death, dying, then passing joyously into the great beyond. It succeeds stunningly, but that's surely in part because, unlike some of Strauss's mystically inclined colleagues, there's a feeling that it doesn't take itself entirely seriously. Of course it's manipulative, but Strauss knows it is. And that, bizarre though it may seem, is part of the pleasure: 'Yes, I'm playing with you,' he seems to say. 'Enjoy it!' Then, after *Till*, comes his 1896 rendering of Friedrich Nietzsche's controversial 'philosophical poem' *Also sprach Zarathustra* ('Thus Spake Zarathustra'), his opening depiction of humanity's 'Dawn of Consciousness' so stupendous that Stanley Kubrick took it for his film *2001: A Space Odyssey*.

Nietzsche's *Zarathustra* famously introduces the idea of the self-overcoming spiritual colossus, the 'Superman'; but the German philosopher was something of a prankster himself – a self-proclaimed 'smasher of idols' – and in this personage Strauss seems to have found a kind of ally. The Superman is heralded stunningly in that famous opening, his spiritual victory then celebrated in a sublime, deliciously schmaltzy waltz; but *Zarathustra's* ending is weirdly ambiguous, as though Strauss had picked out Nietzsche's half-concealed doubts and decided to leave them centre-stage. Significantly, his next tone-poem, *Don Quixote* (1897), is about a tragi-comically deluded would-be Superman. By now Nietzsche himself, like Quixote, had succumbed to insanity. So much for exalted ideals? The prankster has his serious side, after all. Strauss

Strauss caricatured by the Austrian artist Carl Josef Pollak (1877–1937); the caption – 'Der Neurosenkavalier', or The Neurotic Knight – puns on the title of Strauss's opera *Der Rosenkavalier* ('The Knight of the Rose')

may have enjoyed goading purists with his detailed pictorialism in the opulently scored *An Alpine Symphony*, with its wind machine and cowbells. But by 1915, when the score was finished, he knew where Europe was heading and he dreaded it. The image of the mountains is held up as a counterbalance to chaos and destruction, a reminder that some things are timeless and unchanging.

But Strauss can't take himself seriously for long. The opera *Ariadne auf Naxos* ('Ariadne on Naxos', 1911–12) ought to have pleased the modernists with its teasing opera-within-an-opera structure and the way it makes even backstage business and intrigue part of the onstage experience. Yet the final love scene is pure old-fashioned operatic indulgence: the eternal operatic verities hold sway, as they had in that magnificent celebration of Old-World values *Der Rosenkavalier* ('The Knight of the Rose', 1909–10).

There was a time however when, mirroring Till's fate, Nemesis nearly caught up with Strauss. Though privately critical of the Nazis, he was briefly engaged by Joseph Goebbels as head of Hitler's *Reichsmusikkammer* agency. Dismissed when the truth of his opinions came out, he spent most of the war years in a kind of confused half-exile. Strauss turned to Mozart for comfort, as an image of something beyond what Nietzsche called 'all-too-human' violence and stupidity. A rare display of unfiltered, unironic rage flashed out in 1945's *Metamorphosen*, for 23 solo strings – rage at what the 'vandal … criminal' Nazis had done to German culture (rather than to anyone else's, but a legitimate grievance if one takes the longer historical view).

But then came a final masterpiece, the *Four Last Songs* (1948), a sumptuous, tender re-engagement with the Romanticism of his youth and a rare expression in music of love between two old people – Strauss's long marriage to soprano Pauline de Ahna may have had its storms but she was definitely, as he told Mahler, 'what I need'. The new generation of modernists inveighed against it – it was regressive, sentimental, hopelessly bound up with the fatally compromised Old World. Yet, as with *Der Rosenkavalier*, its aggressively forward-looking critics are largely forgotten today, while it endures, popular as ever. Till Eulenspiegel smiles, wryly, one last time. ●

Stephen Johnson is the author of books on Bruckner, Wagner, Mahler and Shostakovich, and a regular contributor to *BBC Music Magazine*. A former presenter of BBC Radio 3's *Discovering Music*, he now works both as a freelance writer and as a composer.

Also sprach Zarathustra
TUESDAY 21 JULY

Death and Transfiguration
THURSDAY 23 JULY

An Alpine Symphony
MONDAY 27 JULY

Ariadne auf Naxos
WEDNESDAY 19 AUGUST

Der Rosenkavalier – suite; Salome – final scene; Ein Heldenleben
WEDNESDAY 26 AUGUST

Four Last Songs
WEDNESDAY 9 SEPTEMBER

Northern Powerhouse

The Black Dyke Band has transcended the demise of its industrial roots in Yorkshire's textile heartland to forge an enviable position on the international stage. **PAUL HINDMARSH** leafs through its history, discovering that where there's pluck, there's brass

The internationally renowned Black Dyke Band belongs to a proud tradition of amateur music-making that sprang from the communities, factories and mines which underpinned so much of this country's wealth and influence in the 19th century. In 1855 John Foster, who built his textile mill high on the hills in the West Yorkshire village of Queensbury, was one of many factory owners to establish a brass band. From his benevolent stewardship evolved what is arguably the most influential brass band on the planet.

Brass bands in England reached a peak – in numbers and reach, if not cultural influence – in the 1920s. However, the past 40 years has seen a seismic shift in the banding culture of this country. The notion of brass bands as 'the working men's orchestra' vanished as the factories and mines that supported so many bands closed in the 1980s and 1990s. By necessity, brass bands had to transform or die. Some disappeared but many survived through the dedication and commitment of their membership. Now run as an independent trust, the Black Dyke Band (formerly Black Dyke Mills Band) has been in the vanguard of transformation within this great British amateur musical tradition, breaking down outdated gender barriers, taking full advantage of new connections with emerging brass band programmes in music colleges and universities across the North, and using the musical experience within the band to open up new pathways for young, aspiring brass players and composers. Twenty years ago the band's Music Director, Nicholas Childs, set up the Yorkshire Youth Band for players aged 11–21, nurturing the next generation of talented players.

◄ Sharp outfit: the Black Dyke Band on the Royal Albert Hall stage at last year's National Brass Band Championships, where it took second place

Cra.g Chapman

> **Over time the Black Dyke Band's unrivalled success in national and international competitions has been a model for others to aspire to, both at home and abroad.**

The band's home since 1885 – now a well-appointed rehearsal and heritage centre – remains at the heart of the town of Queensbury (halfway between Halifax and Bradford), directly facing John Foster's imposing old mill building, which is now a small business centre. Where once most of the players were employed at the mill and lived locally, Black Dyke, like the country's other elite brass bands, now draws its players from a wide catchment area. Being a part of Black Dyke and proudly wearing the iconic black and gold uniform is more than a hobby: it's a life-defining choice.

The recent appointment of a new Principal Cornet is a prime example. This position in the Black Dyke Band is the hottest of hot seats in the banding world, occupied by some of the greatest orchestral trumpeters, such as Maurice Murphy (1935–2010) – whose brilliant high register lives on in the soaring trumpet lines of the *Star Wars* theme by John Williams – as well as legendary cornet players such as the much-recorded Phillip McCann. For the past 20 years the 'end chair' has been graced by Richard Marshall, hailed as one of the greatest cornet players of his generation. Richard stepped down in January to be replaced by another superstar, fellow Yorkshireman and a former student of his at Manchester's Royal Northern College of Music, Tom Hutchinson. Previously Principal Cornet of another great band (and friendly rival), the Cory Band from the Rhondda Valley, South Wales, Tom describes returning to his roots and to Black Dyke as a 'once-in-a-lifetime opportunity'.

Over time the Black Dyke Band's unrivalled success in national and international competitions has been a model for others to aspire to, both at home and abroad. However, if Nicholas Childs describes competitions as 'the sport of banding', concerts, he says, are the 'life-blood'. Generating a wider appreciation of the excellence of brass band music and performance through concerts and recordings has been his guiding principle, building on the band's rich heritage.

The history of the band is punctuated by notable firsts – Black Dyke was the first brass band to appear at the BBC Proms, in 1974 (alongside another famous name, the Grimethorpe Colliery Band), and the first UK brass band to give a concert at Carnegie Hall, New York. Over half a century on, it returns this summer to the Proms for its sixth appearance. And the band is no stranger to the Royal Albert Hall, vying alongside fellow groups in the National Brass Band Championships, which takes place at the Hall each October.

In the 1970s and 1980s the unique warmth and generosity of the 'Black Dyke sound' was a major factor in the export of the British brass band internationally and, whether it's playing to full venues in New York, Tokyo or Birmingham, in the more intimate space of the Royal Northern College of Music for its annual International Festival of Brass, or in the local Victoria Hall in Queensbury, the Black Dyke brand of brass classics, stylish arrangements and new writing never fails to impress. The band's roster of commissions and premieres since the turn of the century – over 100 works and counting – reads like a *Who's Who* of leading composers for the medium, among them multiple Emmy- and Academy Award-winner Bruce Broughton, Sir James MacMillan and professors Peter Graham, Edward Gregson and Philip Wilby. The Black Dyke Band tradition lives proudly on, transformed for the 21st century. •

A former senior producer for BBC Radio 3, Paul Hindmarsh is a freelance journalist, editor and artistic consultant, researching and writing especially on British and band music. In 2005 he received the Iles Medal from the Worshipful Company of Musicians in recognition of his work in the brass band field.

Black Dyke Band
SATURDAY 19 JULY

'Act justly, fear nothing'

Siobhan Edwards, Solo Tenor Horn, offers an insight into life in the Black Dyke Band

Life in the Black Dyke Band is demanding, exhilarating, occasionally exhausting – but utterly addictive. Being part of this band is not simply about performing concerts; it is about belonging to a living tradition, one that respects its heritage while constantly looking forward.

I've been a member of Black Dyke for 10 years now, and in that time I have grown not only as a player but as a person. The band has shaped my musicianship, broadened my horizons and, quite literally, changed my life – as it is also where I met my husband.

Rehearsals are where the band's collective commitment is most keenly felt. There is an unspoken understanding in the room: everyone arrives prepared, focused and ready to give their best. The high standard is constantly inspiring. Under the direction of Nicholas Childs, rehearsals are meticulous and purposeful. Whether it's the music or the deportment, everything is practised with meaning, and every individual's contribution matters.

This approach reflects the band's long-standing motto, *Justum perficito nihil timeto* – 'Act justly, fear nothing'. It's a philosophy that underpins everything we do: striving to do the right thing musically and performing with confidence, courage and conviction on every stage.

A particularly exciting recent development has been our new partnership with an instrument-maker. This gives players the chance to be directly involved in the development of their own instruments, working closely with the makers to refine response, colour and projection.

For most of us, Black Dyke is a passion pursued alongside full-time jobs, yet the long hours of rehearsals, performances, travel and preparation are willingly embraced – we simply wouldn't have it any other way.

Performing is where everything comes together. Walking on stage with Black Dyke brings a unique mix of responsibility and excitement. Over the years the band has performed on some of the world's most iconic stages, from the Sydney Opera House to Carnegie Hall, from the Tokyo Metropolitan Theatre to KKL Lucerne, and even the Glastonbury Pyramid Stage. Wherever we play, there is a deep pride in representing the band.

Yet life in the band extends far beyond rehearsals and performances. The camaraderie within Black Dyke is extraordinary. We spend countless hours together – travelling, rehearsing, sharing meals, conversations and laughter. Even when we have a weekend off from rehearsals or concerts, we're probably still meeting up for some social time together. Over time, colleagues become friends, and friends become something closer to family.

To play in Black Dyke is to carry responsibility – to the music, to our audiences and to those who have worn the same uniform before us. That sense of continuity, paired with a willingness to evolve, is what makes life in the band so special.

Hallé orchestra

Kahchun Wong, Principal Conductor and Artistic Advisor

'Concerts like this one renew one's faith in the ability of British orchestras to flourish, startle and exhilarate.'
The Times

New Manchester season on sale Thu 21 May at halle.co.uk

SIEMENS · GMCA Greater Manchester Combined Authority · MANCHESTER CITY COUNCIL · ARTS COUNCIL ENGLAND

Opera with Opera News — Since 1950—bringing the world's finest performances to life!

'The Monkey King' in San Francisco
Marie Jacquot—top-seeded conductor
Storytelling through lighting design
Hokusai as opera: 'The Great Wave'
Florence Price takes to the stage

Save 50% with code OPERAPR26
Visit opera.escosubs.co.uk or opera.co.uk for more details.

The Purcell School for young musicians
Patron: HM The King

THE FUTURE OF MUSIC BEGINS HERE

TRAINING YOUNG INTERNATIONAL ARTISTS THROUGH:
- CONSERVATOIRE EXCELLENCE
- ELITE INDUSTRY PATHWAYS
- THE WORLD'S GREAT STAGES

APPLICATIONS NOW OPEN FOR 2026 & 2027 ENTRY

Recipient of the UNESCO Mozart Gold Medal

Hands That Do Magic

The rise of the virtuoso in the 19th century saw technical achievements seemingly beyond the limits of body and mind, and the invention of the musician as cult personality. **FLORA WILLSON** delves into a phenomenon that has long been easy to admire but hard to fathom

In July 1837, less than a month after her accession to the throne, the 18-year-old Queen Victoria had a remarkable musical experience. Sigismond Thalberg – 'the most famous pianist in the world', the young queen marvelled in her journal – performed after dinner at Buckingham Palace. 'Never did I hear anything at all like him!' Victoria gushed. 'He combines the most exquisite, delicate and touching feeling with the most wonderful and powerful execution! He is unique and I am quite in ecstasies and raptures with him.'

Thalberg's impact wasn't only driven by what his audiences heard. As the queen explained, 'I sat quite near the piano and it is quite extraordinary to watch his hands, which are large, but fine and graceful.' This was music-making that doubled as visual spectacle. When Thalberg's rival Henri Herz (a pianist nicknamed 'the Semiquaver King' for his flashy fingerwork) played in London three years earlier, he insisted on his instrument being positioned at the very edge of the stage, so the audience could see the keyboard. No trickery here, Herz seemed to brag as he moved, whirlwind-like, around the piano – just technical prowess verging on the superhuman.

In an era of increasingly extravagant musical virtuosity, this was no exaggeration: the ambition of outstripping the human body's conventional limits

◀ Dexterity to dazzle: *The Lute Player* (1917–18) by María Blanchard (1881–1932)

Bridgeman Images

was widespread. Commentators regularly observed that the most celebrated pianists appeared to have three hands or even four. Composer and pianist Robert Schumann – no stranger to virtuosity, though emphatically against its execution for its own sake – sarcastically imagined a future when a new breed of musicians might be born 'with one finger too many on each hand' as an adaptation to the taste for fiendishly difficult passages. And both treatises and orthopaedic contraptions dedicated to 'hand cultivation' promised pianistic hands that would appear 'boneless', 'dissociated' or even 'dead' – subject to physical control from the wrist alone.

No wonder pianists were central to this so-called golden age of the virtuoso. By the 1830s, piano technology had developed radically from the weak-framed fortepianos of the late 18th century. The new, high-tech instruments manufactured by companies such as Érard and Broadwood allowed bigger dynamic contrasts, faster and more precise articulation and more powerful tone to become the norm – even if celebrated pianists still frequently damaged instruments with their heavyweight gymnastics. The same period saw the rise of the solo piano recital, a virtuoso-vehicle closely associated with the Hungarian pianist and composer Franz Liszt, who once supposedly declared 'le concert, c'est moi'. That personal charisma – plus feats such as dispatching the piano reduction of an entire violin concerto while holding a burning cigar, or playing Beethoven's 'Emperor' Piano Concerto without the index finger of his left hand, which he had cut shortly before the concert – inspired Europe-wide 'Lisztomania'. Female audience members were especially afflicted (swooning was a typical symptom). But a male diplomat who attended a recital in Berlin in 1841 reported afterwards that Liszt 'had control of my pulse, and his playing accelerated so much that I became giddy'.

Perhaps the most notorious early 19th-century virtuoso, however, was not a pianist. Nicolò Paganini was a violinist – though his solo performances left many convinced they had also heard a guitarist, thanks to his invention of left-hand pizzicato. (This technique of plucking the strings with the right hand is conventionally an alternative to bowing – Paganini's left-hand version allowed him to bow and pluck simultaneously.) Unlike the piano, the violin was much the same instrument that it had been for a century or more. That familiarity made Paganini's blistering virtuosity all the more shocking. His Paris debut in 1831 left the eminent critic Castil-Blaze casting around for superlatives, describing the performance as 'the most unique, the most extraordinary, the most incredible, the most unexpected that one can imagine'.

So apparently impossible were his technical feats that Paganini was regularly described as a 'magician' or a 'wizard'. But a darker reputation developed, too: rumours circulated that the violinist had been imprisoned for murdering a lover

'Private Practice, or A Solo at Home' (London, 1827), a satirical caricature of Nicolò Paganini – known as 'the Devil's Violinist' – at the height of his London fame

and had used his time behind bars to finesse his technique; or that he had made a pact with the Devil in exchange for his mind-boggling facility. Imaginations ran wild. German music critic Ludwig Rellstab was typical in concluding after one of Paganini's performances: 'There is something demonic about him.'

Such responses say as much about a Europe-wide fascination with the occult at the height of Romanticism as they do about Paganini's violin technique, of course. By the time Paganini died in 1840 tastes were changing and a new critique of musical virtuosity was gathering force. Its tenets were already clear in an obituary for the violinist – penned by none other than Liszt – which urged future musicians to avoid Paganini's 'conceited and egotistical role' and instead 'be the means of virtuosity, and not its end'.

So much for 'le concert, c'est moi'. The fact that virtuoso performers such as Paganini (and Liszt himself) had inspired a cult-following was increasingly diagnosed as the symptom of a musical culture with its priorities all wrong. Romanticism didn't just result in a brief fashion for all things supernatural (including, apparently, Paganini's violin technique): it also produced a lasting new philosophy of music. This new way of thinking prioritised musical works – at their best now understood to be timeless, universal and profound – over individual performers or performances.

In this context, the pursuit of virtuosity risked overshadowing the true value of a composition. As *The Musical World* thundered in 1858, 'It would be a lamentable catastrophe were music to become the exclusive property of a tribe of quasi acrobats … "Virtuosity" is not essentially musical.' It wasn't just the fantasias and technical showpieces with which Paganini, Thalberg and company had entranced their audiences that now came under fire. Even instrumental concertos became suspect for some as the anti-virtuoso faction gathered strength. In 1904, a group lobbied for their exclusion from Paris concerts; in 1918, the American music writer J. N. Burk argued in *The Musical Quarterly* that concertos had had their day, with only 'one or two from Beethoven, Schumann or Brahms' worth saving.

Despite all this, however, virtuosity continued to be valued – and necessary. The opening night of the second ever Proms season, in 1896, included Paganini's Violin Concerto. *The Sunday Times* was left unimpressed by a distinctly un-virtuosic performance: 'If not precisely overweighted by its technical difficulties, [the soloist] failed to overcome them without considerable faultiness of intonation.'

This is where the virtuosity debate finally enters our own musical world. Scattered through the column inches dedicated to musical performance over the past century and more are innumerable comments about musicians' technical powers (or their inadequacy) in relation to the music being performed. After all, virtuosity in the sense of 'exceptional technical skill' – the *Oxford English Dictionary*'s modern definition – is now a baseline requirement for performing whole swathes of the classical repertoire composed since the second half of the 19th century. It is no coincidence that the same period has seen the development and expansion of high-level formal technical training in musical performance at conservatoires all over the world. Or that the establishment and growth of the recording industry has generated a discography of classical studio releases which have normalised a degree of technical 'perfection' that would have been unthinkable during virtuosity's early 19th-century golden age.

The old complaints that a performer's technical wizardry is mechanical, or superficial, or that their fireworks are 'getting in the way of the music' still circulate today. Sometimes, no doubt, with justification. But if you've been lucky enough to attend a live performance in which a pianist's fingers have blurred across the keyboard, in which a violinist seemed to be dancing outside the laws of physics, or in which any musician appeared to merge with their instrument to become a conduit for pure, high-voltage emotion – then you'll also have known the 'ecstasies and raptures' described by the young Queen Victoria: the unique thrill of being swept up and carried along by someone else's extraordinary musical powers. •

Flora Willson is a writer, broadcaster and cultural historian of music. She is one of *The Guardian*'s classical music critics and is a regular contributor to broadcasts on BBC Radio 3.

A View from the Pitch

Former England goalkeeper David James draws the lines between elite performance on the field and onstage

A Proms concert at the Royal Albert Hall is like a football match at Wembley Stadium – they're two of the greatest venues – and at both you'll have a mix in the audience. Some are there for the music or for the team, regardless of anything else; and others, like me in football, might go to see certain individuals. Either way, everyone will come away with their own moments to remember.

There's a thrill in watching people who are at the very top of their game. They have spent thousands of hours gaining their expertise and, though they're doing something others have done before them, they're doing it at such a high level, and also in their individual style. I'm always interested to see how they react in the moment. The technique has to be there – if you let in a goal during a match, you know that you'll be in the highlights reel! – but you have to *feel* it too.

Look at two pianists like Krystian Zimerman and Yuja Wang: they're both brilliant players but they have their own different approaches to the music and the way they use their bodies. They're like Alisson Becker and Gianluigi Donnarumma: two of Europe's greatest goalies, but with different personalities on the pitch.

I'm really envious when I see great musicians on stage. When I was young my grandmother got me playing violin, then double bass, then cello – but I know I couldn't even play a few notes to the standard the great performers can. You know that the soloists you hear at the Proms – and the orchestral players too – are in the premier league.

Preparation is key in both sport and music. There are some games where the goalie doesn't see much action, but you still have to practise for any eventuality. Say if you're playing Arsenal – they're good at set pieces and corners, so you might want to prepare for that. I might imagine Declan Rice going to knock a corner in, so I go through different versions of that in my head. It saves me going out on the field and asking someone to pretend to be Declan Rice for half an hour! A Proms artist might imagine playing in the space of the Royal Albert Hall or feeling the crowd around them or working out if they could cope with a distracting noise in the auditorium. It's to do with external pressures: you might have just had a row, got married, had a baby, but you've still got to perform. Also, you have to find a way of giving your best regardless of how much buzz there is: a friendly match is different to playing in the World Cup, and playing in a small hall is different to playing at the Proms.

Perfection is a funny thing. If you strive for it unrealistically then you can put too much pressure on yourself. What you do is try to be consistently excellent. Playing for England, I'd take a flight, get to the hotel, train on the pitch, play the game and go straight home. Musicians are doing that all the time too. You can't spend the day sightseeing and then rock up to the gig jet-lagged. If you're excellent, very few people know you're not perfect, but if you're average everyone knows, and they're not interested in seeing you again.

Musical Afterlives

EMILY MACGREGOR considers how composers have plumbed the depths to conceive visions of the Beyond, and to express in sound the condition of our souls once the body has departed

Where do we go when we die? Do we go someplace else – Heaven, with a bit of luck, although composers have had a lot of fun with Hell – or do we co-exist with the living, conjured by their memories?

Western classical composers have long exploited the ineffable qualities of music to explore the afterlife, and not only because of its ability emotionally to turn the knife. Alongside sound, one of music's defining components is time – the stuff our mortal bodies are bound by. Just as sound's ephemeral nature gestures to our annoying physical limitations, music plays with our expectations and encourages us to make predictions. In short, just like the afterlife, music is all about what comes next.

And what comes next – at least in the Catholic faith shared by many of the best-known classical composers – is the soul's onward journey from the Last Judgement to (fingers crossed) its ascent to Heaven, a story told in music by the Requiem Mass (also known as the Mass for the Dead). In the 16th century, the set of texts making up the liturgy of the Mass for the Dead was standardised. This offered a tempting proposition for composers, giving rise to many of the classical *Requiem*s regularly heard in concerts today, such as those by Mozart

◀ The path to purification: the Elders, dressed in white and crowned with lilies, on their journey to Paradise; illustration by Gustave Doré (1832–83) for Canto 29 of *Purgatorio* from Dante's *The Divine Comedy*

(1791), Verdi (completed 1874) and Fauré (completed 1893). But, like the *memento mori* in visual art (the decaying apple, the skeleton in the corner of a painting), the Requiem Mass doesn't sugarcoat the truth. It's there to remind you of the certainty of your own death, and the scariness and magnitude of the journey awaiting you. Typical of the genre's emotional range, Mozart's *Requiem*, for instance (which, adding to the aura of legends around it, lay famously incomplete at his death – did he predict his imminent demise?), pinwheels through angst, longing, guilt, fear and hope. Will you be saved or cast down?

> ❝ Western classical composers have long exploited the ineffable qualities of music to explore the afterlife, and not only because of its ability emotionally to turn the knife. ❞

Terrifying though that might sound, Requiems weren't primarily intended for the living – at least, not until the mid-19th century. The clue is in the name: Mass *for the Dead.* Since it was commonly believed that the actions of the living *after* a person's death, like performing a Mass, could affect how the dead would be assessed come Judgement Day, Requiems lobbied for the dear-departed's place in Heaven. For the same reason, the rich left large donations to the Church, specifying that Masses be held regularly in their names. Mozart's *Requiem* is written from the perspective of the soul awaiting Judgement, although it's interspersed with more 'objective' passages depicting what, according to scripture, the dead person will face along the journey, as well as moments where the presence of the divine judge can be perceived in the music.

There's clearly enormous theatrical potential in the form, perhaps never exploited more finely than by Berlioz in his *Grande messe des morts*. 'Extravagant' doesn't come close to describing it. A commission to commemorate soldiers who died in France's 1830 Revolution, it's perhaps the monumental, overpowering sound-world *par excellence* – cower, mere mortals! It calls for a truly vast orchestra (including 18 double basses and eight pairs of timpani), a choir of 210, and – in the first edition, as a treat for fans of the lesser-spotted euphonium-like instrument – Berlioz uses four ophicleides. That's apart from no fewer than four offstage brass choirs for the 'Tuba mirum' (the moment the trumpet call signalling the Last Judgement raises the souls of the dead). Three, clearly, would not suffice. 'If space permits, the chorus may be doubled or tripled and the orchestra proportionately increased,' Berlioz wrote, quite obviously pushing his luck. Complicit in this Gothic spectacle, the writer Alfred de Vigny painted the other-worldly scene of the first performance in true Romantic (with a capital 'R') fashion, 'The church looked beautiful; at the far end, beneath the dome, three long sunbeams fell … and made the chandeliers shine with an unusual light.'

Edward Watson as Dante and Sarah Lamb as Beatrice in the Royal Ballet's premiere production of Thomas Adès's triptych *Dante*, based on *The Divine Comedy*

Things start to shift towards the latter half of the 19th century. Brahms's *A German Requiem* (1865–8), for instance, is not for the souls of the dead, but instead for – and about – the journey of the bereaved. The watchword here is consolation. The altered focus reflected a change in values in the era of Nietzsche and Darwin towards the experience and value of the individual on Earth, alongside a diminishing faith in religious truths as a principle for organising modern life. *A German Requiem* might be considered the first humanist *Requiem* – the word 'German' here equating to something like 'everyman' and referring to the Bible in Luther's German translation, suggesting it's a *Requiem* for everyone. As such it paves the way for those such as Benjamin Britten's 20th-century *War Requiem* (1961–2), which interleaves the Latin Mass for the Dead with poems by the English writer Wilfred Owen. A work such as Mahler's *Kindertotenlieder* (1901–4), the heart-rending setting of Friedrich Rückert's poetry about the death of his children, similarly trades in consolation. It's harrowing to the point that it has made critics pause before accepting a commission to review it.

Not all souls are saved, of course, and there's lots to be scared of in the afterlife. Even more so if you are foolish enough to make a pact with the Devil, as learnt most famously by a certain Herr Doktor Faust. The tale of the scholar who sells his soul to Mephistopheles in exchange for knowledge, Faust's legend has proved irresistible, spawning operas, songs and symphonies from Schumann, Schubert, Gounod, Wagner and Liszt, among others. And then there's Berlioz: ever attracted to dark and excessive theatrics in *The Damnation of Faust* (1845–6), he tells the tale as a 'dramatic legend', a hybrid beast blending oratorio, opera, song and symphony, with four soloists, seven-part chorus, generously sized orchestra and children's choir. Liszt wrote both *A Faust Symphony* (1856) and a set of diabolical waltzes. His raucous *Mephisto Waltz* No. 1 invites us to dance with Faust to the tune of the Devil, animating a rural wedding with a frenzied violinist leading the party – the opening notes paint the intervals of the instrument's open strings. Indeed, such was the hypnotically fiendish virtuosity of Liszt's playing that he, like the violinist Paganini, were half-seriously suspected of satanic pacts themselves. It's hard to shake the notion that talent comes at a price.

Speaking of damnation, it would be remiss not to mention another major cultural touchstone: Dante Alighieri's epic 14th-century poem *The Divine Comedy*, in which a protagonist bearing more than a passing resemblance to Dante himself goes on a journey guided by Virgil through Hell and Purgatory before arriving in Heaven. Liszt saw particular musical potential in the poem, which gave rise first to his 'Dante' Sonata for solo piano (1849), then to his iconic fire-and-brimstone *'Dante' Symphony* (1855–6). In the symphony, Liszt only set *Inferno* and *Purgatorio*, reasoning, after pressure from Wagner, that Paradise was beyond earthly musical imagining. It was an inspired move on the part of Thomas Adès, therefore, in his wildly inventive recent three-part ballet *Dante* (after *The Divine Comedy*), to shapeshift between Liszt's music and his own in its first part, *Inferno*. Liszt is thus metaphorically recast as another Virgil-esque guide through the Underworld: a pleasing bit of music-historical recursiveness. The ballet was first staged complete in 2021, by choreographer Wayne McGregor and the Royal Ballet.

> **Taking us deep into our pasts, music tugs like nothing else at our memories and brings back people we've lost.**

Music can also sometimes evoke, or even grant, a less literal sort of afterlife. Taking us deep into our pasts, music tugs like nothing else at our memories and brings back people we've lost. Nadia Boulanger wrote about this phenomenon, grieving the early death at 24 of her sister, Lili, the first woman to win the coveted Prix de Rome composition prize in 1913, with – incidentally – a take on Faust. Lili's final compositions, especially her *Pie Jesu* (1918), which she dictated to Nadia, but also the meditative *Vieille prière bouddhique* ('Old Buddhist Prayer'; 1914–17), showed an incredible sense of acceptance and hope in the face of her illness. For Nadia – strongly influenced by her Catholic faith as well as by the contemporary obsession with seances that sought to communicate with the dead – a person's music was inextricably linked to their soul.

A lot has happened to funeral music since the days of Mozart's or even Brahms's *Requiem*, and today, at least at secular funerals, the music chosen tends to convey a sense of the personality and essence of the person who's died. Scholars have argued that this is a function of our society's individualism, heading off the existential fear of oblivion. Perhaps. But we can't deny how music draws a strange connection between emotion, memory and our love for those we've lost and the part of ourselves we have lost alongside them. A funeral director told me that the point in a service at which music plays is the moment that people break down in tears. Music can be an unmediated connection to the person who's died. It seems that when we talk about music – even in a modern, secular funeral tradition – we're not too far, once again, from Boulanger's belief that a person's music is connected to their soul.

What did it for me after my father died suddenly was the music I associated with him – the guitar pieces he used to play, such as Isaac Albéniz's *Sevilla* or Heitor Villa-Lobos's Prelude No. 1 in E minor; and the music he loved, such as Miles Davis and John Coltrane. It was the same music that my family reached for when we chose what to play at his funeral. The music that takes me to a place of deep grief isn't the canonical shared experience of a devastating work like *Kindertotenlieder* but instead the cool riffs of Davis's *Kind of Blue*. It's the music that comes closest to bringing my father back, tracing his outline. But it's never enough.

Musical afterlives aren't just about what comes next – they're also about living with loss and about how those who have died live on alongside us. Whenever I can bear it, I put on some Miles Davis and remember my dad. This will be a good year at the Proms for that. And I won't be missing out on all the outrageous Berlioz, either. •

Emily MacGregor is a writer, academic and broadcaster who appears regularly on BBC Radio 3's *Record Review*. She is the author of *While the Music Lasts*, which explores her changed relationship with music following the death of her father, a jazz and classical guitarist.

Boulanger Vieille prière bouddhique
Szymanowski Stabat mater
R. Strauss Death and Transfiguration
Messiaen L'Ascension
THURSDAY 23 JULY

Rossini Stabat mater
FRIDAY 7 AUGUST

Liszt Mephisto Waltz No. 1
Thomas Adès Dante – Part 2: Purgatorio
Berlioz Symphonie fantastique
SATURDAY 8 AUGUST

Thomas Adès Dante – Part 1: Inferno
TUESDAY 11 AUGUST

Berlioz Requiem (Grande messe des morts)
SATURDAY 15 AUGUST

Berlioz The Damnation of Faust
SUNDAY 30 AUGUST

Bach Mass in B minor
THURSDAY 10 SEPTEMBER

A Composer's Life

Two leading Proms composers – Australian **BRETT DEAN** and Franco-American **BETSY JOLAS** – join in conversation to offer an insight into their working lives, influences and musical personalities

We're all familiar with the horror of facing a blank sheet of paper and trying to fill the void. Often we do this to a deadline. The same goes for composers, who also have the task of producing something of artistic worth – of conceiving never-before-heard reverberations and arranging them in never-before-devised sequences. As architects of sound and harnessers of time, composers can project huge vistas or trace lonely voices; they strive for the chance to alter our mood, our day, even our life.

The world-views captured by living composers at this year's BBC Proms are typically wide in scope – from the flutters, rumbles and calls of forest life in Kristine Tjørgersen's *Between Trees* to the buzzing of bees in Dobrinka Tabakova's *Orpheus' Comet*; and from the medieval pilgrimage of Joby Talbot's *Path of Miracles* to the 'grand mystery' of the universe revealed in Édith Canat de Chizy's percussion concerto *Skyline*.

In his new work for the Proms, Brett Dean draws on the dark, witty poems of Carol Ann Duffy's *The World's Wife*, revisiting key women from across time; and Betsy Jolas, like her compatriot Debussy before her, was inspired in *Tales of the Summer Sea* by the symbolism and sensory experience of the waters. In the conversation that follows, they outline the musical influences that shaped them, the performers that inspire them and the artistic principles that drive them.

The creative space

BRETT DEAN: My wife and I have moved out into the country in Wiltshire and I have a nice big room and it's quite spacious. If I'm at home I'll sketch out ideas at the keyboard – or on the viola. That's not to say I haven't sometimes been more efficient when I've been in a much smaller room. But over this past summer I had a very short amount of time to write a string quartet, and that was while on holiday at a beach near Barcelona where I didn't have a keyboard – or a desk, even. And somehow I managed. At this point in my career, I find I can work anywhere if I need to, and I've moved home so many times already that I've had to be flexible. I think the quality of the ideas or the sense of being in an inspired headspace is more important than the room I find myself in.

BETSY JOLAS: For a long time – since I was preparing for studies at the Paris Conservatoire – I've worked in the morning. Now that I'm very old – I'm 99! – I try to have shorter hours: I don't work in the afternoon. In fact, when I wake up, before I get out of bed, I start thinking about the piece I'm working on and trying to find solutions.

For me, I need silence when I work – that's not difficult because I live on my own. And at some point I like to go to the piano and check whether what I heard was OK. But, you know, at the Paris Conservatoire, we had these *mise en loge* exam-preparation periods, where you were confined to a small room with no access to a piano, so that was a useful discipline.

BRETT: I also find early morning walks with our dog can be a useful time. I don't have my sketchbook with me like Beethoven used to, but I do find that getting out into the fresh air is very useful. I also find I can get some useful thinking done in the middle of the night. Almost every night I wake at some point and I quite like being awake for maybe up to an hour because it is so quiet. The silence of the night is a very special time and that's when I might write down some notes or do some thinking.

Musical identity and experiences

BETSY: I was very conscious of what was expected of me as a woman, and especially as, quite frankly, there were many women composers whose music I'm afraid I didn't like at all. It was clear in my mind that either I should be a good composer or I should give up. Very early on I became friends with composers including Pierre Boulez, Iannis Xenakis and Karlheinz Stockhausen. I felt I had to understand how they worked. Sometimes when they tried something new, I'd ask myself, should I try that too? But most times I went somewhere else: I never wanted to imitate anybody.

One of my intentions was to know what I was trying to do. I was never worried about whether I was original or not. I just decided that I was 'Betsy' and if people didn't like my music, that would be too bad. As it happens, it seems to have worked!

BRETT: I totally empathise with that. Of course, sometimes you hear something

Rooms for ruminating: Brett Dean *(above)* and Betsy Jolas at their desks in Wiltshire and Paris

and you think, yes, I should try this as well, but ultimately you have to be true to your own feeling. You have to think what it is that you personally want to say that hasn't already been said.

But unlike you, Betsy, I stumbled into composing almost by accident. I came to it, firstly, through performing, because as a violist I was playing a lot of new music in groups like the Scharoun Ensemble, formed of members of the Berlin Philharmonic, where we would seek out composers and play and commission new works.

I also started improvising with a rock musician friend of mine from Australia. And we began making wacky electronic noises for experimental films. So I was working with film music without really knowing what I was doing but having a lot of fun doing it. And it wasn't until I was quite a few years into that process that I decided to start consciously writing music down. That was an interesting change for me.

BETSY: We are all a product of our own experiences. As a child I studied piano and my mother sang. And very soon I studied the organ: to me the organ was a miracle. I didn't continue playing it for very long but I have written often for it. I was dreaming of Bach's Toccata and Fugue in D minor and said to myself, if you could write anything like that, you would be a real composer! I'm also very familiar with my teacher Olivier Messiaen's organ works.

And I heard orchestral music on our record player, and we were friends with the conductor Désiré-Émile Inghelbrecht – who expected me to be a competent musician. Then, through singing in a choir in New York, I became extremely interested in Renaissance music, especially the works of Orlande de Lassus – and I've arranged a great many works of his for various instruments. I also happen to have a son who is a jazz trumpeter, so that has been an important influence too. Every different type of music that I could hear was extremely enriching for me and that continues today. I keep learning, I keep deciding that I have to be as good as anybody else. That keeps me going.

But like you, Brett, I also fell in love with playing the viola, and through that I fell in love with the music of Berlioz after hearing his 'symphony' for viola and orchestra, *Harold in Italy*. I have since written a number of works for the viola.

brett: Well, although I went to Germany to study viola, I wasn't expecting to spend the next nearly 20 years of my life playing in the viola section of the Berlin Philharmonic. But then, when I got more interested in writing my own music, it was very influenced by this kind of muscular, physical quality of the orchestra's music-making. And I think that has always remained an aspect of the music I want to write for others: it's informed by a performer's view of the world. I often imagine seeing a piece being played and what it looks like in terms of the energy flow of the people that are playing. Also, my wife's a painter, so I've been attuned to how she has found various stimuli. Then, as a cinema-goer, I think film is interesting in the way that it's also a time-limited art form. There are interesting parallels there with how both film directors and composers are expecting people to sit there and put up with how we've decided to curate the next 20 minutes, or two hours, of their lives.

In the hands of the players

BETSY: It's always fascinating when you hear performances of your works. Most of the time it goes better than I expected. I never worry about how the performance will turn out. As the composer, it's my responsibility to get the sounds I want. If I can't do that then I might as well do something else. Also, it's very important for me to know what *didn't* work so that next time I would try to fix it.

BRETT: I share the sentiment of excitement when my music turns into real sounds with real people in a real space. I find first read-throughs and the first rehearsals can be quite tough because, if you don't know the players, you're not sure whether it's your mistake or just the fact that an orchestra is dealing with, in some cases, quite difficult stuff to play. I do share your view that the result is ultimately my responsibility, and I do think that to write music that's simply mind-bogglingly complicated for its own end is not necessarily something I'm into. That said, I do like for musicians to be, in a sense, confronted – but with challenges that they can meet, because then you get the best out of their energy and expertise.

Ludwig van Beethoven

❝ He would walk over hill and dale, sketchbook in hand, never thinking of regular meal-times. Over and over again he would return without his hat … By the middle of August there were thick notebooks full of sketches for the new work.

Anton Schindler, Beethoven's assistant and biographer, recalling the time the composer was working on his Symphony No. 9 in the summer of 1823

Cheryl Frances-Hoad

❝ People think you look at the sky and write notes down, whereas in reality it's hard, frustrating work … When I begin [writing] I panic and usually procrastinate for a week. Once I've got going I'm usually OK, but I need to start well in the morning, otherwise the day goes to pot.

Pyotr Tchaikovsky

❝ When I'm busy no-one, not a single human soul except my servant Alyosha, ever puts in an appearance … I get up at eight, have a bath, drink tea (alone), and then busy myself until breakfast. After breakfast I take a walk, and again work until dinner. After dinner I go for a lengthy stroll, and pass the evening at the big house. There are hardly any guests. In a word, it's very peaceful and quiet here … By virtue of the above, my work is going forward rapidly.

The composer in a letter to his brother Modest while working on his opera *Eugene Onegin* at the estate of a friend in the summer of 1877

Leonard Bernstein

❝ To achieve great things, two things are needed: a plan and not quite enough time.

I do find a great joy in seeing how interpreters – particularly people in whom I have a lot of trust and with whom I've had a long relationship – are able very quickly to get inside your head and work out what you might be wanting. I'm thinking of people like Simon Rattle, who's really championed us both, also Vladimir Jurowski. I've worked with Marin Alsop for quite some years now and she, too, can start to shape things very quickly. The list thankfully goes on of people that I feel can really bring out the best of the piece – and sometimes they understand what it is I'm wanting more clearly than I do myself.

That external perspective can be very helpful, as you can get a bit lost in the fray of so many notes and much else going on. Sometimes it's the case that you perhaps need to cut to the chase a bit more. And it's great when an interpreter, a conductor in particular, who has that overview, can help you get there.

BETSY: I remember when I was writing my Quartet No. 2 [1964] for string trio and soprano that the soprano part was very difficult, and Mady Mesplé did a wonderful job. It can also be the case that nothing is too difficult if you are lucky enough to have a very good musician.

The composer as conductor

BRETT: I find I learn quite a lot about my own pieces by conducting them. It's useful to work out how to get the message across to a larger number of players all at once. I find that a big challenge, but as a result I sometimes see my pieces differently, not only in terms of the mechanics, but also the 'breathing'.

I'd be curious to know, Betsy, have you conducted your own music, and if you have, did it change how you felt about those pieces?

BETSY: I once won a conducting competition but I have rarely conducted my own music.

BRETT: I would have liked to have heard you conduct your music. That would be a very interesting experience, I'm sure.

BETSY: Well, not for me!

BRETT: You're happier listening to others doing it, I understand that: I've now written a third opera and the idea of conducting an opera of mine seems silly. You need to step back and have a bit more objectivity. The sheer challenge of keeping the whole ship afloat would just be too much for me. There are composers who have conducted operas of their own, even large ones – I'm thinking of Thomas Adès, George Benjamin and before them Benjamin Britten – and they've done a magnificent job. I don't know how they do that. I'd get too stuck in the moment, I think.

BETSY: I've written five operas, three of them are chamber operas. I remember conducting the first, *Le pavillon au bord de la rivière*, in Avignon. That was in 1975 and then it went to America. It was quite an experience: I worked with actors who weren't singers by profession, but they learnt as we went along. It turned out to be quite a spectacle.

The future

BETSY: Thinking of what is coming next, I wonder where I am now, even at 99. Am I still writing opera? Is the music still moving? I still need to think about whether my music is going where it should. I remain curious about everything I hear, and there is generally something I want to keep from what I hear. So my ears are open.

BRETT: We can often end up a little glum when we think of the future of classical music. Sure, there are concerns about the position that music holds in our society and the funding of it. But people are still out there doing it. All sorts of creativity is going on, particularly in the area of music theatre, where boundaries between artists are disappearing, and orchestras are becoming more flexible. We may not like the implication of some developments, such as AI, but I think other directions are pointing to a time of great creativity and possibility, including technologically.

BETSY: That's true. I don't worry about that. I say: let's take it as it comes, and let's hope that people will always turn to music. For myself, I know I have to live to the end of my centenary year, as I have pieces on the way! ●

Betsy Jolas Tales of a Summer Sea
TUESDAY 21 JULY

Brett Dean The World's Wife
BBC co-commission: world premiere
WEDNESDAY 29 JULY

A Composer on the Cusp

BBC Young Composer 2023 winner Reese Carly Manglicmot considers her prospects at the start of her career

What is it like being a young composer? I would be dishonest if I said it were an easy path. However, I find an abundance of hope, joy and excitement during this early stage of my career. This would not have come without my involvement in the BBC Young Composer competition.

I entered the competition for the first time in 2021 and was pleasantly surprised to be Highly Commended. This motivated me to apply for a place on a joint degree in Piano Performance and Composition at the Royal Conservatoire of Scotland. There I composed *Rumble*, the solo piano piece I entered into the BBC Young Composer 2023. I was still in the age bracket for Senior entries (ages 17–18) and thought it wouldn't do any harm to enter again. I was not at all expecting a phone call to say I had been chosen as one of the winners.

This was the start of a journey of encounters with incredible tutors, performers and experts from the WWF World Biome Project and UCL's People & Nature Lab. This culminated in the performance and broadcast of my piece *Una voce* by the BBC Concert Orchestra at the Proms in 2024. The learning I gained from this project drove me towards cultivating an artistic voice, and gave me an appetite for writing more orchestral music.

Because of Young Composer, I have become more reflective, pondering upon phenomena and ideas from the world around us. I gained the confidence to experiment with a range of media on larger scales, and explore topics and stimuli which inspire me to compose. This desire to learn and grow has led to some exciting projects since my time on the scheme. I am grateful to have recently won the Walter and Dinah Wolfe Memorial Prize at the conservatoire, which brought a commission to write for the Hebrides Ensemble. I also have plans to write more pieces for myself as a performer, using my experiences as a harpsichordist and collaborative pianist as a starting point. My confidence as an artist has grown, and I have embraced a range of freelance activities, including teaching and playing, as part of a Live Music Now Scotland ensemble.

As I write, I find myself reaching the end of my four-year course at the RCS. When I graduate, I will be navigating a portfolio career involving composing, performing and unexpected in-betweens. I am driven to use the opportunities I have to be an artist for and with others – peers and audiences alike. In any case, in the next stage of my adventure I will need to strike a balance between staying true to my values as an artist and as a person, while being open to new possibilities. Though I don't yet know what opportunities might present themselves, I hope that the way I apply myself as an artist will give back in some way and inspire positive change, however small.

The BBC Young Composer Prom is on 30 August (see page 133). For details of Young Composer Workshops, see page 144. For more information on the competition, search online for 'BBC Young Composer'.

Discover …

EDGAR VARÈSE'S
Amériques

GILLIAN MOORE on a raucous, iconoclastic evocation of New York – complete with sirens and whistles – that is part symphony and part visionary sound-art

In 1915 a French composer in his early thirties arrived as an immigrant in New York City. Edgard Varèse had been medically discharged from the French Army. He'd stored all of his compositions in a Berlin warehouse as the First World War broke out. The warehouse later burnt down and Varèse's life's work up till that point was destroyed.

As he sailed into Manhattan, Varèse saw the first skyscrapers going up. The city rang with the sounds of construction and motor cars, the clatter of the overhead railways, the roar of the subway, the wail of sirens. He said that the last sound he heard as he went to sleep on that first night in New York was the high C sharp of a locomotive whistle.

Stravinsky had already brought the sounds of the industrial 20th century into his 1913 ballet *The Rite of Spring*. That same year, Italian Luigi Russolo had argued in his manifesto *The Art of Noises* that the sounds of aeroplanes and motor cars should be brought into symphony orchestras.

All of this was in Varèse's mind when he wrote his first piece for the New World. *Amériques* ('Americas'; note the plural, suggesting multiple worlds) is a 25-minute symphony for a vast orchestra. And there's plenty of noise in it, with its 10 percussionists, including rattles, bells, two bass drums and a police siren. The clatters, bangs, shrieks, roars and rumbles of New York City are all present and correct.

But in trying to expand the orchestra into the realm of noise, Varèse went far beyond just adding batteries of percussion. He was dreaming about electronic music decades before it was technically possible, calling for the help of 'machinery specialists' to create new instruments. And already in *Amériques* we hear strange new harmonies, masses of sound with richly dissonant overtones: the impression is almost electronic but everything is built up using just strings, winds and brass.

Amériques is full of mystery and awe as well as violence and clamour. Varèse said that the word 'America' suggested 'the unknown, new worlds on this planet, in outer space and in human minds'. For all its noisiness, there is a sense of space – and silence – in *Amériques*. Great orchestral chords or fragments of melodies seem to call out across vast distances; folkloristic dances appear as if called up from the ancient civilisations of the American continents, North and South. Varèse, with his musical past erased, was writing a new kind of music for his new homeland. And, like *The Rite of Spring*, *Amériques* manages to sound simultaneously utterly modern and unfathomably ancient. •

Writer and broadcaster Gillian Moore is the author of *The Rite of Spring: The Music of Modernity* (Apollo, 2019) and co-presenter of *Key Changes: Radio 3's Essential History of Classical Music*. A Board Member of English National Opera, she was appointed CBE in 2022.

Varèse Amériques
SUNDAY 23 AUGUST

◀ Kind of blue: Miles Davis performing at the Newport Jazz Festival in July 1962. Seven years earlier, a performance at the same festival had earned his quintet its first major-label record deal

Miles Ahead

This season the Proms celebrates the centenary of Miles Davis with a concert exploring four of his best-loved albums. **ALYN SHIPTON** traces the great jazz pioneer's musical footsteps, from the cool jazz and hard bop of his breakthrough years to the rock, soul and electronica that he later came to embrace

One of the greatest innovators in jazz, Miles Davis was born on 26 May 1926. His father was a dentist and his grandparents owned land in Arkansas. The family settled in East St Louis on the Illinois side of the Missouri river, and the varied musical life of the greater St Louis area was an excellent place to start a career as a musician. On receiving his first trumpet at the age of 9, Miles studied with Elwood Buchanan, whom his fellow-trumpeter Clark Terry (also from St Louis) regarded as an excellent teacher. The influence of Buchanan and Terry (who was six years older than Davis but befriended him as he developed his playing) led Miles to work on a clear, vibrato-less tone which would become one of his hallmarks.

At 18 he enrolled at New York's Juilliard School, but only stayed there for one year before dropping out. By the time he began the course he had already played with several St Louis bands as well as replacing another trumpeter in the all-star Billy Eckstine big band as it came through his home town. The consequence was a desire to play jazz. In Manhattan he quickly discovered where all the jam sessions happened and where a young instrumentalist could sit in. Many musicians he would later work with were part of the same group of itinerant players, including pianist Thelonious Monk, drummer Kenny Clarke and trombonist J. J. Johnson. But before long Davis was in thrall to the alto saxophonist Charlie Parker, who was recognised as a great innovator. Davis played with Parker before the altoist left for California in late 1945 with trumpeter Dizzy Gillespie. But, significantly, he became a regular recording partner of Parker's in 1947 after his return from the West Coast. This is the first body of work that brought Davis's playing to national attention, and an early piece called *Milestones* comes from one session they recorded together in August that year, for which Miles himself was the leader.

According to Clark Terry, it was Parker who encouraged Miles to use a mute, preferring its effect to his clear, vibrato-less open sound. So much of Davis's later recording career hinges on his muted work that this became another hallmark of his playing. He continued to record with Parker until the end of 1948. By then, however, he had started to lead an experimental nine-piece band at New York's Royal Roost club. This band drew together arrangements by Gil Evans, John Lewis, Johnny Carisi and Gerry Mulligan. When it first broadcast from the club, on 4 September 1948, it was clear that this was unlike any previous jazz ensemble. It had arisen from informal contact between the arrangers (meeting at Evans's apartment) and, as Mulligan told BBC Radio 3, 'Miles was the prime mover. We were thinking of Miles as the lead voice … It's hard to think of other trumpet players having the same effect on the ensemble.' The broadcasts led to a contract with Capitol Records, and the resulting 78rpm records were collected together for an LP under the abiding title: *Birth of the Cool*. Tracks

Davis *(right)* with Gil Evans, the Canadian-born pianist and mastermind behind the big band that recorded three classic Davis albums: *Miles Ahead*, *Sketches of Spain* and *Porgy and Bess*

including *Venus de Milo* and *Boplicity* epitomise the group's ability to set Miles's trumpet and the saxophones of Mulligan and Lee Konitz against rich, polyphonic backdrops, using the timbres of French horn and tuba along with more conventional jazz small-group instruments. Some members of the band, including Lewis and Mulligan, used this as a basis for further musical exploration, but Davis – as he was often to do – moved on to new pastures.

In 1951 Davis signed with Prestige Records in New York, leading a band with Sonny Rollins on tenor saxophone, signalling a move away from the 'cool' nonet towards the 'hard bop' style of the early 1950s. At around this time Davis became addicted to heroin, and it took him until 1954–5 to kick the habit. For some of the intervening years he was neither playing nor practising regularly. Yet, when he did come into the studio, he was still capable of making some fine recordings. A set of 1954 quartets for Prestige with pianist Horace Silver, bassist Percy Heath and drummer Art Blakey stand out, although Horace told me that, as Davis returned to form, his lip was so weak that he limited himself to no more than two takes of just three or four numbers. April the same year saw the creation of a masterpiece as Miles, with trombonist J. J. Johnson and saxophonist Lucky Thompson, made *Walkin'*, also for Prestige. Lasting 13 minutes, it has two great solos from Miles and an extended solo from Lucky. Producer Bob Weinstock told me he waved his stopwatch at Thompson, who ignored him and went on blowing. 'We got one of the greatest tenor solos in history,' Bob reflected, after keeping the tapes rolling.

But it was in the following year that Davis's career truly took off. Following a short imprisonment for failing to pay child maintenance, he was billed at the 1955 Newport Jazz Festival, starring in an ad hoc band of musicians who happened to be available: saxophonists Zoot Sims and Gerry Mulligan, together with Thelonious Monk, Percy Heath and drummer Connie Kay. Their version of Monk's composition *'Round Midnight* was, as Columbia Records producer George Avakian put it, 'spellbinding'. So much so that Avakian signed Miles to this major label forthwith, and set about recording both his quintet with John Coltrane on tenor saxophone plus something that was entirely different from anything Davis had done before: playing as a soloist in a big band, put together by Gil Evans. They created three classic recordings: *Miles Ahead*, *Sketches of Spain* and a jazz version of George Gershwin's opera *Porgy and Bess*.

The end of 1957 saw Miles in Paris. He had been invited to produce a score for Louis Malle's film *Lift to the Scaffold* and decided to assemble a group to improvise to 'rushes' of the film – in other words, creating the music in real time in response to the visual material. He had no more than a few thematic sketches so, effectively, it was a free improvisation project. But with French colleagues René Urtreger (piano), Pierre Michelot (bass) and Barney Wilen (saxophone), plus his old sidekick Kenny Clarke on drums, the results were dramatic.

Back in the USA after a hiatus (during which time Coltrane also quit heroin), Davis led a sextet with Coltrane and altoist Cannonball Adderley, plus pianist Red Garland, bassist Paul Chambers and drummer Philly Joe Jones. Amid more conventional fare, this band explored jazz built on modes (scalar patterns rather than conventional harmonies), and a new piece, *Milestones* (with the same name as his early Parker disc), exemplifies this. Then his personnel changed and Miles went on to record the best-selling jazz album of all time, *Kind of Blue*, in 1959. Adderley, Coltrane and Chambers remained but pianist Bill Evans, then replaced by Wynton Kelly, and drummer Jimmy Cobb were added. Tracks such as *Blue in Green* and *Freddie Freeloader* have become celebrated jazz standards. Adderley left the band soon after this but Davis continued with Coltrane in a quintet, which toured widely through most of 1960. They even recorded together after Coltrane had left to form his own quintet in 1961. In due course Davis recruited what became known as his 'second great quintet' with saxophonist Wayne Shorter, pianist Herbie Hancock, bassist Ron Carter and drummer Tony Williams. This was his staple setting for most of the 1960s, and it gradually moved from playing standard songs to newer pieces that explored different ways of improvising, including remaining on the same harmony while keeping the rhythm going, known as 'time, no changes'. By 1968 this band was also beginning to fuse its jazz playing with ideas drawn from rock, with Ron Carter playing electric bass and Hancock transferring to keyboards, notably on the album *Filles de Kilimanjaro*.

> **Their version of Thelonius Monk's *'Round Midnight* was, as Columbia Records producer George Avakian put it, 'spellbinding'. So much so that Avakian signed Miles to this major label forthwith.**

That band came to an end, and new partners joined Miles in 1969 for his first out-and-out jazz-rock fusion project, *Bitches Brew*. From then on, with producer Teo Macero, Miles tended to assemble different aggregations in the studio from the band with which he toured and played concerts. Albums including *Jack Johnson* and *Live-Evil* had up to a dozen participants but, thanks to *Live in Europe 1969* in Columbia's 'Bootleg' series of releases, we can now also hear the touring band with Davis and Shorter, backed by Chick Corea (keyboards), British-born bassist Dave Holland and drummer Jack DeJohnette, tracking Miles in his final transition from acoustic quintet to all-out fusion.

The early 1970s was a somewhat confused period in Miles's life, not helped by a bad car accident in 1972 that temporarily halted his playing career. Yet albums such as *On the Corner*, with its funk overtones, and *Get Up With It*, which included some very long tracks, came out before he took a complete break from music from 1975 to 1980. Miles's return to playing saw his final albums for Columbia after a 30-year association: *Star People*, *Decoy* and *You're Under Arrest*. All of these showed that his interest in exploring the boundaries between jazz and other forms of music (in this case soul and electronica) were undimmed. From his last period, signed to Warner Bros., his collaborations with multi-instrumentalist and arranger Marcus Miller stand out. *Tutu* (1986) and *Amandla* (1989) both combine traditional playing with contemporary production techniques. Miller was adept at mingling programmed drums and synthesised sounds with multi-tracked instruments, drawing on several different genres of music.

Miles's last significant recording is almost the only retrospective one in his catalogue, playing segments of music from his Gil Evans albums live with Quincy Jones's orchestra at the 1991 Montreux Festival. For the rest of his career, he had always moved on, inexorably, leaving others to explore music he had pioneered. He died on 28 September that year. ●

Alyn Shipton is the presenter of *Jazz Record Requests* on BBC Radio 3, and also a research fellow and lecturer in jazz history at the Royal Academy of Music.

Miles Davis Centenary
THURSDAY 20 AUGUST

Discover …

CARL MARIA VON WEBER'S
Oberon

GEORGE HALL looks forward to the bicentenary revival of a Romantic fairy-tale opera that draws together magical enchantment and heroic adventure

'Through God's grace and help I have this evening had such a complete success as perhaps never before … The overture had to be repeated, and each musical section repeated two or three times and interrupted with the greatest enthusiasm … At the end, a storm of applause – such an honour as England has never before extended to a composer.'

So wrote Carl Maria von Weber to his wife following the premiere on 12 April 1826 at the Theatre Royal, Covent Garden, of his new 'Grand Romantic & Fairy Opera' *Oberon, or the Elf-King's Oath*. It would be his final work: the composer died in London of tuberculosis less than two months later on 5 June at just 39 years of age.

Despite its immense initial success, these days *Oberon* is rarely staged. Covent Garden, its 'home theatre', as it were, last performed it in 1870, and not in English but Italian. The English libretto, by the prolific man of the theatre James Robinson Planché, is usually held responsible for the work's neglect: the score itself, with Weber's extraordinary inventive powers and gift for vivid yet subtle orchestration, has been widely admired. The work can be seen as part of a distinctively English tradition of semi-opera, the best-known examples of which are Purcell's *King Arthur* and *The Fairy Queen*. This Proms performance – conducted by Sir Mark Elder, with the period instruments of the Orchestre Révolutionnaire et Romantique – features a newly commissioned narration that condenses the original dialogue, which was in a style very much of its time.

Audiences at *Oberon*'s premiere in 1826 were treated to a gorgeous visual spectacle in a staging that moved – via transformation scenes and the sheer sonic magic of Weber's music – from the fairy kingdom to Baghdad to Ascalon to a 'desolate' island to the open ocean to Tunis, and finally to Charlemagne's Palace for the finish. We may not see this at the Royal Albert Hall, but a concert performance allows the audience to concentrate on Weber's music, which looks back to Mozart and forward to Mendelssohn, Sullivan and particularly Wagner in its dramatic variety and brilliance.

By the time Weber wrote *Oberon*, he was the internationally acclaimed composer of the darkly supernatural *Der Freischütz* (1817–21) and the equally forward-looking, psychologically intense *Euryanthe* (1822–3). He was at the peak of his powers, and this Proms revival – 200 years after the work's premiere – is surely an event no opera-lover should miss. ●

George Hall writes widely on classical music and especially opera for publications including *The Stage*, *Opera* and *BBC Music Magazine*. As well as authoring numerous programme notes for major companies, he has contributed chapters to the Overture Opera Guides to *Le nozze di Figaro*, *Carmen* and *Simon Boccanegra*.

Carl Maria von Weber Oberon
THURSDAY 6 AUGUST

BBC

RADIO 3 UNWIND

Music to unwind your mind

Listen on smart speaker — SOUNDS

CHARTERHOUSE

Not just playing together – extraordinary together.

A Perfectly Modern British Education.

Listen in

Finland: Savonlinna Opera and the Kuhmo Festival
17 - 24 July 2026

Experience the magic of **THE MARRIAGE OF FIGARO** and **NABUCCO** in a mediaeval castle set on a lake; travel through silver birch and pine forest for chamber music concerts in Kuhmo in Northern Karelia and explore Helsinki on a guided walking tour.

Kudu Travel • 020 8150 3367
www.kudutravel.com/tours/finland-opera-tour

Canterbury Cathedral

*Awe and wonder included
Lose yourself in 1,400 years of living history

Kids Go FREE
Visitor entry.
T&Cs apply

canterbury-cathedral.org
Charity no. 1206913

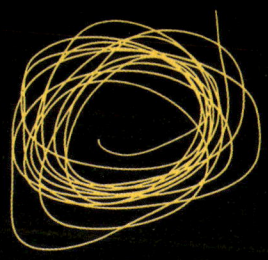

PIERINO

FAMILY RUN ITALIAN RESTAURANT JUST A SHORT STROLL FROM THE ROYAL ALBERT HALL

PROUDLY SERVING TRADITIONAL ITALIAN DISHES

PRE & POST-THEATRE DINING

MONDAY – SUNDAY   12PM – 10PM

37 THURLOE PLACE, SOUTH KENSINGTON, LONDON, SW7 2HP CALL TO BOOK YOUR TABLE: 020 7581 3770

The Proms on TV

The world's greatest classical music festival returns with all the virtuosity, drama and excitement that audiences could want from our BBC television coverage.

Last year the BBC Proms reached its largest-ever audience on BBC iPlayer and Sounds and, for the first time ever, we received a BAFTA nomination for our Last Night of the Proms coverage on TV. This year promises to build on that success, as we put homegrown ensembles at the heart of the Proms story. Britain's finest ensembles, including the Academy of St Martin in the Fields, Sinfonia of London and National Youth Orchestra – not to mention the BBC's own orchestras – will all have starring roles in our TV offering. We also welcome outstanding visiting orchestras including the Los Angeles Philharmonic, The Met Orchestra and Spanish National Orchestra.

World-class soloists such as Leonidas Kavakos, Felix Klieser, Sheku Kanneh-Mason, Jess Gillam and Ben Goldscheider will enjoy their moment in the spotlight. And we range far and wide musically, from much-loved classical favourites to the iconic scores of the Bond films, from the sweet nostalgia of Disney themes to the brilliant innovations of Miles Davis. So here's to a summer of musical magic to enjoy on BBC television.

Suzy Klein
Head of Arts and Classical Music TV

Friday 17 July	First Night of the Proms 2026
Sunday 19 July	Boléro: Rhythms of Spain
Monday 20 July	Beethoven's Ninth
Tuesday 21 July	Also sprach Zarathustra
Friday 24 July	John Wilson Conducts Respighi's 'Roman Trilogy'
Saturday 25 July	Horrible Science: The Big Bang Proms Experiment
Wednesday 29 July	Elgar's First
Sunday 2 August	Kavakos Plays Tchaikovsky
Wednesday 5 August	Under African Skies
Saturday 8 August	Berlioz's 'Symphonie fantastique'
Tuesday 11 August	Dudamel and the LA Phil: Beethoven and Adès
Thursday 20 August	Miles Davis Centenary
Sunday 23 August	Mozart's 'Haffner' Symphony
Monday 24 August	American Classics
Tuesday 25 August	Bond and Beyond
Wednesday 26 August	The Met Orchestra Plays Strauss
Monday 31 August	Enchanted: Alan Menken's Music for Disney
Saturday 5 September	Martha Argerich Plays Beethoven
Sunday 6 September	Dvořák's 'New World' Symphony
Saturday 12 September	Last Night of the Proms 2026

Visit bbc.co.uk/proms for the latest broadcast information

Concert Listings

Full details of all the 2026 BBC Proms concerts – 72 Proms at the Royal Albert Hall, the BBC Young Composer concert at the Royal College of Music, residencies in Gateshead and Bristol and concerts in Middlesbrough, Mold and Sunderland – are listed in these pages, alongside Spotlight interviews with artists.

Proms at the Royal Albert Hall and Royal College of Music *pages 108–139*
Proms in Bristol, Gateshead, Middlesbrough, Mold and Sunderland *pages 140–144*

For an at-a-glance calendar of the whole season, see inside back cover.

Please check the BBC Proms website for the latest information: bbc.co.uk/proms.

We hope you enjoy this summer of world-class music-making.

PROGRAMME CHANGES
Concert details were correct at the time of going to press. The BBC reserves the right to alter artists or programmes as necessary.

Your Summer at the Proms

Book your tickets
Book seated tickets online, in person or by phone from Saturday 16 May. £8 standing tickets are available online on the day. Or, save money by buying Promming Season Passes. *See pages 145–147 for details.*

Enjoy the concerts
These performances are available whether you're attending in person, listening live on Radio 3 or BBC Sounds or watching on BBC TV or iPlayer.

Relive the experience
You can catch up with every Prom on BBC Sounds and all televised Proms on BBC iPlayer.

Friday 17 July
7pm–c9pm • Royal Albert Hall

● £28.52–£89.72 *(including booking fee*)*

DALIA STASEVSKA

First Night of the Proms 2026

Copland Fanfare for the Common Man *3'*
Gershwin An American in Paris *16'*
Ravel Piano Concerto in G major *23'*

INTERVAL

Josephine Stephenson new work *c8'*
BBC commission: world premiere

Finzi For St Cecilia *19'*

Yunchan Lim piano
Thomas Atkins tenor

BBC Singers
BBC Symphony Chorus
BBC Symphony Orchestra
Dalia Stasevska conductor

Dalia Stasevska and massed BBC forces launch the 2026 season with an American accent. The widescreen vision of Copland's *Fanfare for the Common Man* zooms in to teeming city streets in Gershwin's 'rhapsodic ballet' *An American in Paris*, before piano superstar Yunchan Lim performs Ravel's bluesy Concerto in G major, a musical postcard inspired by the composer's time in the States. The second half sees a world premiere from French-British composer Josephine Stephenson, before Finzi's ode to the patron saint of music, premiered in this same Hall nearly 80 years ago. *See pages 14–19.*

📺 *Broadcast live on BBC Two and BBC iPlayer*

Saturday 18 July
7.30pm–c9.45pm • Royal Albert Hall

● £19.34–£71.36 *(including booking fee*)*

ROBERT AMES

Prog Rock: A Fanfare for the Common Man

BBC Concert Orchestra
Robert Ames conductor

There will be one interval

Prog rock exploded the tight boundaries of pop music, amplifying it with new symphonic scope, ambition and influences, and creating spectacular visual and musical statements. The Proms celebrates this pioneering, British-driven movement in a concert celebrating classic tracks on an orchestral scale. Award-winning broadcaster and BBC Radio 6 Music host Stuart Maconie presents brand-new orchestral arrangements of music by ELP, Genesis, Jethro Tull, Mike Oldfield, Renaissance and others. *See pages 26–28.*

Every Prom is broadcast on BBC Radio 3 and BBC Sounds

Sunday 19 July

11am–c1pm • Royal Albert Hall

£14.24–£48.92 (including booking fee')

DAVID CHILDS

Black Dyke Band

Judith Bingham Four Minute Mile 4'

Berlioz, arr. Frank Wright
Overture 'Le carnaval romain' 8'

G. Holst A Moorside Suite 15'

Peter Graham Force of Nature 15'

INTERVAL

Edward Gregson Symphony in
two movements 18'

John Williams, arr. Andrew Duncan
Harry Potter and the Philosopher's
Stone – Hedwig's Theme 3'

Rodrigo, arr. Kevin Bolton
Concierto de Aranjuez – Adagio 5'

Hans Zimmer, arr. Stephen
Roberts Pirates of the Caribbean:
Dead Man's Chest – Wheel of Fortune 5'

Philip Wilby
Paganini Variations 15'

David Childs euphonium

Black Dyke Band
Nicholas Childs conductor

Yorkshire's esteemed Black Dyke Band shows off its virtuosity and versatility in a programme of contemporary pieces, arrangements of popular classics and excerpts from soundtracks by John Williams and Hans Zimmer. *See pages 78–80.*

Sunday 19 July

7pm–c9.15pm • Royal Albert Hall

£16.28–£59.12 (including booking fee')

DAVID AFKHAM

Boléro: Rhythms of Spain

Ravel Alborada del gracioso 8'

Falla, orch. Francisco Coll
Fantasia baetica 12'

Rodrigo Concierto de Aranjuez 21'

INTERVAL

Falla The Three-Cornered Hat –
Suites Nos. 1 & 2 24'

Ravel Boléro 13'

Rafael Aguirre guitar

Spanish National Orchestra
David Afkham conductor

The Spanish National Orchestra makes its Proms debut under Chief Conductor David Afkham, bringing with it a set of heat-soaked musical postcards. Spanish guitar phenomenon Rafael Aguirre joins the ensemble for Rodrigo's much-loved *Concierto de Aranjuez* – an elegant, idealised vision of Spain's past. The orchestra transforms itself into a giant guitar in two Ravel classics: the pulsing seguidilla serenade *Alborada del gracioso* and the hypnotic thrum of *Boléro*. The adventures of a miller, his beautiful young wife and an amorous magistrate become a vivid series of dances in music from Manuel de Falla's ballet *The Three-Cornered Hat. See pages 64–67.*

Recorded for broadcast on BBC TV and BBC iPlayer

Spotlight on …

Rafael Aguirre • 19 July

Rafael Aguirre's mother introduced him to Rodrigo's *Concierto de Aranjuez* when he was a child. As a Spaniard from Malaga, he felt strongly connected to the music before he had even learnt to play the guitar. He identified with its Andalusian influences, from flamenco rhythms to the *saeta* motifs drawn from Spanish Holy Week parades. 'I think Rodrigo was very sensitive to our Spanish traditions, not only from the time that he lived, but from many centuries before,' says Aguirre. 'This is what makes his music so special.'

Aguirre first played the concerto aged 16, on a tour of Andalusia and Morocco with his youth orchestra. It took him just three weeks to learn, because he already knew it so well by ear. After that he played it at competitions across Europe, and at the Verbier Festival, where it launched his musical career. He performed it in the gardens of the Aranjuez Palace, too, surrounded by the sounds of gushing fountains and scents of magnolias that had inspired Rodrigo, who had regularly walked there with his wife. 'The first movement feels like a celebration,' says Aguirre. 'It's alive and joyful. The second is all despair, reflecting how Rodrigo's wife had had a miscarriage. The harmonics at the end show his acceptance and the baby going up to heaven. The third movement represents a very happy time in his life, his love for his wife, and how they used to walk together in the Aranjuez Palace gardens.'

Spotlight on ...
Abel Selaocoe • 20 July

Earlier in his career, Abel Selaocoe played on occasion as an extra for the BBC Philharmonic Orchestra and he found it inspiring to work with top soloists as they brought new works to life. For the Proms this year he's excited to join the orchestra as one of those soloists, in the UK premiere of Jessie Montgomery's cello concerto, *These Righteous Paths*. The piece reflects Selaocoe's love of African and classical music and song and it should, he says, melt the hearts of listeners.

Montgomery's music is based on poems about the Black American experience written by her late mother, the playwright Robbie McCauley. That perspective interests Selaocoe as a South African.

'I think Americans are often looking back, but sometimes they don't know where to look back to,' he says. 'That's what Jessie tries to crystallise here: the sound-world of an American influenced by these small remnants of African culture. Where I come from, we really practise our traditions, and our access to them is not as abstract.' Wrapped within the concerto are Montgomery's memories of her mother murmuring tunefully as they walked hand in hand down a New York street. 'Ancestral connection isn't only an African concept,' says Selaocoe. 'It's to do with the messages that those before you left and what you do with them. That's why this music is for everybody, to reflect: what's my lineage, and how would that sit in a sonic form?'

Monday 20 July
7pm–c9.20pm • Royal Albert Hall

● £19.34–£71.36 *(including booking fee*)*

LEAH HAWKINS

Beethoven's Ninth

J. S. Bach, orch. A. Davis Fantasia and Fugue in G minor, BWV 542   11'
Jessie Montgomery These Righteous Paths   20'
BBC co-commission: UK premiere

INTERVAL

Beethoven Symphony No. 9 in D minor, 'Choral'   65'

Abel Selaocoe *cello*
Leah Hawkins *soprano*
Stephanie Wake-Edwards *mezzo-soprano*
Derek Welton *bass*

Philharmonia Chorus
BBC Philharmonic Orchestra
Gianandrea Noseda *conductor*

Genre-defying South African cellist Abel Selaocoe returns as soloist in the UK premiere of American composer Jessie Montgomery's *These Righteous Paths* – inspired by her late mother, the poet and playwright Robbie McCauley. The concert opens with Bach's mighty Fantasia and Fugue in G minor in Andrew Davis's colourful orchestral arrangement. After the interval comes the monumental power of Beethoven's 'Choral' Symphony: a musical cry for freedom and brotherhood that culminates in the radiant 'Ode to Joy'. *See pages 14–19, 42–43.*

▭ *Recorded for broadcast on BBC TV and BBC iPlayer*

Tuesday 21 July
6pm–c8.10pm • Royal Albert Hall

● £19.34–£71.36 *(including booking fee*)*

JOHN STORGÅRDS

Also sprach Zarathustra

Betsy Jolas Tales of a Summer Sea   15'
UK premiere
Sibelius Violin Concerto in D minor   35'

INTERVAL

R. Strauss Also sprach Zarathustra   33'

Sueye Park *violin*

BBC Philharmonic Orchestra
John Storgårds *conductor*

'Sensational' 2025 Sibelius Competition-winner Sueye Park makes her Proms debut, joining John Storgårds and the BBC Philharmonic Orchestra as soloist in Sibelius's Violin Concerto. All fire and ice, a love song for the composer's own instrument, it's the Romantic concerto *par excellence*: deeply personal and powerfully expressive. Sibelius's Nordic lakes meet the choppy ocean waters of Betsy Jolas's *Tales of a Summer Sea*, and later the dark forests and tectonic stirrings of Strauss's Nietzsche-inspired tone-poem *Also sprach Zarathustra*, its blazing orchestral sunrise made famous by Stanley Kubrick's *2001: A Space Odyssey*. *See pages 74–76, 90–95.*

▭ *Recorded for broadcast on BBC TV and BBC iPlayer*

Tuesday 21 July

10.15pm–c11.30pm • Royal Albert Hall

● £12.20–£30.56 (including booking fee*)

LAURENCE KILSBY

Late Night Baroque

Programme to include:

Dowland
Can she excuse my wrongs? 3'
Now, O now, I needs must part 4'

Purcell
If love's a sweet passion 5'
Strike the viol 4'
Evening Hymn 5'

Handel
Theodora – 'From virtue springs' 8'

Laurence Kilsby tenor
Jupiter Ensemble
Thomas Dunford director/lute

There will be no interval

Formed in 2018 by lutenist Thomas Dunford, the Jupiter Ensemble has enthused audiences around the world. The period-instrument collective makes its Proms debut in a programme celebrating two jewels of the English Renaissance and Baroque – John Dowland (in the 400th anniversary of his death) and the 'British Orpheus' Henry Purcell – as well as 'honorary' Englishman George Frideric Handel, whose dramatic instinct saw his works dominate the London stage. Lending his voice to songs of love's pains and pleasures is British tenor in the ascendant, Laurence Kilsby. *See pages 68–71.*

Wednesday 22 July

7pm–c9.05pm • Royal Albert Hall

● £19.34–£71.36 (including booking fee*)

SAKARI ORAMO

Mahler's 'Tragic' Sixth

György Kurtág Stele 13'

INTERVAL

Mahler Symphony No. 6 in A minor 79'

BBC Symphony Orchestra
Sakari Oramo conductor

Heroes fall but fight on in a programme of monumental soundscapes, poised on the edge of life and death. Sakari Oramo and the BBC Symphony Orchestra celebrate the centenary of Hungary's greatest living composer, György Kurtág, with a rare performance of his powerful orchestral elegy *Stele*, whose kaleidoscopic textures capture the commotion of a battlefield as seen by a wounded man. In Kurtág's own words: 'The fighting rages all around him, but he sees only a very clear, very blue sky.' Written at one of the happiest times of the composer's life, Mahler's premonitory 'Tragic' Symphony No. 6 – haunted by children's voices, dances and marches, by losses and agonies yet to come – broods on human frailty and resilience in music that threatens to burst the banks of the classical symphony.

Spotlight on …

Sueye Park • 21 July

To Sueye Park, Sibelius's Violin Concerto begins as though it comes from nowhere, like icy water seeping into a huge, snowy space. 'I've been to Sibelius's house in Finland,' she says, 'and I can just imagine him composing there all alone, in the middle of nowhere, surrounded by beautiful, wild nature and wanting to express that in this masterwork.' When she plays it she thinks of weather so cold that the ice turns blue, and of the aurora borealis colouring the sky overhead. 'There is also something there that is scalding hot and full of passion,' she says. 'It's like an ice-blue snowball with a fire burning inside.' She feels that particularly strongly in the second movement, when the deep voice of her violin's G string adds to the amazing harmonies of the orchestration.

After the first and second movements Park sometimes finds it hard to continue. 'You need lots of stamina just to get through this concerto,' she says. 'After you've given everything in the first movement, and then again in the second, the third gets even tougher, with all its technical passages.' Experience has taught her that, if she is to endure, Sibelius cannot be rushed. It is music that needs steadiness and backbone, so that it never loses its depth, and the violin is never overwhelmed by the vast orchestration. 'We all breathe together and we just play,' she says. 'I have to adjust to the orchestra, and it's always so exciting, because it's never the same.'

Thursday 23 July

7.30pm–c9.35pm • Royal Albert Hall

● £14.24–£48.92 (including booking fee*)

RYAN BANCROFT

Afterlife: Visions of the Beyond

L. Boulanger Vieille prière bouddhique 7'
Szymanowski Stabat mater 28'

INTERVAL

Messiaen L'Ascension – four symphonic meditations 27'
R. Strauss Death and Transfiguration 23'

Mari Eriksmoen soprano
Paula Murrihy mezzo-soprano
James Way tenor
Szymon Mechliński baritone

BBC National Chorus of Wales
London Philharmonic Choir
BBC National Orchestra of Wales
Ryan Bancroft conductor

Music pierces the veil between heaven and earth in a spiritually charged concert that opens in contemplation and ends in the blaze of ascension and transfiguration. Voices are raised in prayer in Lili Boulanger's haunting *Vieille prière bouddhique*, intensified in the rapt, intimate intercessions of Szymanowski's *Stabat mater*. Unearthly beauty is revealed in Messiaen's *L'Ascension*, before a dying man is raised to heaven in Strauss's *Death and Transfiguration*. See pages 74–76.

Friday 24 July

7.30pm–c10pm • Royal Albert Hall

● £28.52–£89.72 (including booking fee*)

JONATHAN AASGAARD

John Wilson Conducts Respighi's 'Roman Trilogy'

Verdi The Force of Destiny – overture 8'
Walton Cello Concerto 28'

INTERVAL

Respighi
Roman Festivals 25'
Fountains of Rome 15'
Pines of Rome 21'

Jonathan Aasgaard cello

Sinfonia of London
John Wilson conductor

John Wilson and his Sinfonia of London – hailed by critics as 'peerless' and 'simply as good as it gets' – are back for the first of two concerts this season. Ottorino Respighi's love affair with Rome is captured in a trilogy of orchestral tone-poems – heat-soaked, colour-saturated works that invite the listener into the mercurial life of the Eternal City: festivals and dances, misty mornings and scented summer evenings, fanfares and solitary silence. The concert opens with Verdi's much-loved overture to *The Force of Destiny* and Walton's rhapsodic Cello Concerto, its ardent, yearning spirit perhaps a portrait of the composer's own marriage. Norwegian cellist Jonathan Aasgaard is the soloist.

📺 *Recorded for broadcast on BBC TV and BBC iPlayer*

Saturday 25 July

2pm–c4pm & 6pm–c8pm
Royal Albert Hall

● £14.24–£48.92 (including booking fee*)

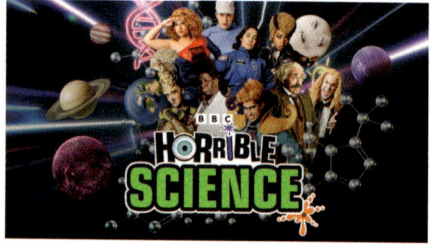

HORRIBLE SCIENCE

Horrible Science: The Big Bang Proms Experiment

Programme to include excerpts from:

Borodin Prince Igor – Polovtsian Dances
G. Holst The Planets
John Williams Star Wars

Richard David Caine
James McNicholas
Jessica Ransom
Inel Tomlinson

BBC National Orchestra of Wales
Karen Ní Bhroin conductor

AD Audio-described by Timna Fibert
BSL British Sign Language-interpreted by Angela Newman
R Relaxed performance

There will be one interval

Join Albert Einstein and Marie Curie as they share the DNA of CBBC's hit comedy sketch show *Horrible Science* live at the Royal Albert Hall with some scientifically proven bangers from the classical canon. They'll be joined by some of the great characters from science to introduce sensational sounds from Holst's *The Planets* to John Williams's *Star Wars*. But will the Prom survive Dr Big Brain's devilish desire to conquer the universe? *For more details about Relaxed Proms, see page 152.*

📺 *Recorded for broadcast on BBC TV and BBC iPlayer*

Sunday 26 July

11am–c12.30pm • Royal Albert Hall

£14.24–£48.92 (including booking fee)

OLIVIER LATRY

Olivier Latry Plays Bach

J. S. Bach
arr. Messerer Partita No. 2 in
D minor, BWV 1004 – Chaconne 17'

transcr. Duruflé Cantata No. 147 –
Chorale 'Jesus bleibet meine Freude' 4'

arr. Widor Bach's Memento –
Mattheus-Final 6'

transcr. Gigout Cantata No. 68 –
Aria 'Mein gläubiges Herze' 3'

J. S. Bach, after Vivaldi
Concerto in A minor, BWV 593 12'

J. S. Bach
Prelude and Fugue in D minor,
BWV 539 8'

Chorale 'Kommst du nun, Jesu,
vom Himmel herunter', BWV 650 4'

Toccata and Fugue in D minor,
BWV 565 10'

Olivier Latry Improvisation on
B-A-C-H c10'

Olivier Latry organ

There will be no interval

Titular Organist of the Grand Organ at Notre-Dame in Paris, Olivier Latry returns for an all-Bach programme with a twist. Hear the Royal Albert Hall's organ put through its paces in arrangements and improvisations on Bach by great organists Widor, Duruflé and Latry himself.

Sunday 26 July

7pm–c9.10pm • Royal Albert Hall

£19.34–£71.36 (including booking fee)

KAZUKI YAMADA

Poulenc and Adams

Poulenc
Sinfonietta 29'
Concerto in D minor for two pianos 20'

INTERVAL

John Adams Harmonium 33'

Lucas and Arthur Jussen pianos
CBSO Chorus
Sydney Philharmonia Chorus
City of Birmingham Symphony Orchestra
Kazuki Yamada conductor

The human voice 'riding upon waves of rippling sound' was the starting point for the glittering, pulsing soundscapes of John Adams's *Harmonium* – one of the American composer's defining works, harnessing the motoric energy of Minimalism to large-scale architectural form and textural richness. Commissioned by the BBC in 1947, Poulenc's *Sinfonietta* is a typically playful, nose-thumbing riff on the traditional symphony, full of wit and brilliance – a mood it shares with the composer's joyful, Mozart-inspired Concerto for two pianos. 'Breathtaking' Dutch siblings Lucas and Arthur Jussen make their Proms debut, joined by the City of Birmingham Symphony Orchestra and Music Director Kazuki Yamada. *See pages 14–19.*

Spotlight on …

Lucas and Arthur Jussen
26 July

'I have never spoken to anybody who doesn't like this piece,' says Arthur Jussen of Poulenc's Concerto for two pianos. 'Poulenc was a master of using elements from other composers in his music, but in the end it always sounds like Poulenc, and that makes it so much fun, and never boring.' Poulenc's musical humour, charm and virtuosic madness, interspersed with moments of enveloping warmth, all appealed to Arthur and his brother Lucas when they began to learn the concerto together aged 10 and 12 respectively. Despite its technical difficulties, musically it always felt very accessible to them. 'It is not hugely intellectual or difficult to digest, so as children it was a piece that we loved very much,' says Lucas. 'We've always played it with a lot of happiness.'

Their bond as siblings has made their connection to it all the stronger. 'We have spent so much time making music together that sometimes we don't even have to look at each other any more,' says Arthur. 'We just feel it.' That has made it easier for them to take risks and have fun on stage – something they are particularly looking forward to doing with conductor Kazuki Yamada. 'Just like us, Kazuki doesn't want to play a piece in a safe way,' says Lucas. 'He wants a little bit of craziness, and that suits us very well. To play this concerto with him and the City of Birmingham Symphony Orchestra for our Proms debut will be a huge joy.'

Spotlight on …
Louise Alder • 27 July

The first time soprano Louise Alder heard Canteloube's *Songs of the Auvergne* – particularly 'Baïlèro', from the first of the collection's five books – she was captivated. 'I heard a recording of Dame Kiri Te Kanawa singing the 'Baïlèro' and I absolutely loved that melody,' she says. 'It's so haunting, and so rich in French history.' Alder has now performed and recorded many of the 27 songs herself, accompanied variously by orchestra, piano and even wind quintet. She finds singing them with an orchestra, as she will do at the Proms, particularly challenging. 'Acoustically a soprano carries across an orchestra very well,' she says, 'but when I've done these songs with full orchestra before we've really had to work on the balance because they are written in the middle of the voice with a lot of very complicated, storytelling text.' It doesn't help that that text is written in Occitan, a difficult and rarely spoken language that lies somewhere between French and Catalan, and which varies from village to village and song to song. Still, she says, 'I think that you can't beat the full orchestral version. There are so many colours in the score, and they give me an amazing palette to work from.' Those colours help her to tell these folk stories of French villages, with all their narratives of local life, animals and landscapes. 'To me, the music really depicts the hot French summer,' she says. 'You can almost feel the heat of the fields, and that is so intoxicating.'

Monday 27 July
7pm–c9pm • Royal Albert Hall

● £19.34–£71.36 (including booking fee*)

EDWARD GARDNER

From the Alps to the Auvergne

Kristine Tjøgersen
Between Trees   15'
UK premiere

Canteloube Songs of the Auvergne – selection   15'

INTERVAL

R. Strauss An Alpine Symphony   47'

Louise Alder soprano
London Philharmonic Orchestra
Edward Gardner conductor

Step into the great outdoors with Edward Gardner and the London Philharmonic Orchestra. Kristine Tjøgersen's *Between Trees* plunges listeners into the mossy shade of a Nordic forest. Childhood walks with his father through the mountains and villages of his native Auvergne inspired Joseph Canteloube's much-loved orchestral songs. 'Glorious' soprano Louise Alder – soloist at last year's Last Night of the Proms – returns, performing these luscious miniatures, not heard at the Proms since 2010. These sonic strolls limber us up for Richard Strauss's epic journey up to a mountain summit. Listeners must traverse glaciers, thickets and pastures, survive storms and cross streams to gain the triumphant orchestral vistas that are the climax to the composer's mighty *An Alpine Symphony*. See pages 74–76.

Tuesday 28 July
7pm–c9.20pm • Royal Albert Hall

● £16.28–£59.12 (including booking fee*)

GUY JOHNSTON

Sibelius's Second

Mark-Anthony Turnage
Festen Suite   21'
BBC co-commission: UK premiere

Britten Cello Symphony   34'

INTERVAL

Sibelius Symphony No. 2 in D major   40'

Guy Johnston cello
BBC Symphony Orchestra
Sakari Oramo conductor

Fifty years since Benjamin Britten's death, former BBC Young Musician winner Guy Johnston brings the composer's Cello Symphony to the Proms. Originally written for Mstislav Rostropovich, it's the composer at his most intense: a *tour de force* for the soloist, set against a brooding, often eerie orchestral backdrop. There's darkness in Sibelius's Symphony No. 2 as well – gloriously thrown aside in the glowing finale – but is it the weight of Russian political oppression or of personal loss? The concert opens with the UK premiere of Mark-Anthony Turnage's *Festen Suite*, adapted from the composer's multi-Olivier-Award-winning 2025 opera. See pages 44–45, 56–60.

Wednesday 29 July

7pm–c9.05pm • Royal Albert Hall

● £14.24–£48.92 (including booking fee*)

CLAIRE BOOTH

Elgar's First

Judith Weir Moon and Star 15'
Brett Dean The World's Wife c20'
BBC co-commission: world premiere

INTERVAL

Elgar Symphony No. 1
in A flat major 50'

Claire Booth soprano
BBC Singers
BBC Scottish Symphony Orchestra
Ryan Wigglesworth conductor

'Human life … and a massive hope in the future': this – no less – is Elgar's sweeping subject for his First Symphony – a work once nicknamed 'Brahms's Fifth' for its close relationship with the German tradition. Exuberant and filled with orchestral colour, an 'immediate and phenomenal success' at its premiere, it's the work of a composer steeped in musical history but looking to the future. Two contemporary works open this concert by Ryan Wigglesworth and the BBC Scottish Symphony Orchestra: Judith Weir's *Moon and Star*, capturing the vastness and strangeness of space through the eyes of New England poet Emily Dickinson; and the world premiere of *The World's Wife* by Brett Dean, setting words by Carol Ann Duffy. See pages 90–95.

▢ *Recorded for broadcast on BBC TV and BBC iPlayer*

Thursday 30 July

7pm–c9pm • Royal Albert Hall

● £16.28–£59.12 (including booking fee*)

ALENA BAEVA

Korngold's Violin Concerto

Dobrinka Tabakova Orpheus' Comet 5'
Korngold Violin Concerto
in D major 24'

INTERVAL

Prokofiev Symphony No. 5
in B flat major 46'

Alena Baeva violin
BBC Scottish Symphony Orchestra
Delyana Lazarova conductor

A symphony 'on the greatness of the human soul' and a cinematic concerto collide in a concert of widescreen orchestral soundscapes. 'Utterly captivating' violinist Alena Baeva is the soloist in Korngold's Violin Concerto – a work imbued with all the sweeping romance and passion of the composer's many film scores. Delyana Lazarova conducts the BBC Scottish Symphony Orchestra in Prokofiev's Symphony No. 5, a musical homecoming featuring one of the composer's most darkly lyrical slow movements. Dobrinka Tabakova's exhilarating fanfare *Orpheus' Comet* launches the evening with a buzzing, fizzing homage to Monteverdi.

Spotlight on …

Delyana Lazarova • 30 July

Prokofiev's Fifth Symphony and Korngold's Violin Concerto make an illuminating pair, says Delyana Lazarova. Though written within a year of each other, at the end of the Second World War, they 'reflect on this moment in history radically differently', she explains. 'Korngold responds with lyricism, memory and inward reflection; Prokofiev gives us tension and a certain monumentality.' Lazarova conducts both works on her second visit to the Proms as Principal Guest Conductor of the BBC SSO. As a trained violinist, she knows Korngold's concerto from the soloist's viewpoint too. 'Hopefully that helps,' she laughs. 'It's such a beautiful work, not only for the violinist, but a *tour de force* for the whole orchestra.' But her starting point for this programme was the Prokofiev, which she thinks speaks to us today 'very clearly but not simply. It's been called a symphony of greatness, of the human spirit, as well as a hymn to free and happy men, but we know that this optimism was state-imposed [in the Soviet Union]. It's supposed to be a triumph but at the end it feels more like survival.'

Opening the Prom is Dobrinka Tabakova's *Orpheus' Comet*. Lazarova is no stranger to her Bulgarian compatriot's music, having recorded this piece with the Hallé. 'It feels like the perfect programme: I'm bringing something from my country, a moment of beauty with Korngold and then Prokofiev's Fifth, which we can maybe see with new eyes.'

Spotlight on …
Jane Mitchell • 1 & 2 August

When you've already played *The Rite of Spring* and Beethoven's Symphony No. 9 from memory, what's next? That was the question facing the Aurora Orchestra, whose memorised performances are always a Proms highlight. 'There's a slightly mysterious process about what's good, possible and worthwhile to memorise,' explains Artistic Director and Principal Flute Jane Mitchell. Ultimately it was decided that Mahler's Symphony No. 1 met all the criteria. 'We've never done any Mahler, and the First finds him at the start of his journey as a symphonist. He was asking if he should write something abstract, in the model of Brahms, or did he need to guide listeners and give titles and explanations,' explains Mitchell.

Actors will join Aurora's players in the first half of the Prom to bring Mahler's creative process to life in a dramatic exploration of the symphony, masterminded by Mitchell. She is excited to take listeners right inside the orchestral writing: 'His symphonies are the ultimate example of orchestral colour,' she says. 'It feels like a playground, in a way. He loved writing about himself and his emotions, and analysing why he did things, so it really feels like you get to know him as a person.' Mitchell, who has been immersed in his letters and writings, was surprised by how openly he writes: 'His music is like that too, but he looks so neat and tidy in his suit in photos – I've had to forget that a little bit.'

Friday 31 July

7.30pm–c9.40pm • Royal Albert Hall

● £19.34–£71.36 *(including booking fee')*

OMER MEIR WELLBER

Bruch's Violin Concerto

Haydn Symphony No. 44 in E minor, 'Trauer' *22'*

Bruch Violin Concerto No. 1 in G minor *24'*

INTERVAL

Schumann Symphony No. 4 in D minor (rev. version, 1851) *29'*

Daniel Lozakovich *violin*

Deutsche Kammerphilharmonie Bremen
Omer Meir Wellber *conductor*

Haydn's Symphony No. 44, written at the height of his fame in Europe – embodies the bracing rhythms, lyrical melodies and dramatic silences typical of the 'Storm and Stress' movement, its nickname – 'Trauer' or 'Mourning' – arising from the suggestion he requested its serene slow movement be played at his funeral. Max Bruch evoked the heyday of Romanticism in his lush, ever-popular First Violin Concerto: young Swedish violinist Daniel Lozakovich returns following his acclaimed Proms debut in 2022. Sketched out in less than a week during a period of white-hot inspiration in 1841, Schumann's Fourth Symphony is the outgoing, extrovert complement to his calmer, recently completed 'Spring' Symphony. Omer Meir Wellber, a former Chief Conductor of the BBC Philharmonic, conducts one of Europe's leading orchestras.

Saturday 1 August

7pm–c9.15pm • Royal Albert Hall

● £19.34–£71.36 *(including booking fee')*

Sunday 2 August

11am–c1.15pm • Royal Albert Hall

● £19.34–£71.36 *(including booking fee')*

Mahler's First by Heart

A musical and dramatic exploration of Mahler's Symphony No. 1 *c45'*

INTERVAL

Mahler Symphony No. 1 in D major (performed from memory) *53'*

Natalie Lewis *mezzo-soprano*

Aurora Orchestra
Nicholas Collon *conductor*

AD Audio-described by Timna Fibert
BSL British Sign Language-interpreted by Kate Green (first half)

'All the floodgates within me have opened … my whole being points me towards this symphony.' Proms favourites Nicholas Collon and the Aurora Orchestra are back to lift the bonnet on another symphonic masterwork. Fifteen years in the making, Mahler's First Symphony was a major statement of intent – a musical distillation of the composer's life in sound, from klezmer bands to the natural world, folk dances to funeral marches, symphony and song united as one. A dramatised first half featuring mezzo-soprano Natalie Lewis introduces both the music and the story behind it, before a complete performance of the symphony after the interval.

Sunday 2 August

7.30pm–c9.45pm • Royal Albert Hall

£16.28–£59.12 (including booking fee*)

PAAVO JÄRVI

Kavakos Plays Tchaikovsky

Dani Howard Concerto for Brass, 'SIGNAL' c18'
BBC co-commission: world premiere

Tchaikovsky Violin Concerto in D major 33'

INTERVAL

Scriabin Symphony No. 2 in C major 41'

Leonidas Kavakos *violin*

BBC Symphony Orchestra
Paavo Järvi *conductor*

'Impeccable' Greek violinist Leonidas Kavakos joins Paavo Järvi and the BBC Symphony Orchestra for one of the great Romantic concertos. Tchaikovsky's Violin Concerto is a deeply personal work, laden with the emotions of a failed marriage. Tender and melancholic, with tempestuous outpourings, it's a piece that wears its heart on its sleeve. Bold colours frame this centrepiece: the world premiere of Dani Howard's Concerto for Brass, 'SIGNAL', showcasing the players of the BBC SO, and Scriabin's Symphony No. 2, with its iconoclastic brilliance and spiritual vision. *See pages 40–41.*

Recorded for broadcast on BBC TV and BBC iPlayer

Monday 3 August

7pm–c9.05pm • Royal Albert Hall

£19.34–£71.36 (including booking fee*)

THOMAS SØNDERGÅRD

Rachmaninov's 'Paganini' Variations

Knussen Flourish with Fireworks 4'
Rachmaninov Rhapsody on a Theme of Paganini 22'

INTERVAL

Shostakovich Symphony No. 11 in G minor, 'The Year 1905' 55'

Kirill Gerstein *piano*

Royal Scottish National Orchestra
Thomas Søndergård *conductor*

Once described as 'a film score without a film', Shostakovich's Symphony No. 11 is subtitled 'The Year 1905'. The work's four movements pay vivid homage to the First Russian Revolution, plunging listeners into the violence of its Bloody Sunday massacre and the grief and anger that followed. Kirill Gerstein is the soloist in Rachmaninov's glittering *Rhapsody on a Theme of Paganini* – a set of virtuoso variations on a devilish theme, while Oliver Knussen pays tribute to Stravinsky in his gilded fanfare *Flourish with Fireworks. See page 72.*

Spotlight on …

Kirill Gerstein • 3 August

'Much as I love all of Rachmaninov's music, the *Rhapsody on a Theme of Paganini* is particularly perfect,' says Kirill Gerstein, who will be playing the piece at this year's Proms. 'It distils and crystallises everything about his music, and he's at the height of his mastery and inspiration.' With dazzling invention Rachmaninov transforms a spiky minor-key theme by the legendary violinist Paganini into a series of variations. 'There's this famous example of when Rachmaninov turns the theme upside down, which gives us the lush, miraculous 18th variation,' explains Gerstein. 'Supposedly he said, "This one's for my manager".'

Yet Rachmaninov was always full of self-doubt, and Gerstein hears this in the *Rhapsody*. 'A second motif enters: the *Dies irae*, the chant of Judgement Day … My theory is that it's his own negative judgement manifesting itself. The themes wrestle with each other,' says Gerstein. And the legend that Paganini sold his soul to the Devil lurks in the background too. 'There's this undercurrent of the macabre and sarcastic.' Given Gerstein's repertoire includes behemoths such as Busoni's Piano Concerto, what challenges does Rachmaninov's more economical *Rhapsody* pose? 'Most of piano playing is there: quick figurations, massive chords, cadenza-like passages. I think the truly great challenge is imitating a *cantabile* – singing – style,' he says. 'It's wonderfully challenging and amusing – and one still needs to practise it!'

Spotlight on …
Elena Schwarz • 4 August

When Elena Schwarz creates a concert programme, she is drawn to the idea of 'dialogue between the music of our time and the main symphonic repertoire'. No surprise, then, that her debut Prom, conducting BBC NOW, is built on this idea, taking as its starting point Zimmermann's seven-movement *Märchen-Suite*. 'I've always adored this piece,' says Schwarz. 'It's so intricate and beautiful in its orchestral writing. It'll be the first time it's heard at the Proms and it's delightful to be able to offer that novelty.' From there, the idea of playing two masterpieces of the 19th century grew organically. 'Dvořák's Seventh is the culmination of the Prom, so we go from Zimmermann's miniature to this large-scale symphonic architecture, and it seemed right as a counterbalance. The symphony is dramatic and sombre and has these undercurrents of tension. In that sense there is a connection with the Zimmermann, because in his music there is always an undercurrent.'

In between comes Mendelssohn's 'perfect' Violin Concerto, which Schwarz sees as a 'ray of sunshine'. It'll be the first time she has worked with violinist Alina Ibragimova, although she has long admired her from afar. 'I love the fantasy in her playing and her qualities as a chamber musician,' she says. 'She has this real capacity for spontaneity, and I really look forward to her fresh interpretation of a beloved piece. She can make us listen in a new way to it.'

Tuesday 4 August

7pm–c9.05pm • Royal Albert Hall

● £16.28–£59.12 *(including booking fee*)*

ALINA IBRAGIMOVA

Dvořák and Mendelssohn

Zimmermann Märchen-Suite (Fairy-Tale Suite) 19'
Mendelssohn Violin Concerto in E minor 26'
INTERVAL
Dvořák Symphony No. 7 in D minor 35'

Alina Ibragimova *violin*

BBC National Orchestra of Wales
Elena Schwarz *conductor*

'Flawless' violinist and Proms regular Alina Ibragimova is back with one of the great Romantic concertos. It may have been seven years in the making, but there's no sense of musical struggle in Mendelssohn's Violin Concerto – only sparkling, lyrical invention and a fleet-footed 'fairy music' finale. Fairy tales are in the spotlight in Zimmermann's evocative 1950 *Fairy-Tale Suite,* with its enchanted castle and propulsive forest ride. Bohemian folk dances and sunshine tug against a powerful undertow of melancholy in Dvořák's passionate Symphony No. 7.

Wednesday 5 August

6pm–c8.10pm • Royal Albert Hall

● £19.34–£71.36 *(including booking fee*)*

KAHCHUN WONG

Rachmaninov's Second

Ravel, orch. Colin Matthews La vallée des cloches 6'
N. Boulanger Fantasy for piano and orchestra 20'
INTERVAL
Rachmaninov Symphony No. 2 in E minor 60'

Alexandra Dariescu *piano*

Hallé
Kahchun Wong *conductor*

Rachmaninov's hard-won Symphony No. 2 – a profoundly personal triumph forged in the failure of his First Symphony over a decade earlier – is the centrepiece of this concert by Manchester's Hallé orchestra and its Principal Conductor Kahchun Wong. Its expansive, late-Romantic lyricism meets the glowing, pealing soundscape of Ravel's 'The Valley of the Bells' from his *Miroirs*, orchestrated by Colin Matthews. Pianist Alexandra Dariescu makes her Proms debut in Nadia Boulanger's boldly poetic 1912 Fantasy for piano and orchestra, with its eclectic nods to Franck, Fauré and Stravinsky.

Wednesday 5 August

10.15pm–c11.30pm • Royal Albert Hall

● £14.24–£39.74 (including booking fee*)

LADYSMITH BLACK MAMBAZO

Under African Skies

Ladysmith Black Mambazo

Nu Civilisation Orchestra
Peter Edwards director

There will be no interval

Five-time Grammy Award-winners Ladysmith Black Mambazo bring their uplifting voices to a concert exploring the music of South Africa. The group makes its Royal Albert Hall Proms debut 50 years on from the Soweto Uprising and 40 years since the release of Paul Simon's era-defining album *Graceland*, which was recorded during the cultural backlash against Apartheid in South Africa and brought the group to international attention. They are joined by the Nu Civilisation Orchestra and director Peter Edwards, plus special guests.

▣ *Recorded for broadcast on BBC TV and BBC iPlayer*

£8 Promming tickets available for every concert

Thursday 6 August

7pm–c9.30pm • Royal Albert Hall

● £19.34–£71.36 (including booking fee*)

SIR MARK ELDER

Elder Conducts Weber's 'Oberon'

Weber Oberon   120'
(semi-staged; sung in English, with English surtitles)

Nicky Spence *Oberon*
Jennifer Davis *Reiza*
Charles Castronovo *Sir Huon of Bordeaux*
Yannick Debus *Sherasmin*
Rachael Wilson *Fatima*
Jasmin White *Puck*
Charlotte Bowden *Mermaid*
Jessica Cale *Mermaid*

Monteverdi Choir
Orchestre Révolutionnaire et Romantique
Sir Mark Elder conductor

AD *Audio-described by Timna Fibert*

There will be one interval

Described as 'one of the most remarkable combinations of fantasy and technical skill in music', Weber's final opera – first performed 200 years ago – follows the battle of wills between Fairy King and Queen Oberon and Titania. A new narration brings fresh life and wit to this chivalric fantasy of shipwrecks and magic horns, all set to a ravishing Romantic score. Sir Mark Elder makes his debut conducting the Monteverdi Choir, performing alongside an all-star cast. *See pages 68–71, 102.*

Spotlight on …

Alexandra Dariescu
5 August

Nadia Boulanger is remembered as one of the great music pedagogues of the 20th century, having taught everyone from Copland to Philip Glass. But 'her own compositional voice is just so powerful and original,' says Alexandra Dariescu. 'It deserves to be heard.' Proms audiences will have that chance this summer when the Romanian pianist brings Boulanger's Fantasy for piano and orchestra to the festival. It's a work 'full of vibrant energy and daring harmonic language. There are influences from Fauré, Stravinsky, Rachmaninov – but the voice is unmistakably hers,' says Dariescu. 'It's poetic, dramatic and utterly compelling.' Dariescu gave the UK premiere of the Fantasy in 2019 and has performed it in many other countries since. After a new manuscript was recently found, an updated edition has been prepared – and it's this version that Dariescu brings to the Proms.

'Performing this piece around the world, I find that audiences say, "Why have we not heard this before?",' says Dariescu, who has made championing music by female composers a mission, and will herself be the first female Romanian pianist to appear at the Proms. 'It's a journey of discovery for me and it's incredibly meaningful.' And she's seen the impact of inclusive programming: 'It brings a younger generation into the concert hall. If audiences see themselves represented in the music we perform, then it becomes a lot more accessible.'

Friday 7 August

7pm–*c***9pm • Royal Albert Hall**

● £16.28–£59.12 (including booking fee*)

NIL VENDITTI

Rossini's 'Stabat mater'

Respighi Church Windows   27'

INTERVAL

Rossini Stabat mater   61'

Federica Lombardi *soprano*
Chiara Amarù *mezzo-soprano*
René Barbera *tenor*
Nicola Ulivieri *bass*

Epiphoni Consort
BBC Symphony Chorus
BBC Symphony Orchestra
Nil Venditti *conductor*

Fragments of Gregorian chant are reassembled in the jewel-toned mosaic that is Respighi's 1927 *Church Windows* – given its Proms debut by Nil Venditti and the BBC Symphony Orchestra. Four richly scored orchestral movements each depict a different scene in sound: a shimmering nocturne for 'The Flight into Egypt', a luminous portrait of St Clare and explosive martial conflict for 'The Archangel Saint Michael'. Ancient musical models also inspired Rossini's operatic *Stabat mater* – a powerful spiritual statement from the master of secular drama. *See pages 86–89.*

Saturday 8 August

7.30pm–*c***9.40pm • Royal Albert Hall**

● £19.34–£71.36 (including booking fee*)

THOMAS ADÈS

Berlioz's 'Symphonie fantastique'

Liszt Mephisto Waltz No. 1   11'
Thomas Adès Dante – Part 2: Purgatorio   24'

INTERVAL

Berlioz Symphonie fantastique   49'

National Youth Orchestra
Thomas Adès *conductor*

Does the Devil really have all the best tunes? When it comes to classical music, he just might. Thomas Adès conducts the National Youth Orchestra – over 150 of Britain's most talented teenagers – in a thrilling musical journey to Hell and back. Follow Faust into the irresistible, whirling dance of Liszt's Mephisto Waltz No. 1; contemplate Purgatory, 'a sort of pre-dawn, before the sun of Paradise', in *Purgatorio* – the central panel of Adès's own Grammy Award-winning, Dante-inspired ballet; and surrender to the vast soundscapes and phantasmagoria of Berlioz's *Symphonie fantastique*, culminating in a horrifying 'Witches' Sabbath'. *See pages 86–89.*

▢ *Recorded for broadcast on BBC TV and BBC iPlayer*

Sunday 9 August

11am–*c***12pm • Royal Albert Hall**   ☀

● £13.24–£33.64 (including booking fee*)

TOM FETHERSTONHAUGH

Relaxed Prom

Programme to include:

Vaughan Williams arr. R. Douglas
Serenade to Music   14'

Radiohead, arr. Simon Hale
Pyramid Song   5'

Meredith Monk Panda Chant 2   2'

Duke Ellington, arr. Harry Baker
It Don't Mean a Thing (if It Ain't Got that Swing)   5'

BBC Singers
Fantasia Orchestra
Tom Fetherstonhaugh *conductor*

[AD] Audio-described by Timna Fibert
[BSL] British Sign Language-interpreted by Sean Chandler
[R] Relaxed performance

There will be no interval

An informal, Transatlantic-themed matinee in the year we celebrate the 250th anniversary of America's Declaration of Independence. *For more details about Relaxed Proms, see page 152.*

Sunday 9 August

7pm–c9pm • Royal Albert Hall

● £19.34–£71.36 (including booking fee)

ERIN MORLEY

The OAE Plays Mozart and Haydn

Zelenka Miserere in C minor 14'
Mozart
Masonic Funeral Music 5'
Aria 'Schon lacht der holde Frühling' 8'
Aria 'Vorrei spiegarvi, oh Dio!' 6'

INTERVAL

Haydn Mass in D minor, 'Nelson Mass' 42'

Erin Morley *soprano*
Helen Charlston *mezzo-soprano*
Guy Cutting *tenor*
William Thomas *bass*

Choir of the Enlightenment
Orchestra of the Age of Enlightenment
Peter Whelan *conductor*

A musical postcard from 18th-century Vienna. The threat to Austria from Napoleon's army is vividly rendered in the turbulent opening of Haydn's choral *tour de force* the 'Nelson Mass', but it's Nelson's victory we hear in the celebratory ending. There's brooding spiritual darkness from Zelenka's *Miserere* and Mozart's *Masonic Funeral Music* – written in response to the deaths of two of the composer's fellow Freemasons. Soprano Erin Morley is the soloist in two of Mozart's showstopping 'insertion' arias. *See pages 68–71.*

Monday 10 August

7pm–c9.15pm • Royal Albert Hall

● £16.28–£59.12 (including booking fee)

ESA-PEKKA SALONEN

Salonen Conducts 20th-Century Classics

Stravinsky Symphony in Three Movements 22'
Berg Violin Concerto 22'

INTERVAL

Bartók Concerto for Orchestra 36'

Vilde Frang *violin*

Juilliard Orchestra
Royal Academy of Music Symphony Orchestra
Esa-Pekka Salonen *conductor*

Esa-Pekka Salonen conducts the combined orchestras of London's Royal Academy of Music and New York's Juilliard School in three 20th-century orchestral masterworks. Award-winning Norwegian violinist Vilde Frang is the soloist in Berg's heartbreaking elegy of a Violin Concerto, with its embedded Bach chorale, dedicated 'to the memory of an angel'. Completed in the dying days of the Second World War, Stravinsky's *Symphony in Three Movements* offers a 'cinematographic impression of the war' – jagged and convulsively rhythmic. Moving 'from austerity to the affirmation of life', Bartók's 1943 *Concerto for Orchestra* responds more optimistically to war, defiant in its folk-inspired melodies and collective virtuosity. *See page 24.*

Spotlight on …
Vilde Frang • 10 August

For Vilde Frang, Berg's Violin Concerto is, quite simply, 'one of the greatest concertos written for violin in the 20th century'. It has beauty, elegance and charm, says the Norwegian, but above all it offers incredible drama. 'It's one of those pieces that feels like you are living it rather than playing it.' That drama is one of life and death. Dedicated 'to the memory of an angel', the piece was written to mourn Manon Gropius, Alma Mahler's 18-year-old daughter. 'I've been wondering about the personality of this young girl who left such an impression on Berg,' reflects Frang. 'Her personality comes to the fore in the first movement's expressive language. The second movement is almost like a tango with death, and she finally ascends to the stars. It's a cosmic ending.'

Yet despite the work's deeply moving backstory, for years Frang saw it as 'a very intellectual piece'. It was only during the Covid-19 pandemic, which she sees as 'an existential time', that it made sense to her: 'I think it was meant to reach me then. It was a very emotional experience when I finally got it. I discovered the music is crystal clear.' From that point on she has felt compelled to champion the piece. 'When I take on a new concerto, it's like learning a new language that's calling out to me. The message is so strong that I have to uncover it,' she says. 'I need to tell its story, and I have a mission to share it with other people.'

Spotlight on …
Evelyn Glennie
11 August

Dame Evelyn Glennie has several Proms records to her name. In 1989 she became the first percussionist to give a recital at the festival. Three years later she was the first Proms soloist to play a percussion concerto – James MacMillan's *Veni, veni Emmanuel*. Then, in 1994, she became the first percussion soloist at the Last Night. This year she adds a personal first to the tally by performing at a Late Night Prom. 'It's quite a different vibe musically,' she says, 'and I think we can stretch the boundaries a little.' She offers a tantalising glimpse of what that means: 'My role will be more to do with playing things that are slightly unexpected, such as Vincent Ho's *Sandman's Castle* for tam-tam.'

Glennie will be joining forces with the Fantasia Orchestra and conductor Tom Fetherstonhaugh, who gave their Proms debut in the 2024. 'I love playing with this orchestra. It's open and everyone has a voice,' she says. 'That's very important when you're working with any group of musicians.' They'll be performing a sequence of bespoke arrangements of music by, among others, John Coltrane, Duke Ellington and Radiohead. 'Arrangers are truly extraordinary because they have to take something already written, that could be really great, and do something great with it again,' says Glennie. 'If it's being arranged for percussion, you almost have to imagine it's the original version by the composer. When it works well, an arranger is worth their weight in gold.'

Tuesday 11 August

6pm–c8.10pm • Royal Albert Hall

● £19.34–£71.36 (including booking fee*)

GUSTAVO DUDAMEL

Dudamel and the LA Phil: Beethoven and Adès

Beethoven Symphony No. 6 in F major, 'Pastoral' 39'

INTERVAL

Thomas Adès Dante – Part 1: Inferno 45'

Los Angeles Philharmonic
Gustavo Dudamel *conductor*

The Los Angeles Philharmonic returns to the Proms for the first time in over two decades, conducted by Music Director Gustavo Dudamel. Pastoral peace meets infernal horrors in two vividly descriptive orchestral classics. Cuckoos and nightingales call, a brook gently gurgles and tavern musicians strike up a dance in Beethoven's 'Pastoral' Symphony. Thomas Adès paints a bleaker landscape in *Inferno* – the first panel of his *Dante* ballet (hear part two, *Purgatorio*, performed by the National Youth Orchestra on 8 August). 'Physical, vivid and grotesque', it's a score that finds strange beauty in horror. See pages 86–89.

Recorded for broadcast on BBC TV and BBC iPlayer

Tuesday 11 August

10.15pm–c11.30pm • Royal Albert Hall

● £14.24–£39.74 (including booking fee*)

TOM FETHERSTONHAUGH

Evelyn Glennie and the Fantasia Orchestra

Programme to include:

Caroline Shaw Partita – Sarabande 5'

Héloïse Werner new work c5'
BBC commission: world premiere

Vaughan Williams, arr. R. Douglas
Serenade to Music 14'

Radiohead, arr. Simon Hale
Pyramid Song 5'

and works by John Coltrane, Duke Ellington, Vincent Ho and Philip Sheppard

Evelyn Glennie *percussion*
BBC Singers
Fantasia Orchestra
Tom Fetherstonhaugh *conductor*

BSL *British Sign Language-interpreted by Sean Chandler*

There will be no interval

Grammy Award-winning percussionist Dame Evelyn Glennie joins the Fantasia Orchestra and BBC Singers for a genre-busting programme connecting Vaughan Williams's lyrical *Serenade for Music* – written for Proms founder-conductor Henry Wood – via Radiohead and the jazz of John Coltrane and Duke Ellington to the exhilarating invention of Caroline Shaw's Pulitzer Prize-winning *Partita*.

Wednesday 12 August

7pm–c9pm • Royal Albert Hall

● £19.34–£71.36 (including booking fee*)

GUSTAVO DUDAMEL

Dudamel and the LA Phil: Beethoven and Ortiz

Beethoven Symphony No. 7 in A major   36'

INTERVAL

Gabriela Ortiz Revolución diamantina   42'
UK premiere

Los Angeles Master Chorale (upper voices)
Los Angeles Philharmonic
Gustavo Dudamel conductor

In the second of their two Proms, the Los Angeles Philharmonic and its Music Director Gustavo Dudamel again pair a Beethoven symphony with a contemporary ballet. The obsessive, often wild rhythms of Beethoven's Symphony No. 7 – famously described by Wagner as 'the apotheosis of the dance' – meet the politically charged pulse of Gabriela Ortiz's *Revolución diamantina*: music 'full of visceral primeval rhythms and mysterious, soulful sound-worlds'. Taking Mexico's 2019 Glitter Revolution as its starting point, this groove-driven, urgent score – 'a ritual in motion' – roars against female oppression in music of fierce, hypnotic beauty. *See page 62.*

Thursday 13 August

7pm–c9.15pm • Royal Albert Hall

● £16.28–£59.12 (including booking fee*)

JAMES GAFFIGAN

Gershwin's Piano Concerto

Wynton Marsalis Concerto for Orchestra   36'
BBC co-commission: UK premiere

INTERVAL

Gershwin Piano Concerto in F major   31'
Barber Symphony No. 1 in One Movement   21'

Yeol Eum Son piano
BBC Symphony Orchestra
James Gaffigan conductor

James Gaffigan and the BBC Symphony Orchestra mark the 250th anniversary of the US Declaration of Independence with 100 years of American music. South Korean pianist Yeol Eum Son joins the orchestra for Gershwin's Piano Concerto in F major – its Charleston rhythms and songful slow-movement capturing the energy of 20th-century New York. Samuel Barber's rarely heard Symphony No. 1 in One Movement marries the lyrical intensity of the composer's beloved *Adagio* with taut structural drama. The concert opens with the UK premiere of contemporary jazz great Wynton Marsalis's mercurial, kaleidoscopic *Concerto for Orchestra*. *See pages 14–19.*

Spotlight on …

Yeol Eum Son • 13 August

When pianist Yeol Eum Son made her Proms debut in 2019 she chose a concerto by Mozart, a composer with whom she's made her name. Her prize-winning performance of his Concerto No. 21, for example, has had over 28 million views online. But for her return to the Proms this summer Son has picked a contrasting piece: Gershwin's jazz-infused Piano Concerto in F major. 'It is one of my favourites,' she says, 'it's so well written and uplifting. I've loved it since I was very young and always dreamt of playing it.'

Son fell in love with the work in her teens, when she heard a recording of it by Earl Wild. 'I listened to it, I don't know, 500 times,' she says. 'It's always been my favourite. And then I started to play the piece myself and the more I play it, the more I love it.' That's thanks, in part, to Gershwin's rich melting pot of styles. 'It's not only jazz and classical – there's a lot of folk in there too. Some scenes are like musicals, some like operas. You feel like you're hearing many different things at the same time. It's very attractive.'

'Should it be more jazzy? More classical? That's always been my question,' says Son of her approach to the piece. 'But I think actually it is more of a classical concerto.' And she can't wait to perform it at the Royal Albert Hall: 'It's like a stadium – you're surrounded by so many people. It's been six years since I was last at the Proms but I remember it like it was yesterday.'

Spotlight on …
Martin Fröst • 16 August

Martin Fröst returns to the Proms this summer as both a solo clarinettist and Chief Conductor of the Swedish Chamber Orchestra. As if that wasn't enough, the multi-talented Swedish musician is also the creative force behind the 'DNA Project', which he hopes 'will hint at how art forms can touch each other – how light relates to movement, movement to dance and dance to music'.

The project's centrepiece is Beethoven's Seventh Symphony, once dubbed 'the apotheosis of the dance' by Wagner. Its rhythmic energy is the springboard for a programme that features the composers who inspired Beethoven, explains Fröst – as well as 'music based on the same dances and rhythmic motifs' as the symphony.

Many of the pieces have been arranged by Hans Ek, who 'sometimes writes as if using the same ideas as modern electronic dance music,' says Fröst. A new piece by Swedish composer Jacob Mühlrad adds another contemporary perspective, while Fröst has also joined forces with his viola-playing brother Goran to create *Nomadic Dances*, based on Beethovenian building blocks.

And how does Fröst balance clarinet playing and conducting? 'It feels like the interplay of music-making in the first half extends into conducting and this different type of communication in the second,' he says, 'but hopefully it retains the same sort of music-making'.

Friday 14 August
7pm–c9.15pm • Royal Albert Hall

● £16.28–£59.12 *(including booking fee*)*

EDWIN OUTWATER

BBC Concert Orchestra and Edwin Outwater

BBC Concert Orchestra
Edwin Outwater *conductor*

There will be one interval

A musical omnivore equally at home conducting prestigious international orchestras or working with pop and rock artists, Edwin Outwater is as fleet-footed as the BBC Concert Orchestra itself, of which he is Principal Guest Conductor and Curator. Together at the Proms they have collaborated with Cynthia Erivo and celebrated the work of Henry Mancini and Bernard Herrmann. Tonight brings another genre-bending symphonic adventure.

Every Prom is broadcast on BBC Radio 3 and BBC Sounds

Saturday 15 August
7.30pm–c9pm • Royal Albert Hall

● £28.52–£89.72 *(including booking fee*)*

SIR ANTONIO PAPPANO

Pappano Conducts Berlioz's 'Requiem'

Berlioz Requiem (Grande messe des morts) *82'*

tenor to be announced

BBC Symphony Chorus
London Symphony Chorus
London Symphony Orchestra
Sir Antonio Pappano *conductor*

There will be no interval

Sir Antonio Pappano conducts the London Symphony Orchestra in one of the repertoire's most monumental musical statements. Premiered in 1837 with 450 performers, Berlioz's *Requiem* is a colossal, cinematic statement of faith, fear and hope – a sonic portrait of 'mankind gathered together on the last day'. Demanding 10 timpanists and with four separate brass groups, it sends the shockwaves of the Day of Judgement right through listeners, insisting on the majesty, the fragility and the terrifying spectacle of death and resurrection. *See pages 86–89.*

Sunday 16 August

11am–c1pm • Royal Albert Hall

● £16.28–£59.12 (including booking fee*)

MARTIN FRÖST

Swedish Chamber Orchestra: Beethoven and Baroque

Jacob Mühlrad Helix c5'
BBC commission: world premiere

Hans Ek DNA Suite 20'
orchestrations of pieces by Rameau, J. S. Bach and Handel, plus transitions
UK premiere

Göran and Martin Fröst
Nomadic Dances 5'

INTERVAL

Beethoven Symphony No. 7 in A major 38'

Swedish Chamber Orchestra
Martin Fröst conductor/clarinet

Maverick clarinet virtuoso Martin Fröst – praised for his 'unsurpassed musicianship' by *The New York Times* – explores the evolution of dance in a wide-ranging programme that contrasts the courtly with the rustic and climaxes in Beethoven's Symphony No. 7: dance unleashed as never before. The courtly dances of Rameau and Handel give way to Bach's contrapuntal invention and folk music's instinctive pulse, transformed into something provocative and dynamic in works by contemporary Swedish composers Hans Ek and Jacob Mühlrad.
See pages 68–71.

Sunday 16 August

7.30pm–c9.30pm • Royal Albert Hall

● £19.34–£71.36 (including booking fee*)

VASILY PETRENKO

Elgar's Cello Concerto

Webern Passacaglia 11'
Elgar Cello Concerto in E minor 30'

INTERVAL

Walton Symphony No. 2 28'

Pablo Ferrández cello
Royal Philharmonic Orchestra
Vasily Petrenko conductor

Le Figaro called him a 'new cello genius'. Now prize-winning Spanish cellist Pablo Ferrández makes his Proms debut with Elgar's achingly passionate concerto. He joins Vasily Petrenko and the Royal Philharmonic Orchestra for a programme that measures out the griefs, conflicts and shifting identities of the 20th century – opening with Webern's lushly Romantic 1908 *Passacaglia*, whose sequence of intricate variations finds a ghostly echo in the finale of Walton's Second Symphony. Premiered in 1960, the latter work looks back rather than forwards, rejecting the avant-garde in favour of a dense, Expressionistic intensity.

Spotlight on …

Pablo Ferrández • 16 August

When Pablo Ferrández makes his Proms debut this summer he will have already played out the moment dozens of times in his mind. 'I like to visualise, when I'm preparing, so I will imagine myself playing in such a large space and how to fill it,' the Spanish cellist says. 'It's something I enjoy doing and I think it helps.' Naturally he is, he says, 'very excited' about the Prom, which sees him play one of the best-loved cello concertos – and his own personal favourite, Elgar's great E minor.

But, he admits, it wasn't love at first sight. 'I loved the recordings I heard but when I started to work on it as a teenager I found it wasn't as easy to understand and perform as I'd imagined.' It was only when his international career took off in his twenties that the concerto fell into place. 'I think I used to overdo the drama,' he says. 'Every movement is so different, and the challenge is to get into all these characters. Now I love performing it. It gives you so many possibilities to express many things.'

The key to the Elgar lies in embracing its contrasts, Ferrández has found. 'There's the darkness and passion of the first movement, the lightness and warmth of the second and the incredible beauty of the finale.' Playing the concerto on his 'Archinto' Stradivarius cello ('the love of my life') at the Proms, where he joins forces with the Royal Philharmonic Orchestra and conductor Vasily Petrenko, will be, he says, 'a dream come true'.

Spotlight on …
Anthony McGill • 17 August

When composer Gabriel Kahane went to a concert given by the New York Philharmonic a few years ago he was drawn in particular to the sound of the orchestra's Principal Clarinet, Anthony McGill. 'Gabriel messaged me on social media and said he really liked my playing, and I thought that was awesome because I love his music too,' says McGill. 'He said we should do something. And that's how it all started.'

The result: a Clarinet Concerto, which McGill brings to the Proms this summer for its European premiere. 'We first got together in Portland where Gabriel lives and discussed an initial idea,' says McGill. 'He's Jewish American and I'm Black American and we'd been talking about the relationship between our cultures over the years. Then he stumbled over a quote by James Baldwin – "If love will not swing wide the gates" – and decided he would take a more universal theme of love and humanity.'

The concerto is, says McGill, 'a joy to play'. 'The first movement starts very beautifully, and there are lots of different textures in the orchestra, and fast, challenging rhythmic figures,' he says. 'In the second movement he uses an upright, muted piano and the clarinet plays a melody with it. It's like I'm singing in some smoky little café. I love it. And the third movement has this playful melody that just dances.' Above all, McGill loves the concerto's 'magical moments – a few are just stunning to play. And that's what I live for.'

Monday 17 August
7pm–c9.05pm • Royal Albert Hall

● £14.24–£48.92 (including booking fee*)

RYAN BANCROFT

Copland and Stravinsky

Copland Billy the Kid – suite 22'
Gabriel Kahane Clarinet Concerto, 'If love will not swing wide the gates' 22'
BBC co-commission: European premiere

INTERVAL

Stravinsky Petrushka (1947 version) 34'

Anthony McGill clarinet
BBC National Orchestra of Wales
Ryan Bancroft conductor

Two 20th-century ballets lie at the heart of this colourful concert by Ryan Bancroft and the BBC National Orchestra of Wales. Puppets come to life at a bustling Shrovetide Fair in Stravinsky's *Petrushka* – a giddy musical collage of folk tunes and modernist invention – while cowboy songs swirl through the score of Copland's *Billy the Kid*: a musical portrait of the infamous outlaw. Dedicatee Anthony McGill is the soloist in a new Clarinet Concerto, 'If love will not swing wide the gates', by Portland-based composer and songwriter Gabriel Kahane. A collaborator of Sufjan Stevens and Rufus Wainright, Kahane blends classical forms with folk-pop influences in his melodic, anthemic writing. *See pages 14–19.*

Tuesday 18 August
7pm–c8.50pm • Royal Albert Hall

● £14.24–£48.92 (including booking fee*)

CRISTIAN MĂCELARU

Shostakovich's Tenth

Édith Canat de Chizy Skyline (Concerto for three percussionists, timpani and orchestra) 20'
BBC co-commission: UK premiere

INTERVAL

Shostakovich Symphony No. 10 in E minor 55'

BBC Symphony Orchestra
Cristian Măcelaru conductor

Cristian Măcelaru, whose own childhood was spent in communist Romania, conducts the BBC Symphony Orchestra in Shostakovich's devastatingly powerful Symphony No. 10. Premiered after Stalin's death in 1953, it's a work whose fierce rage, violence and grief tell a terrifying story of life in the dictator's Russia – a painfully personal history, and one shot through with the composer's own musical signature: DSCH. The concert opens with the UK premiere of Édith Canat de Chizy's intricately textured *Skyline* for three percussionists, timpani and orchestra – a musical vision of the cosmos, from void to teeming, multiplying musical life.

Wednesday 19 August

7pm–c9.35pm • Royal Albert Hall

● £28.52–£89.72 (including booking fee*)

RACHEL WILLIS-SØRENSEN

'Ariadne auf Naxos' from Glyndebourne

R. Strauss Ariadne auf Naxos *120'*
(semi-staged; sung in German, with English surtitles)

Rachel Willis-Sørensen Ariadne
David Butt Philip Bacchus
Alina Wunderlin Zerbinetta
Mikhail Timoshenko Harlequin
Caspar Singh Scaramuccio
Liam James Karai Truffaldino
Liam Bonthrone Brighella
Samantha Hankey Composer
Michael Kraus Music Master
Ru Charlesworth Dancing Master
Anna Denisova Naiad
Ekaterina Chayka-Rubinstein Dryad
Eirin Rognerud Echo

Glyndebourne Festival Opera
London Philharmonic Orchestra
Robin Ticciati conductor

AD Audio-described by Timna Fibert

There will be one interval

The richest man in Vienna has commissioned an evening's entertainment. But when an opera and a comedy troupe are forced to share the same stage, all bets are off. Strauss's *Ariadne auf Naxos* is part farce, part dream-like fantasy, set to one of the composer's most luscious scores. It comes fresh from the Glyndebourne Festival, performed complete at the Proms for the first time in nearly half a century. *See pages 74–76.*

Thursday 20 August

7pm–c9.15pm • Royal Albert Hall

● £19.34–£71.36 (including booking fee*)

AMBROSE AKINMUSIRE

Miles Davis Centenary

Programme to include new arrangements of excerpts from 'Miles Ahead', 'Porgy and Bess', 'Sketches of Spain' and 'Quiet Nights'

Ambrose Akinmusire trumpet
Sam Harris piano
Harish Raghavan bass
Justin Brown drums

BBC Concert Orchestra
Miho Hazama conductor

There will be one interval

Trumpeter, bandleader and composer Miles Davis transformed modern jazz with music that embraced the world around him – a new and exhilarating collage of modal scales, electronic and classical influences, expansive new structures and, of course, technical virtuosity. The Proms marks Davis's centenary with a concert that combines the musician's influences – works by Rodrigo and Gershwin – with his own hits. 'Incandescent' American jazz trumpeter Ambrose Akinmusire joins the BBC Concert Orchestra and Miho Hazama for a celebration of a jazz legend. *See pages 98–101.*

▯ *Recorded for broadcast on BBC TV and BBC iPlayer*

Spotlight on …

Miho Hazama • 20 August

'This is a big year for jazz musicians,' says Miho Hazama. 'It's the centenary of both the great trumpet player and composer Miles Davis and the great saxophonist John Coltrane.' The Japanese-born, New York-based conductor, composer and arranger will be leading the Davis celebrations at the Proms this year in a concert exploring his collaborations with another jazz great, the pianist Gil Evans. 'They made jazz history together,' she says. 'Without their collaboration we basically don't exist as jazz musicians and composers. I have so much respect for them.' Hazama discovered the duo when she was a classical composition student playing in a college big band. She already loved Gershwin's *Porgy and Bess*, then found out that they had arranged songs from the opera for a joint album. 'It was a sensational discovery for me,' she says – so it's no surprise these songs sit at the heart of this year's Prom: 'It's my "dream come true" moment,' she says.

The Prom will also feature music from the peak of Evans and Davis's collaboration, during the late 1950s and early 1960s. Hazama is orchestrating the tracks herself, and plans to let her imagination take flight. 'I grew up listening to classical symphonic music, so that's the natural sound in my head,' she says. And she can't wait to show off Davis's genius. 'He had such a great sense of discovery and making something new with jazz. He kept making history.'

Spotlight on …
Jonathon Heyward
22 August

Jonathon Heyward has strong reasons for opening his Prom with music by American composer and bandleader Edmund Thornton Jenkins. 'He was born in Charleston, South Carolina, where I'm from; he set his sights on Europe, as I did; and studied at the Royal Academy of Music in London, where I attended,' the conductor says. 'He is a composer dear to my heart because of our life connections.'

In the 1920s Jenkins gravitated to Paris – 'where his musical development would flourish' – and began work on a ballet but died before he could complete it. The *Dance Suite* is the result of the combined scholarship and imagination of Heyward and Tuffus Zimbabwe – Jenkins's great-nephew. 'We are performing sketches, some orchestration and some completion of the material. It's amazing to think what this piece could have been.'

Also on the programme are Samuel Barber's *Knoxville: Summer of 1915* and Dvořák's Symphony No. 8 – two works steeped in nostalgia and wonder. In between, soprano Angel Blue presents a selection of favourite American songs, including one by Margaret Bonds (1913–72). 'Bonds wrote these beautiful songs that are hardly ever played and have never been arranged for orchestra,' says Heyward.

He has worked with the Chineke! Orchestra since it was founded in 2015. 'It's great to come back again with them at the Proms.'

Friday 21 August
7pm–c9.45pm • Royal Albert Hall

● £16.28–£59.12 (including booking fee*)

ANJA BIHLMAIER

Mahler's 'Song of the Earth'

Bushra El-Turk Mosaic 8'
Haydn Symphony No. 45 in F sharp minor, 'Farewell' 28'

INTERVAL

Mahler Das Lied von der Erde 68'

Jamie Barton *mezzo-soprano*
Clay Hilley *tenor*
BBC Philharmonic Orchestra
Anja Bihlmaier *conductor*

'How should I describe such a colossal crisis?' Mahler wrote in 1909. 'Yet I am thirstier than ever for life …' Personal and professional loss had taken the composer to the brink, but even as he faced tragedy he experienced the pleasures of living with renewed intensity. It's this strange, urgent ecstasy that runs through *Das Lied von der Erde* ('The Song of the Earth') – a collision of symphony and song, life and loss. This epic musical farewell meets the witty musical parting of Haydn's 'Farewell' Symphony, with its famous final movement of ever-shrinking forces. Bushra El-Turk's *Mosaic* opens the concert with nods to *Das Lied*, in a meditation on identity, otherness and exoticism.

Saturday 22 August
7.30pm–c9.35pm • Royal Albert Hall

● £19.34–£71.36 (including booking fee*)

JONATHON HEYWARD

Chineke! Orchestra with Angel Blue

Edmund Thornton Jenkins reconstr. & arr. Tuffus Zimbabwe Dance Suite c15'
world premiere

Barber Knoxville: Summer of 1915 15'

New arrangements of songs by Harold Arlen, Irving Berlin, Margaret Bonds, George Gershwin and Richard Rodgers 18'

INTERVAL

Dvořák Symphony No. 8 in G major 34'

Angel Blue *soprano*
Chineke! Orchestra
Jonathon Heyward *conductor*

Europe's first majority-Black and ethnically diverse orchestra Chineke! is back. It opens with the premiere of a suite drawn from music for a ballet left incomplete by the South Carolina-born Edmund Thornton Jenkins, who died aged only 32. American soprano Angel Blue sings Samuel Barber's *Knoxville: Summer of 1915* – a child's all-encompassing vision of life in a teeming urban centre – as well as new arrangements of songs by some of 20th-century America's greatest tunesmiths. After the interval we swap cities for forests and fields in the ecstatic nature hymn that is Dvořák's Symphony No. 8.

Sunday 23 August

11am–c1pm • Royal Albert Hall

£16.28–£59.12 (including booking fee')

FELIX KLIESER

Mozart's 'Haffner' Symphony

Britten Simple Symphony	17'
Mozart Horn Concerto No. 3 in E flat major	16'

INTERVAL

Thea Musgrave Bassoon Concerto, 'Out of the Darkness'	c12'
BBC commission: world premiere	
Elgar Romance for bassoon and orchestra	5'
Mozart Symphony No. 35 in D major, 'Haffner'	18'

Felix Klieser *horn*
Amy Harman *bassoon*

Academy of St Martin in the Fields
Benjamin Marquise Gilmore *director/leader*

The Academy of St Martin in the Fields spotlights the French horn and bassoon in two concertos: one classic, one contemporary. The ink is still wet on veteran Scottish composer Thea Musgrave's new Bassoon Concerto, 'Out of the Darkness', receiving its world premiere. Mozart's good-natured Horn Concerto No. 3 ends with a rollicking Allegro that's hard to resist. There are more dancing rhythms from Britten's playful *Simple Symphony* – based on themes written by the composer before the age of 12. *See pages 56–60.*

Recorded for broadcast on BBC TV and BBC iPlayer

Sunday 23 August

7.30pm–c9.45pm • Royal Albert Hall

£19.34–£71.36 (including booking fee')

ALAIN ALTINOGLU

Capuçon Plays Dvořák's Cello Concerto

Stravinsky Symphonies of Wind Instruments (1947 version)	12'
Dvořák Cello Concerto in B minor	40'

INTERVAL

Debussy Prélude à l'après-midi d'un faune	10'
Varèse Amériques	26'

Gautier Capuçon *cello*

BBC Symphony Orchestra
Alain Altinoglu *conductor*

One hundred years since wailing siren, whip and wind machine announced the arrival of Varèse's *Amériques* in the concert hall, the Proms celebrates this exhilarating urban hymn to the composer's adopted home of New York City. Alain Altinoglu traces the vibrant dialogue between Europe and America, pairing music from the Old World and the New. The languorous sensuality of Debussy's *Prélude à l'après-midi d'un faune* contrasts with the clean architectural lines of Stravinsky's *Symphonies of Wind Instruments* – at once ancient and modern. Composed during his time in the USA, Dvořák's Cello Concerto is a nostalgic homage to his Bohemian roots. *See page 96.*

Spotlight on …
Amy Harman • 23 August

British bassoonist Amy Harman had been planning a sabbatical when she was offered a dream opportunity: to perform the world premiere at the BBC Proms of a new concerto written for her by the Scottish-American composer Thea Musgrave. 'The bassoon has rarely featured as a solo instrument at the Proms, and we don't have many concertos, so this is gold dust,' says Harman. The two then met in London and from their interactions Musgrave filled the piece with 'lots of amazing fast passages, lots of staccato, and lots of low register – rich and dark'. The concerto reflects a journey from darkness to light both 'musically and physically', the bassoonist says. 'It begins with me at the back of the stage in the dark, playing in the low register alongside the low-registered instruments. As the music unfolds, I move through the orchestra, playing with the different sections. Then I hear the first violinist playing the melody – representing the light – and I must get to them in order to reach the light myself.'

Harman will be joined by the Academy of St Martin in the Fields, and together they will also perform Elgar's Romance for bassoon and orchestra. 'Musgrave and Elgar have the same intensity and skill in writing for the bassoon,' says Harman. 'The Romance is very melancholic and, while there are moments of hope, it ends mournfully. "Out of the Darkness" ends in the light – so it's a good juxtaposition.'

Monday 24 August

7pm–c9.30pm • Royal Albert Hall

● £19.34–£71.36 (including booking fee*)

MARIN ALSOP

American Classics

Joan Tower Fanfare for the
Uncommon Woman 3'

Bernstein Symphonic Dances
from 'West Side Story' 24'

Gershwin, orch. Grofé
Rhapsody in Blue 16'

INTERVAL

Moross The Big Country – prelude 3'

Copland
Appalachian Spring – suite 23'

Still Three Visions – No. 2:
Summerland 5'

Bernstein On the Town – Three
Dance Episodes 11'

**Marcus Roberts Trio
Philharmonia Orchestra
Marin Alsop** conductor

An all-American celebration, from the urban rhythms of Bernstein's *West Side Story* and *On the Town* to Copland's barn dances and Gershwin's jazz-infused *Rhapsody in Blue*. To these are added all-American landscapes in *The Big Country* and *Appalachian Spring*, as well as a fanfare dedicated to tonight's conductor, Marin Alsop. See pages 14–19.

🖵 Recorded for broadcast on BBC TV and BBC iPlayer

Tuesday 25 August

7pm–c9.15pm • Royal Albert Hall

● £16.28–£59.12 (including booking fee*)

DANIEL BARTHOLOMEW-POYSER

Bond and Beyond

**BBC Concert Orchestra
Daniel Bartholomew-Poyser** conductor

No character in cinema history has a more instantly recognisable theme tune, or has inspired more classic pop songs, than James Bond. Daniel Bartholomew-Poyser conducts the BBC Concert Orchestra in a musical homage to Ian Fleming's suave spy. Together with special guests they train their sights on the greatest hits from *Skyfall*, *The Spy Who Loved Me* and others, promising to leave you stirred, not shaken.

🖵 Recorded for broadcast on BBC TV and BBC iPlayer

£8 Promming tickets available for every concert

Wednesday 26 August

7pm–c9.15pm • Royal Albert Hall

● £35.66–£114.20 (including booking fee*)

ELZA VAN DEN HEEVER

The Met Orchestra Plays Strauss

R. Strauss, arr. attrib. A. Rodziński
Der Rosenkavalier – suite 26'

R. Strauss Salome – final scene 18'

INTERVAL

R. Strauss Ein Heldenleben 46'

Elza van den Heever soprano

**The Met Orchestra
Yannick Nézet-Séguin** conductor

A long-awaited Proms debut for the Metropolitan Opera's Met Orchestra – praised for its 'white-hot musical drama' – under Music Director Yannick Nézet-Séguin. A sumptuous all-Strauss programme includes a suite from *Der Rosenkavalier* – a ravishing homage to Vienna's golden age – as well as the autobiographical drama of *Ein Heldenleben* – a striving, battling 'Hero's Life' brought to vivid orchestral life. Celebrated South African soprano Elza van den Heever joins the orchestra for the final scene of the composer's *Salome* – a searing centrepiece for one of the world's great opera orchestras. See pages 74–76.

🖵 Recorded for broadcast on BBC TV and BBC iPlayer

Thursday 27 August

6pm–c8.10pm • Royal Albert Hall

● £35.66–£114.20 (including booking fee*)

YANNICK NÉZET-SÉGUIN

The Met Orchestra Plays Mahler

Saariaho Lumière et pesanteur   7'
Mahler Rückert-Lieder   20'
INTERVAL
Mahler Symphony No. 4 in G major   57'

Joyce DiDonato mezzo-soprano

The Met Orchestra
Yannick Nézet-Séguin conductor

Star mezzo-soprano and former Last Night of the Proms soloist Joyce DiDonato joins Yannick Nézet-Séguin and The Met Orchestra for their second concert of the season. Mahler is in the spotlight celebrating the wonder of nature, innocence and faith in his Symphony No. 4 – lively with birdsong and sleigh bells – and looking beyond in the contemplative meditations – on life, death and transcendence – of his *Rückert-Lieder*. The same spirit runs through the swelling, breathing orchestral arcs of the late Kaija Saariaho's *Lumière et pesanteur* ('Light and Gravity') – luminescent music adapted from the composer's oratorio *La Passion de Simone*.

Thursday 27 August

10.15pm–c11.30pm • Royal Albert Hall ☾

● £12.20–£30.56 (including booking fee*)

ERLAND COOPER

Ultimate Calm

Erland Cooper presenter

Ultimate Calm has been taking listeners on immersive and reflective journeys through classical and ambient music since the show launched in 2022, with presenters including Ólafur Arnalds, Hania Rani and now Erland Cooper. This late-night Prom includea music by Cooper, originally from the Orkney Islands and whose work explores the themes of nature and landscape, along with guest artists, atmospheric soundscapes and electronic elements. A serene and escapist concert for the night hours.

📻 Broadcast live on BBC Radio 3 and Radio 3 Unwind

Spotlight on …

Joyce DiDonato • 27 August

'Each time I revisit this cycle, I'm singing the same words, notes, dynamics and articulation, but the inner journey always brings me to a different corner of the human experience. Having access to that journey as a singer, and then offering it to an audience, allows for them to also take a unique and highly personal journey alongside us musicians.' Joyce DiDonato is describing her relationship with Mahler's *Rückert-Lieder*. As she goes on to explain, communicating these enchanting, emotionally complex songs must begin with an 'absolute adherence' to the composer's meticulous directions. 'Mahler was incredibly specific in his markings in the score, and these are both the starting and ending points for a performer. However, there is also ample space to deeply personalise what these immense pieces mean to you: the struggle of faith and doubt ("Mitternacht"), the perfection and bliss of being alive in the world ("Ich atmet …"), the deep meaning of pure love ("Liebst du um Schönheit") and the sheer transcendence of "Ich bin der welt".'

The Prom ends with Mahler's Symphony No. 4, which incorporates into its finale the song 'Das himmlische Leben'. The poem upon which the song is based offers a child's vision of heaven, and DiDonato's approach is 'simply to be joyfully angelic. There is a childlike innocence and playful abandon in the text and vocal line, all pointing to angelic revelry and joy.'

Spotlight on …
Jakob Lehmann • 30 August

'The nature of the work is such that the imagination of the audience will do it the most justice,' says conductor Jakob Lehmann of Berlioz's visionary and unclassifiable masterpiece *The Damnation of Faust*, with which he makes his Proms debut. 'I think of it as a sort of audio drama, because the switches in time and place are quite abrupt at times, and the narrative is not chronological – some consecutive pieces happen at the same time in the plot.' Based on Goethe's two-part dramatic text, *Faust* divided audiences when it premiered in 1846. Berlioz described this part-opera, part-cantata as a 'dramatic legend' but Lehmann says audiences today 'appreciate its many idiosyncratic qualities: the unconventional narrative, the combination of styles and genres and the big contrasts between its chamber music-like moments and *tutti* outbursts. It is best enjoyed by letting the experience wash over oneself.'

Lehmann is joined by French ensemble Les Siècles – 'a group so flexible and versatile in its approach to any sort of repertoire,' he says. 'Even in music that is close to them, such as Berlioz, the players bring so many ideas to the table. The use of historical instruments clearly shows how Berlioz was pushing what was possible at that time. My hope is that the audience gets a sense of how physical and almost primal this music is. Performing with this orchestra and this extraordinary cast of singers is going to be a highlight of my career.'

Friday 28 August
7.30pm–c9pm • Royal Albert Hall

● £16.28–£59.12 (including booking fee*)

ALTIN GÜN

Altın Gün

BBC Symphony Orchestra
Jules Buckley conductor

There will be no interval

Grammy-nominated Dutch-Turkish band Altın Gün brings its unique blend of psychedelic folk-rock to the BBC Proms for the first time, drawing on its recent Anatolian rock album *Garip* ('Strange'), a tribute to the great Turkish folk musician Neşet Ertaş. The band joins forces with Jules Buckley and the BBC Symphony Orchestra to turn cool riffs and Anatolian folk textures into rich orchestral colours.

Saturday 29 August
7.30pm–c9.45pm • Royal Albert Hall

● £19.34–£71.36 (including booking fee*)

PATRICIA KOPATCHINSKAJA

Stravinsky and Prokofiev with the Oslo Philharmonic

Øyvind Torvund Symphonic Poem No. 1, 'Forest Morning' 12'
Stravinsky Violin Concerto 22'

INTERVAL

Prokofiev Romeo and Juliet – excerpts 42'

Patricia Kopatchinskaja violin

Oslo Philharmonic
Mirga Gražinytė-Tyla conductor

Powerhouse conductor Mirga Gražinytė-Tyla and the Oslo Philharmonic team up with maverick virtuoso Patricia Kopatchinskaja for Stravinsky's Bach-inspired Violin Concerto – a ferociously demanding work that showcases all the violinist's signature 'beauty, passion and imagination'. Shakespeare's warring families and passionate young lovers come to life in excerpts from Prokofiev's *Romeo and Juliet*, and the concert opens with Norwegian composer Øyvind Torvund's symphonic poem 'Forest Morning' for orchestra and electronics, in which idyllic birdsong is gradually taken over by the sounds of traffic and urban bustle.

Sunday 30 August

4.30pm–c5.30pm • Royal College of Music ☀

Tickets: free. For ticket information, see bbc.co.uk/promstickets

TESS JACKSON

BBC Young Composer

New works by:

Oskar Wit Baldyga
Luca Boston
Gerard Coutain
Noah Hacking
Nemunis Jusionis-Vila
Jixuan Li

BBC Concert Orchestra
Tess Jackson conductor

There will be no interval

Be first to hear pieces composed by the most recent winners of the BBC Young Composer competition, performed by the BBC Concert Orchestra. Mentored by Gavin Higgins, Helen Grime and Lloyd Coleman, these young composers have written new pieces that reflect and celebrate their own generation.

Every Prom is broadcast on BBC Radio 3 and BBC Sounds

Sunday 30 August

7pm–c9.30pm • Royal Albert Hall

● £19.34–£71.36 *(including booking fee*)*

VÉRONIQUE GENS

Berlioz's 'The Damnation of Faust'

Berlioz The Damnation of Faust 130'
(concert performance; sung in French, with English surtitles)

John Osborn Faust
Véronique Gens Marguerite
Gerald Finley Méphistophélès
Thomas Dolié Brander

Maîtrise de Radio France
Chœur de Radio France
Les Siècles
Jakob Lehmann conductor

There will be one interval

Berlioz's 'Dramatic Legend' *The Damnation of Faust* is an operatic thrill-ride, a *tour de force* for orchestra, chorus and soloists that throws all of music's capacity at one simple question: what is the price of the human soul? A story of heaven and hell, of demons and angels is best staged in sound and imagination – too cinematic for the confines of the stage. Jakob Lehmann and the period musicians of Les Siècles bring it to life in a concert performance with an international cast of soloists, including American tenor John Osborn in the title-role, Gerald Finley and Véronique Gens. *See pages 86–89.*

Monday 31 August

7pm–c9.30pm • Royal Albert Hall

● £28.52–£89.72 *(including booking fee*)*

BEAUTY AND THE BEAST

Enchanted: Alan Menken's Music for Disney

National Youth Music Theatre
BBC Philharmonic Orchestra
Anthony Parnther conductor

BSL *British Sign Language-interpreted by Kate Green*

There will be one interval

Only 21 people in the world are EGOTs – winners of the coveted quartet of Emmy, Grammy, Oscar and Tony Awards. One of those is Alan Menken, the American composer whose acclaimed catalogue of shows, songs and scores includes so many of Disney's greatest hits. Anthony Parnther conducts the BBC Philharmonic Orchestra, joined by special guests and performers from the National Youth Music Theatre in a celebration of this classic songwriter, including sets from *The Little Mermaid*, *Aladdin*, *Beauty and the Beast* and *Enchanted*. So why not 'Be our guest' …! *See pages 45–48.*

📺 *Recorded for broadcast on BBC TV and BBC iPlayer*

Spotlight on ...
Jakub Hrůša • 1 September

'The *Suita rustica* is a fresh, bold work that immediately makes a sympathetic impact. It is inspired by the same French-tinged modernism that composers such as Stravinsky and Prokofiev drew upon or directly helped to shape, while at the same time we hear very clearly echoes of folk music. It is a highly communicative piece.' Czech conductor Jakub Hrůša is describing the opening work of his Prom, which he performs with the BBC Symphony Orchestra. Its creator, the Czech composer Vítězslava Kaprálová, was on the cusp of an international career when she died tragically young, aged 25. The *Suita rustica* emerged two years before her death, by which time her qualities as both a composer and conductor were attracting the attention of critics and public alike.

The programme concludes with Janáček's final orchestral work, the *Sinfonietta*. This year marks the centenary of its composition, yet for Hrůša the piece 'fits our own time wonderfully well, because it is concise, direct, extraordinarily striking and effective. It is one of the finest works by our most original [Czech] creator and one of the most remarkable figures in the history of music.' He continues: 'For Janáček, the *Sinfonietta* may have been a lighter, occasional piece, yet in its effect it is utterly overwhelming. It is also a work that suits the Royal Albert Hall marvellously because it has a ceremonial brass character that calls for a vast space.'

Tuesday 1 September
7.30pm–c9.35pm • Royal Albert Hall

● £19.34–£71.36 (including booking fee*)

LUKÁŠ VONDRÁČEK

Rachmaninov's Third Piano Concerto

Kaprálová Suita rustica 16'
Rachmaninov Piano Concerto No. 3 in D minor 40'
INTERVAL
Janáček Sinfonietta 24'

Lukáš Vondráček *piano*
BBC Symphony Orchestra
Jakub Hrůša *conductor*

An afternoon spent listening to a military band in a Bohemian park inspired the arresting fanfares and jagged folk-rhythms of Janáček's last and best-loved orchestral work, composed 100 years ago, the *Sinfonietta*: less a conventional symphony than a sequence of sonic frescoes. Jakub Hrůša and the BBC Symphony Orchestra are joined by 'extraordinary' Czech pianist Lukáš Vondráček for the Everest of Romantic piano concertos – Rachmaninov's Third, for many years performed only by the composer himself. The concert opens with the haunting folk melodies and dancing rhythms of Kaprálová's *Suita rustica*.

Wednesday 2 September
6.30pm–c8.25pm • Royal Albert Hall

● £35.66–£114.20 (including booking fee*)

KIRILL PETRENKO

Berlin Philharmonic Plays Elgar and Tchaikovsky

Elgar 'Enigma' Variations 31'
INTERVAL
Tchaikovsky Symphony No. 4 in F minor 44'

Berlin Philharmonic
Kirill Petrenko *conductor*

'An artist lives a double life,' Tchaikovsky wrote. The Berlin Philharmonic and Chief Conductor Kirill Petrenko return to the Proms with a concert of concealed identities and confessions, musical secrets and hidden selves, explored in two Romantic orchestral classics. The secret theme concealed within Elgar's *'Enigma' Variations* remains elusive, but the heart-on-sleeve appeal of the composer's wistful, warmly personal musical sketches of his friends is anything but. The personal conflicts that lie beneath the tumultuous surface of Tchaikovsky's Symphony No. 4 are darker: Fate assails the listener before the music casts off its grip in a defiantly joyous finale. *See pages 36–39.*

Wednesday 2 September

10.15pm–c11.30pm • Royal Albert Hall

● £14.24–£39.74 (including booking fee*)

COLIN CURRIE

Steve Reich at 90

Early sacred choral music by composers including Hildegard of Bingen, Machaut, Josquin and Pérotin   35'

Steve Reich Tehillim   30'

The Gesualdo Six
Owain Park director

Colin Currie Group
Colin Currie conductor

There will be no interval

Vivid percussion-and-voice rhythms of the 20th century contrast with the choral consolation of the ancient. The Gesualdo Six and the Colin Currie Group come together for a Late-Night Prom that combines the Christian meditations of the Renaissance – choral works by composers including Hildegard of Bingen, Machaut, Josquin and Pérotin – with Steve Reich's take on traditional Hebrew Psalms, in his ecstatic, deeply moving *Tehillim*.

£8 Promming tickets available for every concert

Thursday 3 September

7pm–c9.15pm • Royal Albert Hall

● £35.66–£114.20 (including booking fee*)

AUGUSTIN HADELICH

Berlin Philharmonic Plays Beethoven and Scriabin

Beethoven Violin Concerto in D major   42'

INTERVAL

Scriabin Symphony No. 3 in C minor, 'The Divine Poem'   50'

Augustin Hadelich violin

Berlin Philharmonic
Kirill Petrenko conductor

The 'sumptuous' and 'sublime' Berlin Philharmonic and Chief Conductor Kirill Petrenko pair Beethoven's Violin Concerto – with the singing lyricism of its slow movement and exuberant dancing Rondo – with the rapturous musical tussle of Scriabin's Third Symphony: worldly pleasure and spiritual enlightenment locked in an intoxicating, mystical battle of wills, 'A joyful and liberating affirmation of … liberty and unity with the universe'. Grammy Award-winning violinist Augustin Hadelich returns to the Proms following his 'intimate, poised and heartbreakingly direct' performance of Mendelssohn's Violin Concerto last season.

Friday 4 September

7pm–c9.15pm • Royal Albert Hall

● £16.28–£59.12 (including booking fee*)

SIMONE LAMSMA

Vaughan Williams's 'Fantasia' and Symphony No. 9

Vaughan Williams Fantasia on a Theme by Thomas Tallis   15'

Britten Violin Concerto   32'

INTERVAL

Carmel Smickersgill A Brick Thrown with Love   c10'
BBC co-commission: world premiere

Vaughan Williams Symphony No. 9 in E minor   33'

Simone Lamsma violin

Royal Liverpool Philharmonic Orchestra
Andrew Manze conductor

Andrew Manze conducts the Royal Liverpool Philharmonic Orchestra in a celebration of English music, including a commission from Carmel Smickersgill exploring resilience in the face of tragedy. The starkly beautiful landscape of Thomas Hardy's Wessex haunts the score of Vaughan Williams's Symphony No. 9 – pastoral yearning tinged with darker wartime memories and fears, a contrast to the radiant spiritual affirmation of the composer's *Fantasia on a Theme by Thomas Tallis*, with its shimmering clouds of strings. 'Eloquent' Dutch violinist Simone Lamsma makes her Proms debut in Benjamin Britten's Violin Concerto, another work steeped in thoughts of war and hopes of peace. *See pages 56–60.*

Saturday 5 September

7pm–c9.15pm • Royal Albert Hall

● £28.52–£89.72 *(including booking fee*)*

MARTHA ARGERICH

Martha Argerich Plays Beethoven

Farrenc Overture No. 2 — 7'
Beethoven Piano Concerto No. 2 in B flat major — 28'

INTERVAL

Brahms Symphony No. 4 in E minor — 46'

Martha Argerich *piano*
Munich Philharmonic
Lahav Shani *conductor*

Yuja Wang calls her the 'pure goddess' of the piano, to others she's simply the world's greatest living pianist: Martha Argerich is back at the Proms, joining Lahav Shani and the Munich Philharmonic for the singing beauty and light-hearted delight of Beethoven's Second Piano Concerto. Brahms's final symphony offers glimpses of warmth and joy, but always shrouded in melancholy. One critic compared the work to gazing into a deep well: 'The longer we look into it, the more brightly the stars shine back …' The concert opens with Louise Farrenc's dramatic Overture No. 2.

🖥 *Recorded for broadcast on BBC TV and BBC iPlayer*

Sunday 6 September

11am–c1pm • Royal Albert Hall ☀

● £16.28–£59.12 *(including booking fee*)*

JOHN WILSON

John Wilson Conducts the Sinfonia of London Strings

L. Berkeley Serenade for Strings — 13'
Bridge Lament — 4'
Britten Les illuminations — 22'

INTERVAL

I. Holst Suite for String Orchestra — 16'
Britten Variations on a Theme of Frank Bridge — 26'

Julie Roset *soprano*
Sinfonia of London *(strings)*
John Wilson *conductor*

'I alone hold the key to this wild parade.' Benjamin Britten is the keystone of this second concert by John Wilson and the Sinfonia of London *(see 24 July)*, a family tree of English music. The shimmering, kaleidoscopic visions of the composer's orchestral song-cycle *Les illuminations* – performed by rising-star soprano Julie Roset – and the taut, witty invention of his *Variations on a Theme of Frank Bridge* are framed by works by members of Britten's circle: teachers, friends and colleagues. Imogen Holst's *Suite for String Orchestra* – her homage to England's musical past and vision for its future – receives its Proms premiere. *See pages 56–60.*

Sunday 6 September

7.30pm–c9.25pm • Royal Albert Hall

● £19.34–£71.36 *(including booking fee*)*

SHEKU KANNEH-MASON

Dvořák's 'New World' Symphony

Britten The Young Person's Guide to the Orchestra — 18'
Gwilym Simcock Triple Concerto for Soprano Saxophone, Horn and Cello — c20'
BBC co-commission: world premiere

INTERVAL

Dvořák Symphony No. 9 in E minor, 'From the New World' — 40'

Jess Gillam *saxophone*
Ben Goldscheider *horn*
Sheku Kanneh-Mason *cello*
BBC Symphony Orchestra
Sakari Oramo *conductor*

BBC Young Musician has launched many classical careers since it began in 1978. Three of its 2016 finalists – Jess Gillam, Ben Goldscheider and Sheku Kanneh-Mason – are reunited a decade on in a specially commissioned Triple Concerto by former BBC Radio 3 New Generation Artist Gwilym Simcock, full of rhythmic energy and joy. Britten's colourful *The Young Person's Guide to the Orchestra* and the folk-inspired warmth of Dvořák's 'New World' Symphony complete a vibrant programme. *See pages 14–19, 56–60.*

🖥 *Recorded for broadcast on BBC TV and BBC iPlayer*

Monday 7 September

7pm–c9.15pm • Royal Albert Hall

£28.52–£89.72 (including booking fee*)

ISABELLE FAUST

Rattle Conducts Schumann

Schumann
Genoveva – overture 10'
Violin Concerto in D minor 33'

INTERVAL

Symphony No. 2 in C major 38'

Isabelle Faust *violin*

Freiburg Baroque Orchestra
Sir Simon Rattle *conductor*

The elusive, troubled visionary Robert Schumann is in the spotlight for Sir Simon Rattle and the Freiburg Baroque Orchestra – 'one of the most polished period-instrument ensembles in the world' – which brings its distinctive tang and timbre to three of the composer's best-loved works. Joy and despair, sanity and madness are in constant conflict through Schumann's music, a battle that yields a glorious C major resolution in the overture from *Genoveva* and a profound, resilient optimism in the rich Second Symphony. But peace is harder to come by in the enigmatic Violin Concerto, composed on the brink of the composer's final mental collapse. Isabelle Faust is the soloist. *See pages 68–71.*

Tuesday 8 September

6.30pm–c8.15pm • Royal Albert Hall

£16.28–£59.12 (including booking fee*)

RYAN WIGGLESWORTH

Rachmaninov, Bartók and Varèse

Varèse Density 21.5 3'
Bartók Music for Strings, Percussion and Celesta 28'

INTERVAL

Rachmaninov Symphony No. 3 in A minor 39'

Matthew Higham *flute*

BBC Scottish Symphony Orchestra
Ryan Wigglesworth *conductor*

The BBC Scottish Symphony Orchestra and Ryan Wigglesworth celebrate the orchestra's 90th anniversary with a snapshot of a golden year in musical history: 1936 was a turning point, producing not only Rachmaninov's final symphony – the Romantic, death-haunted No. 3 – but also Bartók's electrifying fusion of folk and modernity, his *Music for Strings, Percussion and Celesta*, with its two duelling string orchestras and barrage of percussion forces. Varèse tests the limits of sound and space in *Density 21.5* – named for the density of platinum – for solo flute, performed by the orchestra's Principal Flute Matthew Higham.

Tuesday 8 September

10.15pm–c11.30pm • Royal Albert Hall

£14.24–£39.74 (including booking fee*)

JULES BUCKLEY

Jules Buckley Orchestra

Jules Buckley *conductor*

There will be no interval

Jules Buckley's collaborations with an array of artists mark him out as a musician with no bounds. At the Proms he has appeared with Laura Mvula, Jacob Collier, Anoushka Shankar, Florence + The Machine and St. Vincent, and led celebrations of Quincy Jones, Nina Simone, Aretha Franklin and Nick Drake. For this, his 26th Proms appearance, he returns with his own ensemble in a new collaboration – a typically imaginative meeting of musical minds in an intimate late-night setting.

Every Prom is broadcast on BBC Radio 3 and BBC Sounds

Spotlight on …
Nicky Spence • 12 September

'The Proms has been a very happy thread through my life, so coming back for the Last Night feels rather like being handed the keys to the kingdom,' says the Scottish tenor Nicky Spence. 'It's a real arrival moment for a singer – one of those evenings you grow up watching and dare not imagine yourself in, as it's too delicious!' Spence has performed several times at the Proms in recent years, and in 2024 he joined presenter Katie Derham and guests in the commentary box at the Last Night of the Proms. 'Having been part of the presenting gang, I know there's nothing quite like the atmosphere in the Royal Albert Hall: grand, joyful, and just a tiny bit mischievous. I feel hugely grateful to be part of it. True to tradition, there will be one or two surprises in store. It is the Last Night, after all.'

Spence, who made his Proms debut over a decade ago, is looking forward to performing with the BBC Symphony Orchestra and conductor Sakari Oramo. 'They are a dream to work with: curious, generous, and wonderfully alive to colour. Sakari has that rare combination of razor-sharp clarity and complete bear-hug warmth. He knows exactly what he wants, but he creates such a spirit of trust that you feel brave enough to try things. It never feels like a conductor and soloist dynamic; it feels like music-making among friends. I'm a very lucky lad to be joining them for such a big celebration of music.'

Wednesday 9 September
7pm–c8.55pm • Royal Albert Hall

● £16.28–£59.12 (including booking fee*)

PAWEŁ KAPUŁA

Strauss's 'Four Last Songs'

Henze Erlkönig – orchestral fantasy 6'
Schubert Symphony No. 8 in B minor, 'Unfinished' 25'

INTERVAL

Mahler, arr. Britten What the Wild Flowers Tell Me 10'
R. Strauss Four Last Songs 24'

Natalya Romaniw soprano

BBC Scottish Symphony Orchestra
Paweł Kapuła conductor

Schubert's 'Unfinished', one of at least three symphonies he left incomplete at his death, is one of his most popular, combining private drama with lyrical sweetness. The same composer's alarming song 'Erlkönig' inspired Hans Werner Henze to create his vivid orchestral fantasy evoking a terrifying, supernatural night-ride. 'My new god' was what Benjamin Britten discovered on hearing his first Mahler symphony soon after leaving school. His arrangement of 'What the Wild Flowers Tell Me', the second movement of Mahler's Third Symphony, reclothes a piece inspired by the abundant blooms around the Austrian composer's lakeside composing hut by the Swiss Alps. First performed at the Royal Albert Hall in 1950, Richard Strauss's *Four Last Songs* is the composer's achingly nostalgic musical farewell.

Thursday 10 September
7pm–c9.30pm • Royal Albert Hall

● £28.52–£89.72 (including booking fee*)

JEANINE DE BIQUE

Bach's Mass in B minor with Arcangelo

J. S. Bach Mass in B minor 115'

Jeanine De Bique soprano
Eva Zaïcik soprano
Hugh Cutting counter-tenor
Nick Pritchard tenor
Florian Störtz bass-baritone

Arcangelo
Jonathan Cohen director/harpsichord

There will be one interval

The spiritual and musical summation of a life, J. S. Bach's Mass in B minor is one of the most powerful and universal statements in art, as well as one of the most joyous musical experiences of the repertoire. This compendium of styles and textures – thrilling contrapuntal choruses, virtuosic and emotive arias and duets, brilliantly inventive orchestral writing – comes together in a deeply moving musical epic. Continuing their 'tremendous' Proms performances of sacred Baroque masterpieces, Arcangelo and Music Director Jonathan Cohen return with an exciting team of soloists that includes soprano Jeanine De Bique and counter-tenor Hugh Cutting. *See page 12.*

Friday 11 September

8pm–c9.30pm • Royal Albert Hall

● £19.34–£71.36 (including booking fee*)

PHILIPP VON STEINAECKER

Mahler's Ninth with the Mahler Academy Orchestra

Mahler Symphony No. 9 81'

Mahler Academy Orchestra
Philipp von Steinaecker *conductor*

There will be no interval

Death haunts Mahler's monumental Ninth Symphony, woven right through it from the brooding farewell of a first movement – 'the greatest Mahler ever composed', according to Alban Berg – to the finale's radiant, distant vision of a world beyond. Musicians from across Europe come together under Philipp von Steinaecker in the Mahler Academy Orchestra's Proms debut. This pioneering project combines student players with professionals from Europe's best ensembles to explore and recreate the instruments Mahler himself would have known, generating a performance as close as possible to the work's original sound and style. *See pages 68–71.*

£8 Promming tickets available for every concert

Saturday 12 September

7.15pm–c10.30pm • Royal Albert Hall

● £53–£185.60 (including booking fee*)

NICKY SPENCE

YUJA WANG

Last Night of the Proms 2026

Programme to include:

arr. Wood Fantasia on British Sea-Songs 13'

Arne, arr. Sargent Rule, Britannia! 5'

Elgar Pomp and Circumstance March No. 1 in D major ('Land of Hope and Glory') 8'

Parry, orch. Elgar Jerusalem 2'

arr. Britten The National Anthem 2'

Trad., arr. P. Campbell Auld lang syne 2'

Nicky Spence *tenor*
Yuja Wang *piano*

BBC Singers
BBC Symphony Chorus
BBC Symphony Orchestra
Sakari Oramo *conductor*

There will be one interval

The culmination of a summer of over 80 concerts – including at venues around the country – classical music's greatest international party draws the 2026 Proms to a close while echoing some of the themes of the season. Superstar pianist Yuja Wang returns following her last appearance here in 2023. Her talents are matched by the vocal and stage prowess of charismatic Scottish tenor Nicky Spence, whose repertoire ranges from operatic roles by Britten and Janáček to the witty, urbane numbers of Noël Coward. As ever, BBC forces flood the stage of the Royal Albert, all marshalled by Sakari Oramo, returning for his fifth Prom this summer – including an appearance as violinist in Bristol – and his seventh Last Night. *See pages 14–19.*

📺 *Broadcast live on BBC Two (first half), BBC One (second half) and BBC iPlayer*

Every Prom is broadcast on BBC Radio 3 and BBC Sounds

Proms North East

Thursday 23 July
MIDDLESBROUGH TOWN HALL
7.30pm–c9.30pm

ROYAL NORTHERN SINFONIA

Royal Northern Sinfonia Presents …

Royal Northern Sinfonia
There will be one interval

Following the success of last year's 'homecoming' Prom with JADE (described as 'a love letter to the region') and earlier collaborations with Jordan Rakei and Self Esteem, the ever-eclectic Royal Northern Sinfonia feeds its appetite for explorations into new musical dialogues.

 *Recorded for future broadcast on BBC Radio 3*

Proms Gateshead

Thursday 23 July
THE GLASSHOUSE INTERNATIONAL CENTRE FOR MUSIC
8pm–c10pm • Sage Two

SHAKK

BBC Introducing from The Glasshouse: Live at the Proms

Shakk *presenter*
There will be no interval

A celebration of musicians who have launched their careers under the groundbreaking BBC Introducing scheme. Catch up with brilliant emerging and independent artists making waves in the North East and beyond. This special BBC Proms edition promises a line-up of fresh performers that you'll want to tell friends you saw here first.

Friday 24 July
THE GLASSHOUSE INTERNATIONAL CENTRE FOR MUSIC
7pm–c8.35pm • Sage Two

DINIS SOUSA

Crippled Symmetry

Feldman Crippled Symmetry 90'

Helena Gourd *flute/bass flute*
Jude Carlton *percussion*
Dinis Sousa *piano/celesta*
There will be no interval

The intricate patterns of Turkish rugs – conjured from the memory of the women who wove them – inspired the mesmerising meditation that is centenary composer Morton Feldman's *Crippled Symmetry*. Scored for flutes, percussion, piano and the glassy-toned celesta, this is music that seems to float, at once absolutely controlled and left freely to chance – its hypnotic patterns forming and reforming like a mobile, suspended in the air. The Royal Northern Sinfonia's Music Director Dinis Sousa is joined by principal musicians Jude Carlton and Helena Gourd.

Recorded for future broadcast on BBC Radio 3

FOR VENUE DETAILS, SEE PAGES 149–50

Friday 24 July

THE GLASSHOUSE INTERNATIONAL CENTRE FOR MUSIC
9pm–c11pm • Concourse

NADINE SHAH

Nadine Shah and Royal Northern Sinfonia

Nadine Shah

Royal Northern Sinfonia
Ellie Slorach conductor

There will be one interval

With her subjects including grief, womanhood and addiction, and melodies inspired by Sufi singer Abida Parveen, Nadine Shah is a powerful voice in the UK indie-rock scene. The Mercury Prize-nominated South Tyneside-born singer-songwriter collaborates with the Royal Northern Sinfonia in the latest of the orchestra's series of bold musical dialogues.

Saturday 25 July

THE GLASSHOUSE INTERNATIONAL CENTRE FOR MUSIC
4pm–c7pm • Concourse

VOICES OF THE RIVER'S EDGE

Choirs on the Concourse

Programme to include:

Parry Songs of Farewell – selection
Tavener Song for Athene

Jess Gillam saxophone

BBC Singers
Voices of the River's Edge
Chorus of Royal Northern Sinfonia
Sofi Jeannin conductor

There will be two intervals

A mini choral convention, shining a spotlight on voices from the North East as well as on the BBC Singers. The event includes a selection from Parry's set of motets written during the First World War, as well as Tavener's heart-rending memorial for a family friend who died tragically young in a cycling accident.

🎙 *Recorded for future broadcast on BBC Radio 3*

Saturday 25 July

THE FIRE STATION, SUNDERLAND
7.30pm–c9.30pm

MARIA WŁOSZCZOWSKA

Mozart and Mendelssohn

Bacewicz Divertimento 7'
Mendelssohn Concerto for Violin, Piano and Strings in D minor 37'

INTERVAL

Mozart Symphony No. 39 in E flat major 29'

Christian Ihle Hadland piano

Royal Northern Sinfonia
Maria Włoszczowska director/violin

Polish violinist Maria Włoszczowska directs the Royal Northern Sinfonia in a programme of musical innovations and provocations. Grażyna Bacewicz turns an 18th-century entertainment into a witty, piquant and often densely beautiful miniature. The 14-year-old Mendelssohn had no model for his unusual Concerto for Violin, Piano and Strings but combined his two soloists with ingenious and eloquent results. At the other end of his career, Mozart took the symphony to new heights in his final three efforts in the genre, beginning with the vivacious Symphony No. 39, whose brilliance veers on the cusp of darkness.

Proms Bristol

Friday 7 August
BRISTOL BEACON
7.30pm–c8.45pm • Beacon Hall

PARAORCHESTRA

Steve Reich at 90

Steve Reich
Music for 18 Musicians　　65'

Paraorchestra
Charles Hazlewood director
Faye Stoeser director

AD *Audio-described*

There will be no interval

Paraorchestra, the bold collective of disabled and non-disabled musicians, brings an immersive take on Steve Reich's *Music for 18 Musicians*. When it was first performed 50 years ago, the work made Reich a household name and propelled Minimalism into the mainstream. Here it's performed with the players distributed on plinths across Beacon Hall, breaking the barrier between audience and performers and allowing you to explore the work's sublime shifting phases as you move among pulsing marimbas, pianos and vocals, or simply remain still and allow yourself to be enveloped. *See pages 14–19.*

📻 *Recorded for future broadcast on BBC Radio 3*

Saturday 8 August
BRISTOL BEACON
5pm–c7.10pm • Beacon Hall

ADAM HICKOX

Russian Classics

Shostakovich
Festive Overture　　7'
Cello Concerto No. 1 in E flat major　　30'

INTERVAL

Gubaidulina Fairy-Tale Poem　　12'
Rachmaninov
Symphonic Dances　　35'

Max Hornung cello

Bournemouth Symphony Orchestra
Adam Hickox conductor

BSL *British Sign Language-interpreted*

Rachmaninov's *Symphonic Dances* is a summation of his career, a whirling phantasmagoria of rhythm and melody. The Russian spirit also runs through both Shostakovich's *Festive Overture* and his sardonically witty Cello Concerto No. 1. Gubaidulina's *Fairy-Tale Poem* introduces a whimsical element, a sumptuous musical fantasy about the adventures of a piece of chalk.

Saturday 8 August
BRISTOL BEACON
8pm–c10pm • Lantern Hall

JOHN COLTRANE

'Round Midnight

There will be one interval

A special live edition of the acclaimed late-night Radio 3 jazz show *'Round Midnight*. Following last year's Proms celebration of Oscar Peterson in Sunderland, this year the focus turns to the centenary artist John Coltrane and his 1965 album *A Love Supreme*, which not only reflected the jazz legend's own spiritual journey but also deeply resonated with the struggles of America's Civil Rights Movement.

📻 *Recorded for future broadcast on BBC Radio 3*

Sunday 9 August

BRISTOL BEACON
2.30pm–c3.30pm • Beacon Hall

Relaxed Prom

Price, arr. Rhian Davies Symphony No. 1 in E minor – Juba Dance 3'

Oliver Cross, arr. Liam Taylor-West Barriers 7'

Vivaldi, arr. Rhian Davies The Four Seasons – excerpts 14'

Michael Betteridge, arr. Julia Koelmans Soaring Through Sparks (Clarion Concerto) 3'

Charlotte Harding, arr. Liam Taylor-West The Orchestra: A Young Person's Guide 12'
BBC commission

Alessandro Vazzana *clarion*
National Open Youth Orchestra
Members of the BBC National Orchestra of Wales
Alice Farnham *conductor*

BSL *British Sign Language-interpreted*
R *Relaxed performance*
There will be no interval

The National Open Youth Orchestra – the world's first disabled-led national youth ensemble – and members of BBC NOW perform music spanning the sound-pictures of Vivaldi's *The Four Seasons* to Florence Price's toe-tapping Juba Dance and Michael Betteridge's concerto for Clarion, an accessible instrument. *See pages 52–55. For more details about Relaxed Proms, see page 152.*

Recorded for future broadcast on BBC Radio 3

Sunday 9 August

ST GEORGE'S BRISTOL
4pm–c5.20pm

TENEBRAE

Path of Miracles

Joby Talbot Path of Miracles 70'

Tenebrae
Nigel Short *conductor*
There will be no interval

Follow the Camino – the ancient pilgrim route – to Spain's Santiago de Compostela in the spiritually charged choral ecstasy of Joby Talbot's *Path of Miracles*: a pilgrimage in sound. The 500-mile musical journey starts at the Abbey of Roncesvalles at the foot of the Pyrenees, travelling across country via the great cathedrals of Burgos and León in music whose Minimalist patterns meet the beauty of plainchant and bell chimes. Nigel Short conducts his award-winning choir Tenebrae – the work's 'magnificent' commissioners – in this Proms premiere.

Sunday 9 August

BRISTOL BEACON
6pm–c7.05pm • Lantern Hall

ANU KOMSI

Kafka Fragments

György Kurtág Kafka Fragments 60'

Anu Komsi *soprano*
Sakari Oramo *violin*
There will be no interval

Part song-cycle, part personal diary, at once a duet and a duel between soprano and violin, György Kurtág's *Kafka Fragments* is a collection of musical aphorisms – an armful of miniatures that both provoke and defy interpretation. Fragile and hauntingly lyrical, violent and sensual, these distilled works – few of them longer than a minute – explore the strange kinship between composer and author in music haunted by the ghosts of Bach, Bartók, Schumann and more. Celebrated Finnish musicians Anu Komsi and Sakari Oramo perform this intimate recital as part of the composer's 100th-birthday celebrations.

Recorded for future broadcast on BBC Radio 3

Saturday 29 August

THEATR CLWYD, MOLD
4pm–c5.30pm

IWAN DAVIES

Words and Music

Sinfonia Cymru
Iwan Davies conductor

BSL *British Sign Language-interpreted*
There will be no interval

An afternoon sequence exploring the connections and communicative powers of words and music, inspired by the themes of legend and folklore. Among the prose and poetry excerpts in English and Welsh lies an excursion into the fantastical medieval folk tales of *The Mabinogion*. A moment to spark the imagination and a shared experience to transcend the everyday.

BBC Young Composer Workshops

BBC PROMS YOUNG COMPOSER WORKSHOP, 2024

myplace, Middlesbrough
Thursday 23 July

Bristol Beacon
Saturday 8 August

Theatre Clwyd, Mold
Saturday 29 August

Our free BBC Young Composer workshops offer young music-makers the chance to develop their own original music with support from experienced composers and musicians. Through a range of creative activities, these workshops provide a space to build confidence, try out new ideas, sharpen skills and learn from professionals working in the industry. The workshops, which take place in Bristol, Middlesbrough and Mold, are designed for young people already making their own music across any style or genre.

BBC Young Composer aims to nurture and develop the next generation of young composers, creating opportunities and resources for 12- to 18-year-olds across the UK who make their own original music. It holds a nationwide competition every two years. Past winners include Kristina Arakelyan, Grace-Evangeline Mason, Shiva Feshareki, Mark Simpson and Asteryth Sloane.

The initiative offers a wealth of composition resources for both teachers and young people, and was conceived with the hope of inspiring more young people to get creative with music and to consider a career in the music industry.

For further information and current opportunities, visit bbc.co.uk/youngcomposer

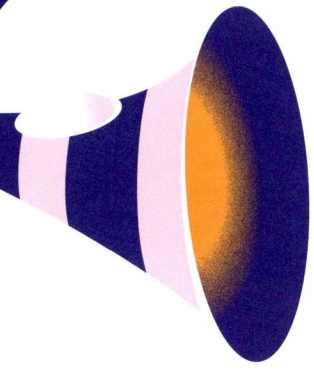

Booking at the Royal Albert Hall

Online
royalalberthall.com or
bbc.co.uk/promstickets

By phone
on 020 7070 4441*
9am–5pm, weekdays, plus:
Saturday 16 May: 9am–8pm
Sunday 17 May: 9am–5pm

In person
at the Royal Albert Hall
Box Office (Door 12)
9am–9pm, daily; please note:
until 17 July, on days where there is
no evening performance at the Hall,
the Box Office will close at 5pm

21 April
Create your Proms Plan online

From 9am on Tuesday 21 April, go to bbc.co.uk/promstickets and fill in your Proms Planner. You must complete and submit your Plan by 11.59pm on Friday 15 May in order to make a booking. Creating a Plan does not by itself result in a booking.

14 May
Book your Promming Passes

From 9am on Thursday 14 May, book your Season and Weekend Promming (standing) Passes for the Royal Albert Hall. (These passes are not bookable in the Proms Planner.)

15 May
Booking opens for the Horrible Science Proms and the Relaxed Prom

From 9am on Friday 15 May, book your tickets for the Horrible Science Proms (25 July) and Relaxed Prom (9 August). (These tickets are not bookable in the Proms Planner.)

16 May
General booking opens

From 9am on Saturday 16 May, submit your Proms Plan; or book online via bbc.co.uk/promstickets, in person or by phone. See bbc.co.uk/promstickets for details of how to book.

TICKETS FOR CONCERTS AT OTHER VENUES
Tickets for concerts in Bristol, Gateshead, Middlesbrough, Mold and Sunderland will be available directly from each venue, not the Royal Albert Hall. (These tickets are not bookable via the Proms Planner.) See pages 149–150 for details of these venues.

* CALL COSTS
Standard geographic charges from landlines and mobiles apply. All calls may be recorded and monitored for training and quality-control purposes.

Royal Albert Hall ticket prices

Seated ticket price bands are shown at the top of each concert listing on pages 108–144. The prices shown below include a fee of 2% of the total value – plus £2 per ticket (£1 per ticket for the Relaxed Prom) up to a maximum of £25. This applies to all bookings (including Season and Weekend Promming Passes) made online and by telephone. Bookings made in person at the Royal Albert Hall do not incur fees. See bbc.co.uk/promstickets for full details. Promming (standing) tickets are available on the day of each concert for just £8 (including a £1.14 booking fee, whether tickets are bought online or in person). See opposite for details.

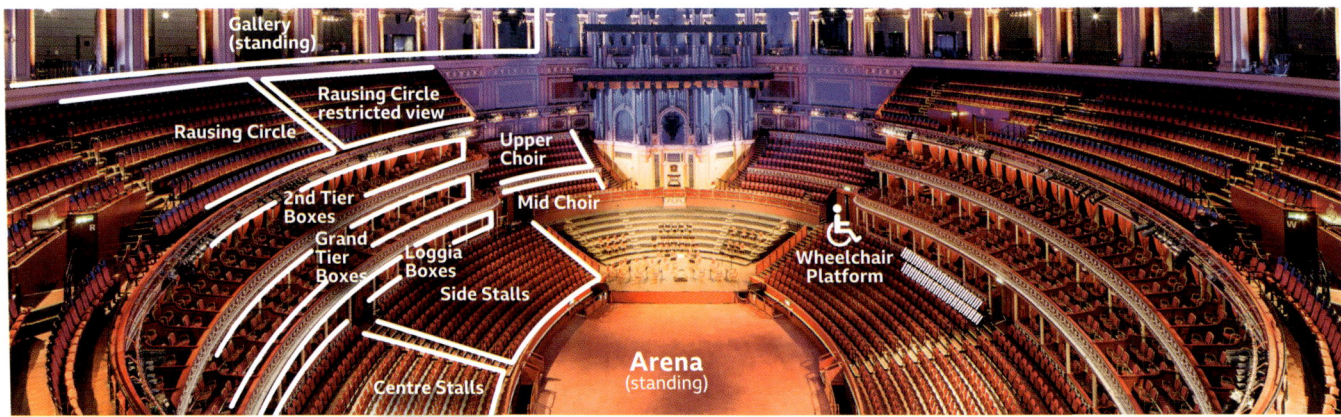

PRICE BANDS	🔵	🟢	🔴	🟠	🩷	🟩	🟣	🩷	🟡
GRAND TIER BOXES 12 seats, price per seat *	£33.64	£30.56	£39.74	£48.92	£59.12	£71.36	£89.72	£114.20	£185.60
LOGGIA AND 2ND TIER BOXES Loggia: 8 seats, price per seat 2nd Tier: 5 seats, price per seat	£31.60	£30.56	£39.74	£44.84	£55.04	£69.32	£85.64	£104	£175.40
CENTRE STALLS	£28.54	£27.50	£36.68	£40.76	£50.96	£67.28	£81.56	£101.96	£165.20
SIDE STALLS	£25.48	£27.50	£36.68	£36.68	£48.92	£63.20	£77.48	£93.80	£155
MID CHOIR	£23.44	£26.48	£34.64	£30.56	£34.64	£40.76	£54.02	£65.24	£104
UPPER CHOIR	£19.36	£21.38	£26.48	£25.46	£28.52	£34.64	£47.90	£59.12	£98.90
RAUSING CIRCLE FRONT	£21.40	£23.42	£28.52	£28.52	£31.58	£37.70	£51.98	£62.18	£101.96
RAUSING CIRCLE MID	£19.36	£20.36	£26.48	£24.44	£26.48	£32.60	£42.80	£49.94	£83.60
RAUSING CIRCLE REAR	£16.30	£18.32	£23.42	£19.34	£21.38	£28.52	£36.68	£42.80	£78.50
RAUSING CIRCLE RESTRICTED VIEW	£13.24	£12.20	£14.24	£14.24	£16.28	£19.34	£28.52	£35.66	£53

£8 Promming (standing) tickets

An optional £1.50 levy will be added to tickets for Proms at the Royal Albert Hall. *As most Grand Tier Boxes are privately owned, availability is limited.

There's a Prom for every music-lover, whether you're a first-timer or a seasoned regular. For the season calendar, see the inside back cover. Seats start from just £10 (plus booking fee) – and you can Prom (stand) for only £8 (including booking fee).

If you cannot use your ticket
Tickets cannot be refunded or exchanged after purchase. But, if you cannot use a ticket for any reason and want to try to resell it, we recommend using Twickets – an ethical ticket resale marketplace, enabling concert-goers to sell tickets at no more than face value.

Promming on the day
The popular tradition of Promming (standing in the Arena or Gallery areas of the Royal Albert Hall) is central to the unique atmosphere of the BBC Proms. Around 1,000 standing places in the Arena and Gallery are available on the day of each concert for just £8 (including booking fee). You can book up to two tickets online from 9.30am on the day of the concert. If you are unable to book online, you may be able to book in person at the Royal Albert Hall Box Office (Door 12), subject to availability. Visit bbc.co.uk/proms for details.

Save money by buying a Season Promming Pass for £287.60. These offer priority access to standing places in the Arena or Gallery throughout the season (excluding the Horrible Science Proms, Relaxed Prom and a second performance of the Aurora Prom) plus savings on individual ticket prices, as well as guaranteed admission to the Last Night of the Proms. Weekend Promming Passes are also available. Visit bbc.co.uk/proms for full details.

For information on Promming tickets for non-Royal Albert Hall concerts, see bbc.co.uk/promstickets.

A limited number of seats are available either at the back of the Arena or in the Choir or Gallery for those Prommers who are unable to stand for an entire concert. These can be booked online. See bbc.co.uk/proms for details.

Online booking
The 'Select Your Own Seat' option is not available via the Proms Planner or during the first few days that Proms tickets are on sale. You will be allocated the best available places within your chosen seating area. During this time it is also not possible to book an entire box online. If you would like to book a complete box, call the Box Office on 020 7070 4441.

18s and under go half-price
Tickets for people aged 18 and under can be bought at half-price in any seating area of the Royal Albert Hall (not including Promming tickets or tickets for the Last Night).

Great savings for groups
Groups of 10 or more attending Royal Albert Hall concerts can claim a 5% discount on the price of selected tickets (not including the Last Night). For details, call the Group Booking Information Line on 020 7070 4408.

Concerts across the UK
For information regarding tickets for non-Royal Albert Hall concerts, see bbc.co.uk/promstickets.

Last Night of the Proms
Owing to high demand, the majority of seated tickets for the Last Night are allocated by ballot, as follows:

The Five-Concert Ballot
Customers who purchase tickets for at least five other concerts at the Royal Albert Hall are eligible to enter the Five-Concert Ballot. For details on how to enter, see bbc.co.uk/promstickets. The Five-Concert Ballot closes at midnight on Thursday 4 June.

If you require a wheelchair space for the Last Night, you will still need to book for five other concerts, but you must phone the Access Information Line (020 7070 4410) before 5pm on Thursday 4 June to enter the separate ballot for wheelchair spaces.

The Open Ballot
One hundred Centre Stalls seats (priced £160 each, plus booking fee) and 100 Front Circle seats (priced £98 each, plus booking fee) for the Last Night will be allocated by Open Ballot, which closes at midnight on Thursday 9 July. Please enter the ballot online or complete the official ballot form at bbc.co.uk/promstickets.

General availability for the Last Night
Any remaining tickets for the Last Night will go on sale at 9am on Friday 17 July by phone or online only. Only one application (for a maximum of two tickets) can be made per household. Demand for Last Night tickets is exceptionally high, but returns occasionally become available.

Promming (standing) at the Last Night
Season Promming Passes include admission to the Last Night. A limited allocation of Last Night standing tickets (priced £8, including booking fee) are also reserved for Prommers who have attended five or more concerts. They are eligible to purchase one ticket each for the Last Night on presentation of their used tickets (which will be retained) at the Box Office. For details, see bbc.co.uk/promstickets.

A limited number of Promming tickets are available on the Last Night itself (priced £8, including booking fee, one per person). No previous ticket purchases are necessary.

Royal Albert Hall

Kensington Gore, London SW7 2AP
www.royalalberthall.com • 020 7070 4441

The Royal Albert Hall of Arts and Sciences was officially opened by Queen Victoria on 29 March 1871. When, in 1867, Victoria laid the foundation stone for the building, she announced that it was to be named after her husband, Prince Albert, who had died six years earlier.

The Hall has hosted 25 suffragette meetings, and many of the world's leading figures in music, dance, sport and politics have appeared on its stage. These include Winston Churchill, Emmeline Pankhurst, the Dalai Lama and Nelson Mandela, as well as members of the royal family and world leaders.

The BBC Proms has called the Royal Albert Hall its home since 1941, after the Queen's Hall was gutted by fire in an air-raid. The Hall has since hosted nearly 5,000 Proms concerts.

Latecomers
Latecomers will only be admitted if and when there is a suitable break in the performance.

Security
Please note that certain items are not permitted inside the Royal Albert Hall. We recommend checking the full list in advance to ensure a smooth and enjoyable visit. Further details can be found at royalalberthall.com/visit/general-information/your-safety

- South Kensington (Piccadilly, Circle & District Lines); Gloucester Road (Piccadilly, Circle & District Lines); High Street Kensington (Circle & District Lines)

- Enjoy a wide range of food and drink from two hours before each concert – see royalalberthall.com

Please do not bring large bags to the Royal Albert Hall. All bags and visitors will be subject to security checks as a condition of entry.

It is not permitted to bring food or drink into the Royal Albert Hall. However, there are bars, cafes and restaurants on-site. Find out more at royalalberthall.com/visit/food-and-drink.

Children under 5
Children of all ages are welcome at the Horrible Science Proms (25 July) and the Relaxed Prom (9 August). Out of consideration for audience and artists, we recommend that children attending other Proms are aged 5 and over.

Dress code
Come as you are: there is no dress code at the Proms.

Proms merchandise and programmes
Merchandise is available at Doors 6 and 12 and on the Rausing Circle level at Doors 4 and 8. Programmes are on sale throughout the building. Merchandise can be pre-ordered online at shop.royalalberthall.com. You can pre-order programmes when booking your tickets (if booking after the onsale day) or via the link on your Print at Home tickets.

Access
See page 151 for access details.

- Cloakroom available. A £2 charge per item applies. Cloakroom season tickets are also available for £30. *(conditions apply – see royalalberthall.com)*

Middlesbrough Town Hall
23 July

Albert Road, Middlesbrough TS1 2QJ
www.boxoffice.middlesbrough.gov.uk • 01642 729729

- Middlesbrough (National Rail)
- Bar on site; food and drink available
- Cloakroom available
- Wheelchair-accessible
- Guide and assistance dogs welcome

The Glasshouse International Centre for Music
23–25 July

St Mary's Square, Gateshead NE8 2JR
www.theglasshouseicm.org • 0191 443 4661

- Newcastle Central (National Rail; Metro); Gateshead (Metro)
- Bars on site; food and drink available
- Cloakroom available
- Wheelchair-accessible
- Guide and assistance dogs welcome

The Fire Station, Sunderland
25 July

High Street West, Sunderland SR1 3HA
www.thefirestation.org.uk • 0191 570 0007

- Sunderland
- Bars on site; food and drink available
- Cloakroom available
- Wheelchair-accessible
- Guide and assistance dogs welcome; please let venue know in advance
- **ALS** Assisted listening system

Bristol Beacon
7–9 August

Trenchard Street, Bristol BS1 5AR
www.bristolbeacon.org • 0117 203 4040

- Bristol Temple Meads (National Rail); city centre bus stops, where most bus services stop, are 250m from the venue
- Bars on site; food and drink available
- Cloakroom available
- Wheelchair-accessible
- Guide and assistance dogs welcome
- Hearing loop system

David Allen (The Fire Station)

Venues

St George's Bristol
9 August

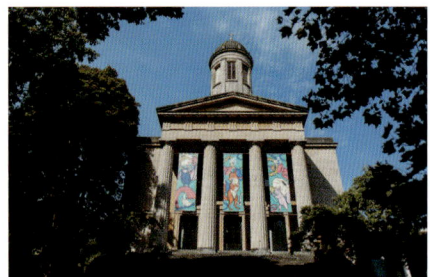

Great George Street, Bristol BS1 5RR
www.stgeorgesbristol.co.uk • 0117 929 4929

- Clifton Down; Bristol Temple Meads (National Rail)
- Bars on site; food and drink available
- Wheelchair-accessible
- Guide and assistance dogs welcome
- Hearing loop system

Theatr Clwyd, Mold
29 August

Raikes Lane, Mold CH7 1YA
www.theatrclwyd.com • 01352 344101

- Buckley, Shotton, Flint, Chester (National Rail); town bus stops, where most bus services stop, are 450m from the venue
- Bar and restaurant on site; food and drink available
- Wheelchair-accessible
- Guide and assistance dogs welcome
- Hearing loop system

Royal College of Music
30 August

Prince Consort Road, London SW7 2BS
www.rcm.ac.uk • 020 7591 4300

- South Kensington (Piccadilly, Circle & District Lines); Gloucester Road (Piccadilly, Circle & District Lines); High Street Kensington (Circle & District Lines)
- Wheelchair-accessible
- Guide and assistance dogs welcome

Ruby Walker (St George's Bristol); Mark Carline (Theatr Clwyd)

Access at the Royal Albert Hall

Disabled concert-goers (and one companion) receive a 50% discount on all Proms tickets (excluding £8 Promming tickets). To book, call the Access Information Line *(see next column)* or purchase in person at the Royal Albert Hall.

♿	**Wheelchair spaces**	All Proms
🐕	**Assistance dogs welcome**	All Proms
AD	**Audio description**	25 July (Horrible Science, 2pm & 6pm) 1 & 2 August (Mahler's First by Heart) 6 August (Weber's 'Oberon') 9 August (Relaxed Prom) 19 August (Ariadne auf Naxos)
BSL	**British Sign Language-interpreted Proms**	25 July (Horrible Science, 2pm & 6pm) 1 & 2 August (Mahler's First by Heart) 9 August (Relaxed Prom) 11 August (Fantasia Orchestra) 31 August (Menken's Music for Disney)
R	**Relaxed performances**	25 July (Horrible Science, 2pm & 6pm) 9 August (Relaxed Prom)
ALS	**Assisted listening service**	All Proms
LP	**Large-print programmes**	All Proms; large-print programmes must be pre-ordered *(see page 153)*

ACCESS INFORMATION LINE

020 7070 4410 (weekdays: 9am–5pm, plus Saturday 16 May: 9am–8pm and Sunday 17 May: 9am–5pm)

♿ Full information on access facilities offered at the Royal Albert Hall, including an Access Guide, is available at royalalberthall.com or by calling the Access Information Line. The Hall has a Bronze award from the Attitude is Everything Charter of Best Practice.

Throughout the Proms season at the Royal Albert Hall 12 spaces will be available to book for wheelchair-users and companions on a designated wheelchair platform situated in front of Loggia Boxes 31–33. Depending on the Prom, between 18 and 25 additional spaces for wheelchair-users and companions will be available in the Stalls and the Circle. To book, call the Access Information Line or visit the Royal Albert Hall Box Office in person.

For information on wheelchair spaces available for the Last Night of the Proms via the Five-Concert Ballot, see page 147. The Gallery can accommodate up to four wheelchair-users. Some accessible seats in the Arena, Choir and Gallery (£8, including booking fee) are available to Prommers who are unable to stand. See bbc.co.uk/proms for details. Ramped venue access is available at Doors 1, 3, 8, 9 and 12. The most convenient set-down point for vehicle arrival is near Door 3. Public lifts are located at Doors 1 and 8. All bars and restaurants are wheelchair-accessible.

Unisex wheelchair-accessible toilets are located as follows: *Level -1*: Door 1 and Door 8; *Ground Floor*: Door 4 porch, Door 8 porch and Door 12; *Level 1*: Door 4; *Level 2*: Door 4; *Level 3*: Door 8; *Level 5*: Door 1.

Transfer wheelchairs are available for customer use, subject to availability. The Hall has busy corridors and therefore visitors using mobility scooters are asked to enter via Door 3 or Door 8 and will be offered a transfer wheelchair on arrival.

Mobility scooters can be stored in designated places. The Hall is unable to offer charging facilities for scooters.

🚗 A limited number of car parking spaces close to the Hall can be reserved by disabled concert-goers; contact the Access Information Line to book.

🐕 Assistance dogs are welcome. The Hall's stewards will be happy to look after your dog during a concert. This service is by prior arrangement and subject to availability. Please tell the Hall in advance so that it can be arranged.

To request any of the above services, call the Access Information Line or complete an accessibility request form online at royalalberthall.com 48 hours before you attend. Alternatively you can make a request upon arrival at the Information Desk at Door 6, subject to availability.

British Sign Language-interpreted Proms

BSL Five Proms at the Royal Albert Hall (see page 151 table for details) will be BSL-interpreted. You can book tickets for these online in the usual way. If you require good visibility of the signer, choose the Stalls Signer Area when selecting tickets, or request by calling the Access Information Line.

Relaxed Proms

R BBC Proms relaxed performances are designed to suit people who feel more comfortable attending concerts in an informal environment – including those with sensory and communication needs, learning disabilities, or who are neurodivergent; and for family members of all ages. There is a relaxed attitude to noise and movement, and audience members are free to leave and re-enter the auditorium at any point. Chill-out areas offer a space for anyone who needs some quiet time before or during the performance. For details of the adjustments planned for these events, visit bbc.co.uk/proms. Visual Information Guides for these concerts will be made available closer to the start of the season on the individual concert event pages. Visit bbc.co.uk/proms for details.

Assisted listening service and audio-described Proms

ALS **AD** The Royal Albert Hall is equipped with a digital assisted listening system, delivering high-quality, reliable and interference-free audio to every seat in the auditorium. Five Proms at the Royal Albert Hall (see page 151 table for details) will be audio-described. Receiver packs and headphones for assisted listening services and audio-described performances are available from the Door 6 Information Desk. Customers are also welcome to use their own headphones (3.5mm minijack required).

See pages 149–150 for access information regarding Proms not at the Royal Albert Hall

> ❝ Having a dedicated wheelchair platform makes visiting the Proms so enjoyable and easy. From arrival at the Royal Albert Hall to getting to your 'seat', everything you need is nearby and really accessible, and the staff at the Hall are so helpful. I am very much looking forward to next season.

Antonia Stoneman, Proms audience member

Wheelchair platform in front of Loggia Boxes 31–33 at at the Royal Albert Hall

For further information, please visit bbc.co.uk/proms. If you would like to discuss additional access requirements, call the Access Information Line (020 7070 4410; 9am–5pm, weekdays).

Chris Christodoulou/BBC

Braille and Large-Print Publications

BBC Proms Festival Guide – Braille and large-print formats

Braille versions of this Festival Guide are available in two parts, 'Articles' and 'Concert Listings/Booking Information', priced £5 each. For more information and to order, call the RNIB Helpline on 0303 123 9999.

LP A text-only large-print version of this Festival Guide is available, priced £9.99. To order, call 07716 225658, or email PromsPublications@bbc.co.uk. (Please allow 10 working days for delivery.)

The Guide is also available to purchase as an eBook from Amazon, and as both an eBook and ePDF from Bloomsbury. Both formats are compatible with screen readers and text-to-speech software. Visit amazon.co.uk or bloomsbury.com/uk for details.

Concert programmes in large print

LP Large-print concert programmes can be pre-ordered for collection on the night (at the same price as standard programmes), if ordered at least five working days in advance.

Large-print sung texts and librettos (where applicable) are available with the purchase of a standard programme, if ordered at least five working days in advance. This excludes surtitled Proms, for which librettos are not printed.

To order, call 07716 225658, or email PromsPublications@bbc.co.uk. Programmes and texts will be left for collection at the Door 6 Merchandise Desk one hour before the concert begins.

A Royal Albert Hall steward will be happy to read the concert programme to visually impaired visitors. Call the Access Information Line (020 7070 4410) or complete an accessibility request form online at royalalberthall.com 48 hours before you attend.

Access on BBC TV and iPlayer

A number of televised Proms, including the Horrible Science Prom, will be broadcast with audio description and British Sign Language. Please see bbc.co.uk/proms for details.

Accessible Performances in Bristol and Mold

British Sign Language-interpreted and audio-described Proms

BSL Two concerts in Bristol and one in Mold will be BSL-interpreted: Russian Classics (8 August, Bristol), the Relaxed Prom (9 August, Bristol) and Words and Music (29 August, Mold). One concert in Bristol will be audio-described: Steve Reich at 90 (7 August, Bristol). For details of these venues, see pages 149–150. For details regarding tickets for non-Royal Albert Hall Proms concerts, see bbc.co.uk/promstickets.

Relaxed Prom

R One Prom in Bristol will be a Relaxed performance (9 August). Please see opposite for details.

A NIGHT OF RHYTHM AND MEWS

In this wry little story, a composer and his cat create a musical extravaganza for a concert like no other.

View an extract at

http://www.anightofrhythmandmews.com

ISBN 978-1-9161166-1-0   *Price £9.99*   *Raincliffe Books*

Handel's Serse

ACADEMY of ANCIENT MUSIC

Friday 19 June | 7.00pm
Barbican Hall, London

On sale now **aam.co.uk**

WORTH SCHOOL

Education with Heart and Soul in Sussex's glorious countryside
35 minutes by train from central London

"This school has everything going for it"
The Good Schools Guide

www.worthschool.org.uk

WINNER — INDEPENDENT SCHOOLS OF THE YEAR — BOARDING SCHOOL OF THE YEAR

Catholic co-educational school Pupils aged 11-18 years. Day, boarding and flexible boarding Qualifications include GCSE/IGCSE, A-levels and BTEC or IB

A CURZON FILM

"A TRIUMPH"
LOUD AND CLEAR

VIVALDI SOUGHT ETERNITY...
SHE JUST WANTED TO BE HEARD

Primavera

A FILM BY DAMIANO MICHIELETTO

IN CINEMAS 24 APRIL

CURZON

GARSINGTON OPERA
AT WORMSLEY

2026 Season

Experience world-class opera in the breathtaking natural beauty of the Chiltern Hills, featuring the Philharmonia and The English Concert. Our 2026 Season spans nearly 400 years of opera, from Monteverdi's depiction of Homer's Odyssey to Gerald Barry's hilarious reimagination of Oscar Wilde's classic play.

Less than an hour from London, and just 25 minutes from Oxford.

garsingtonopera.org | 01494 376037

La Traviata — Giuseppe Verdi — 27 May – 24 July

Der Rosenkavalier — Richard Strauss — 28 May – 29 June

Il Ritorno d'Ulisse — Claudio Monteverdi — 12 June – 25 July

The Importance of Being Earnest — Gerald Barry — 10 – 23 July

SUPPORTING MUSICIANS IN NEED SINCE 1738

RSM provides vital financial assistance, advice and guidance to music professionals impacted by physical or mental ill health.

Help us help musicians in need today. Thank you.

www.rsmgb.org

Registered Charity No. 208879

THE ROYAL SOCIETY OF MUSICIANS

2026 CONCERTS

CHINEKE! ORCHESTRA

Championing change and celebrating diversity in classical music

Coleridge-Taylor Violin Concerto Sun 7 Jun
Anthem of Unity Sun 11 Oct
Concierto de Aranjuez for guitar Fri 27 Nov
Romeo & Juliet Fri 29 Jan 2027

Queen Elizabeth Hall - Southbank Centre

chineke.org

HAFLIÐI HALLGRÍMSSON

Lebensfries

SSENS TRIO

LAWO CLASSICS

Hafliði Hallgrímsson's **Lebensfries** with the Ssens Trio will be released digitally on **27 March**. The physical CD follows in **June 2026**, marking a striking new addition to the trio's chamber catalogue.

OPEN UP MUSIC

> 'It has changed my life - not only musically.'
> Evie, Clarion player

Leave a lasting legacy through music

Music enriches our lives in ways few things can. Yet talented young disabled musicians face barriers to **learning and performing**.

Thanks to music lovers like you, we **create opportunities**, including the National Open Youth Orchestra and the Clarion, our accessible instrument.

By leaving a gift in your Will to Open Up Music, you can help **ensure music is open to future generations**.

Ensure music lives on - for everyone

Registered with **FUNDRAISING REGULATOR**

Registered Charity No. 1167028

openupmusic.org/legacy

BBC Get Singing

Engaging new resources for teachers and vocal leaders to get 11–14-year-olds singing together.

Start your singing journey at
bbc.co.uk/getsinging

BBC young composer

Nurturing the next generation of composers, championing new music across diverse genres. Opportunities and resources for young people and teachers, inspiring creativity, original music-making and opening up pathways into the music industry.

Find out more
bbc.co.uk/youngcomposer

Peregrine's Pianos

Award-winning Piano Dealer

Music Rehearsal Rooms

Domestic Piano Hire

Pianos for Concert Hire

Acoustic Piano Sales

Visit us for: **Music Rehearsal Rooms** - the first choice for orchestras, opera companies, teachers and independent musicians. **Domestic Piano Hire** - a superb range of pianos available on a six monthly home hire agreement. **Pianos for Concert Hire** - a unique line-up of Schimmel upright and grand pianos for countrywide concerts and musical events. **Acoustic Piano Sales** - selling quality pianos is a major part of our 'raison d'être' and we are proud of the instruments that we present.

Peregrine's Pianos is the exclusive London dealer for August Förster and Schimmel, two of the finest German piano manufacturers.

Peregrine's Pianos, 137A Grays Inn Road, London WC1X 8TU
www.peregrines-pianos.com
Telephone: 020 7242 9865

ROYAL ALBERT HALL

FILMS IN CONCERT

with a live symphony orchestra

La La Land, How to Train Your Dragon 2, Casino Royale, Matilda with Danny Devito, Black Panther and more

Book now
RoyalAlbertHall.com

®,™& ©2025 Lions Gate Entertainment Inc. and related companies. All Rights Reserved

Index of Artists

Bold italic figures refer to Prom dates

P@ refers to 'Proms Across the UK' (see pages 140–144)
    P@Middlesbrough Thursday 23 July
    P@Gateshead Thursday 23 – Saturday 25 July
    P@Sunderland Saturday 25 July
    P@Bristol Friday 7 – Sunday 9 August
    P@Mold Saturday 29 August

*first appearance at a BBC Henry Wood Promenade Concert
† former member of BBC Radio 3's New Generation Artists scheme

— A

Jonathan Aasgaard* cello ***24 July***
Thomas Adès conductor ***8 August***
David Afkham* conductor ***19 July***
Rafael Aguirre* guitar ***19 July***
Ambrose Akinmusire* trumpet ***20 August***
Louise Alder soprano ***27 July***
Marin Alsop conductor ***24 August***
Alain Altinoglu conductor ***23 August***
Chiara Amarù mezzo-soprano ***7 August***
Robert Ames conductor ***18 July***
Martha Argerich piano ***5 September***
Thomas Atkins tenor ***17 July***

— B

Alena Baeva violin ***30 July***
Ryan Bancroft conductor ***23 July, 17 August***
René Barbera* tenor ***7 August***
Daniel Bartholomew-Poyser conductor ***25 August***
Jamie Barton mezzo-soprano ***21 August***
Anja Bihlmaier conductor ***21 August***
Angel Blue soprano ***22 August***
Liam Bonthrone tenor ***19 August***
Claire Booth soprano ***29 July***
Charlotte Bowden* soprano ***6 August***
Justin Brown* drums ***20 August***
Jules Buckley conductor ***28 August, 8 September***

— C

Richard David Caine conductor ***25 July***
Jessica Cale* soprano ***6 August***
Gautier Capuçon cello ***23 August***
Jude Carlton* percussion *P@Gateshead*
Charles Castronovo tenor ***6 August***
Ru Charlesworth* tenor ***19 August***
Helen Charlston † mezzo-soprano ***9 August***
Ekaterina Chayka-Rubinstein* mezzo-soprano ***19 August***
David Childs euphonium ***19 July***
Nicholas Childs conductor ***19 July***
Jonathan Cohen director/harpsichord ***10 September***
Nicholas Collon conductor ***1, 2 August***
Erland Cooper* presenter ***27 August***
Colin Currie † conductor ***2 September***
Guy Cutting tenor ***9 August***
Hugh Cutting † counter-tenor ***10 September***

— D

Alexandra Dariescu* piano ***5 August***
Iwan Davies* conductor *P@Bristol*
Jennifer Davis soprano ***5 August***
Jeanine De Bique soprano ***10 September***
Yannick Debus* baritone ***6 August***
Anna Denisova* soprano ***19 August***
Joyce DiDonato mezzo-soprano ***27 August***
Thomas Dolié* bass ***30 August***
Gustavo Dudamel conductor ***11, 12 August***
Thomas Dunford* director/lute ***21 July***

— E

Peter Edwards director ***5 August***
Sir Mark Elder conductor ***6 August***
Mari Eriksmoen soprano ***23 July***

— F

Alice Farnham conductor *P@Bristol*
Isabelle Faust violin ***7 September***
Pablo Ferrández* cello ***16 August***
Tom Fetherstonhaugh conductor ***9, 11 August***
Gerald Finley baritone ***30 August***
Vilde Frang violin ***10 August***
Martin Fröst conductor/clarinet ***16 August***

— G

James Gaffigan conductor ***13 August***
Edward Gardner conductor ***27 July***
Véronique Gens soprano ***30 August***
Kirill Gerstein piano ***3 August***
Jess Gillam saxophone ***6 September,*** *P@Gateshead*
Evelyn Glennie percussion ***11 August***
Ben Goldscheider horn ***6 September***
Helena Gourd* flute/bass flute *P@Gateshead*
Mirga Gražinytė-Tyla conductor ***29 August***

— H

Augustin Hadelich violin ***3 September***
Christian Ihle Hadland † piano *P@Sunderland*
Samantha Hankey* mezzo-soprano ***19 August***
Amy Harman bassoon ***23 August***
Sam Harris* piano ***20 August***
Leah Hawkins* soprano ***20 July***
Miho Hazama conductor ***20 August***
Charles Hazlewood director *P@Bristol*
Elza van den Heever* soprano ***26 August***
Jonathon Heyward conductor ***22 August***
Adam Hickox* conductor *P@Bristol*
Matthew Higham* flute ***8 September***
Clay Hilley* tenor ***21 August***
Max Hornung* cello *P@Bristol*
Jakub Hrůša conductor ***1 September***

— I

Alina Ibragimova † violin ***4 August***

— J

Tess Jackson conductor ***30 August***
Paavo Järvi conductor ***2 August***
Sofi Jeannin conductor *P@Gateshead*
Guy Johnston cello ***28 July***
Lucas and Arthur Jussen* pianos ***26 July***

— K

Sheku Kanneh-Mason cello ***6 September***
Paweł Kapuła* conductor ***9 September***
Liam James Karai* bass-baritone ***19 August***
Leonidas Kavakos violin ***2 August***
Laurence Kilsby tenor ***21 July***
Felix Klieser horn ***23 August***
Anu Komsi soprano *P@Bristol*
Patricia Kopatchinskaja violin ***29 August***
Michael Kraus baritone ***19 August***

— L

Simone Lamsma* violin ***4 September***
Olivier Latry organ ***26 July***
Delyana Lazarova conductor ***30 July***
Jakob Lehmann* conductor ***30 August***
Natalie Lewis* mezzo-soprano ***1, 2 August***
Yunchan Lim piano ***17 July***
Federica Lombardi* soprano ***7 August***
Daniel Lozakovich violin ***31 July***

— M

Cristian Măcelaru conductor ***18 August***
Andrew Manze conductor ***4 September***
Benjamin Marquise Gilmore* director/leader ***23 August***
Anthony McGill clarinet ***17 August***
James McNicholas conductor ***25 July***
Szymon Mechliński* baritone ***23 July***
Erin Morley soprano ***9 August***
Paula Murrihy mezzo-soprano ***23 July***

— N

Yannick Nézet-Séguin conductor ***26, 27 August***
Karen Ní Bhroin conductor ***25 July***
Gianandrea Noseda conductor ***20 July***

— O

Sakari Oramo conductor ***22, 28 July, 6, 12 September,*** *P@Bristol*
John Osborn tenor ***30 August***
Edwin Outwater conductor ***14 August***

— P

Sir Antonio Pappano conductor ***15 August***
Owain Park director ***2 September***
Sueye Park violin ***21 July***

Index of Artists

Anthony Parnther *conductor* 31 August
Kirill Petrenko *conductor* 2, 3 September
Vasily Petrenko *conductor* 16 August
David Butt Philip *tenor* 19 August
Nick Pritchard *tenor* 10 September

— R
Harish Raghavan* *bass* 20 August
Jessica Ransom 25 July
Sir Simon Rattle *conductor* 7 September
Eirin Rognerud* *soprano* 19 August
Natalya Romaniw *soprano* 9 September
Julie Roset* *soprano* 6 September

— S
Esa-Pekka Salonen *conductor* 10 August
Elena Schwarz* *conductor* 4 August
Abel Selaocoe *cello* 20 July
Nadine Shah* P@Gateshead
Shakk* *presenter* P@Gateshead
Lahav Shani *conductor* 5 September
Nigel Short *conductor* P@Bristol
Caspar Singh *tenor* 19 August
Ellie Slorach *conductor* P@Gateshead
Yeol Eum Son *piano* 13 August
Thomas Søndergård *conductor* 3 August
Dinis Sousa *piano/celesta* P@Sunderland
Nicky Spence *tenor* 6 August, 12 September
Dalia Stasevska *conductor* 17 July
Philipp von Steinaecker* *conductor* 11 September
Faye Stoeser* *director* P@Bristol
John Storgårds *conductor* 21 July
Florian Störtz* *bass-baritone* 10 September

— T
William Thomas† *bass* 9 August
Robin Ticciati *conductor* 19 August
Mikhail Timoshenko* *baritone* 19 August
Inel Tomlinson 25 July

— U
Nicola Ulivieri* *bass* 7 August

— V
Alessandro Vazzana* *clarion* P@Bristol
Nil Venditti *conductor* 7 August
Lukáš Vondráček* *piano* 1 September

— W
Stephanie Wake-Edwards *mezzo-soprano* 20 July
Yuja Wang *piano* 12 September
James Way *tenor* 23 July
Omer Meir Wellber *conductor* 31 July
Derek Welton *bass* 20 July
Peter Whelan *conductor* 9 August
Jasmin White *contralto* 6 August
Ryan Wigglesworth *conductor* 29 July, 8 September
Rachel Willis-Sørensen* *soprano* 19 August
John Wilson *conductor* 24 July, 6 September
Rachael Wilson* *mezzo-soprano* 6 August
Maria Włoszczowska *director/violin* P@Sunderland
Kahchun Wong *conductor* 5 August
Alina Wunderlin* *soprano* 19 August

— Y
Kazuki Yamada *conductor* 26 July

— Z
Eva Zaïcik *soprano* 10 September

GROUPS
Academy of St Martin in the Fields 23 August
Altın Gün* 28 August
Arcangelo 10 September
Aurora Orchestra 1, 2 August
BBC Concert Orchestra 18 July, 14, 20, 25, 30 August
BBC National Chorus of Wales 23 July
BBC National Orchestra of Wales 23, 25 July, 4, 17 August, P@Bristol
BBC Philharmonic Orchestra 20, 21 July, 21, 31 August
BBC Scottish Symphony Orchestra 29, 30 July, 8, 9 September
BBC Singers 17, 29 July, 9, 11 August, 12 September, P@Gateshead
BBC Symphony Chorus 17 July, 7, 15 August, 12 September
BBC Symphony Orchestra 17, 22, 28 July, 2, 7, 13, 18, 23, 28 August, 1, 6, 12 September
Berlin Philharmonic 2, 3 September
Black Dyke Band 19 July
Bournemouth Symphony Orchestra P@Bristol
CBSO Chorus 26 July
Chineke! Orchestra 22 August
Choeur de Radio France* 30 August
Choir of the Enlightenment 9 August
Chorus of Royal Northern Sinfonia P@Gateshead
City of Birmingham Symphony Orchestra 26 July
Colin Currie Group* 2 September
Deutsche Kammerphilharmonie Bremen 31 July
Epiphoni Consort* 7 August
Fantasia Orchestra 9, 11 August
Freiburg Baroque Orchestra 7 September
The Gesualdo Six 2 September
Glyndebourne Festival Opera 19 August
Hallé 5 August
Juilliard Orchestra 10 August
Jules Buckley Orchestra 8 September
Jupiter Ensemble* 21 July
Ladysmith Black Mambazo* 5 August
London Philharmonic Choir 23 July
London Philharmonic Orchestra 27 July, 19 August
London Symphony Chorus 15 August
London Symphony Orchestra 15 August
Los Angeles Master Chorale (upper voices)* 12 August
Los Angeles Philharmonic 11, 12 August
Mahler Academy Orchestra* 11 September
Maîtrise de Radio France* 30 August
Marcus Roberts Trio 24 August
The Met Orchestra* 26, 27 August
Monteverdi Choir 6 August
Munich Philharmonic 5 September
National Open Youth Orchestra* P@Bristol
National Youth Music Theatre* 31 August
National Youth Orchestra 8 August
Nu Civilisation Orchestra 5 August
Orchestra of the Age of Enlightenment 9 August
Orchestre Révolutionnaire et Romantique 6 August
Oslo Philharmonic 29 August
Paraorchestra P@Bristol
Philharmonia Chorus 20 July
Philharmonia Orchestra 24 August
Royal Academy of Music Symphony Orchestra 10 August
Royal Liverpool Philharmonic Orchestra 4 September
Royal Northern Sinfonia P@Middlesbrough, P@Gateshead, P@Sunderland
Royal Philharmonic Orchestra 16 August
Royal Scottish National Orchestra 3 August
Les Siècles 30 August
Sinfonia Cymru* P@Mold
Sinfonia of London 24 July, 6 September
Spanish National Orchestra* 19 July
Swedish Chamber Orchestra 16 August
Sydney Philharmonia Chorus 26 July
Tenebrae P@Bristol
Voices of the River's Edge P@Gateshead

Index of Works

P@ refers to 'Proms Across the UK' (see pages 140–144)
P@Gateshead Thursday 23 – Saturday 25 July
P@Sunderland Saturday 25 July
P@Bristol Friday 7 – Sunday 9 August
P@Mold Saturday 29 August

*first performance at a BBC Henry Wood Promenade Concert

— A

John Adams (born 1947)
Harmonium **26 July**
Thomas Adès (born 1971)
Dante – Part 1: Inferno* **11 August**
Dante – Part 2: Purgatorio* **8 August**
Thomas Arne (1710–78)
Rule, Britannia! (arr. Sargent) **12 September**

— B

Grażyna Bacewicz (1909–69)
Divertimento* **P@Sunderland**
Johann Sebastian Bach (1685–1750)
Bach's Memento – Mattheus-Final (arr. Widor)* **26 July**
Cantata No. 68 – Aria 'Mein gläubiges Herze' (transcr. Gigout*) **26 July**
Cantata No. 147 – Chorale 'Jesus bleibet meine Freude' (transcr. Duruflé*) **26 July**
Chorale 'Kommst du nun, Jesu, vom Himmel herunter', BWV 650* **26 July**
Concerto in A minor, BWV 593 (after Vivaldi)* **26 July**
Fantasia and Fugue in G minor, BWV 542 (orch. A. Davis*) **20 July**
Mass in B minor **10 September**
Partita No. 2 in D minor, BWV 1004 – Chaconne (arr. Messerer*) **26 July**
Prelude and Fugue in D minor, BWV 539 **26 July**
Toccata and Fugue in D minor, BWV 565 **26 July**
Samuel Barber (1910–81)
Knoxville: Summer of 1915 **22 August**
Symphony No. 1 in One Movement **13 August**
Béla Bartók (1881–1945)
Concerto for Orchestra **10 August**
Music for Strings, Percussion and Celesta **8 September**
Ludwig van Beethoven (1770–1827)
Piano Concerto No. 2 in B flat major **5 September**
Symphony No. 6 in F major, 'Pastoral' **11 August**
Symphony No. 7 in A major **12, 16 August**
Symphony No. 9 in D minor, 'Choral' **20 July**
Violin Concerto in D major **3 September**
Alban Berg (1885–1935)
Violin Concerto **10 August**
Lennox Berkeley (1903–89)
Serenade for Strings **6 September**
Hector Berlioz (1803–69)
The Damnation of Faust **30 August**
Overture 'Le carnaval romain' (arr. Frank Wright*) **19 July**
Requiem (Grande messe des morts) **15 August**
Symphonie fantastique **8 August**
Leonard Bernstein (1918–90)
On the Town – Three Dance Episodes **24 August**
Symphonic Dances from 'West Side Story' **24 August**
Michael Betteridge (born 1988)
Soaring Through Sparks (Clarion Concerto) (arr. Julia Koelmans)* **P@Bristol**
Judith Bingham (born 1952)
Four Minute Mile* **19 July**
Alexander Borodin (1833–87)
Prince Igor – Polovtsian Dances (excerpts) **25 July**
Lili Boulanger (1893–1918)
Vieille prière bouddhique **23 July**
Nadia Boulanger (1887–1979)
Fantasy for piano and orchestra* **5 August**
Johannes Brahms (1833–97)
Symphony No. 4 in E minor **5 September**
Frank Bridge (1879–1941)
Lament **6 September**
Benjamin Britten (1913–76)
Cello Symphony **28 July**
Les illuminations **6 September**
Simple Symphony **23 August**
Variations on a Theme of Frank Bridge **6 September**
Violin Concerto **4 September**
The Young Person's Guide to the Orchestra **6 September**
Max Bruch (1838–1920)
Violin Concerto No. 1 in G minor **31 July**

— C

Édith Canat de Chizy (born 1950)
Skyline (Concerto for three percussionists, timpani and orchestra)* BBC co-commission: UK premiere
Joseph Canteloube (1879–1957)
Songs of the Auvergne – selection **27 July**
Aaron Copland (1900–90)
Appalachian Spring – suite **24 August**
Billy the Kid – suite **17 August**
Fanfare for the Common Man **17 July**
Oliver Cross (born 1996)
Barriers (arr. Liam Taylor-West)* **P@Bristol**

— D

Brett Dean (born 1961)
The World's Wife* BBC co-commission: world premiere **29 July**
Claude Debussy (1862–1918)
Prélude à l'après-midi d'un faune **23 August**
John Dowland (1563–1626)
Can she excuse my wrongs? **21 July**
Now, O now, I needs must part* **21 July**
Antonín Dvořák (1841–1904)
Cello Concerto in B minor **23 August**
Symphony No. 7 in D minor **4 August**
Symphony No. 8 in G major **22 August**
Symphony No. 9 in E minor, 'From the New World' **6 September**

— E

Hans Ek (born 1964)
DNA Suite* UK premiere **16 August**
Edward Elgar (1857–1934)
Cello Concerto in E minor **16 August**
'Enigma' Variations **2 September**
Pomp and Circumstance March No. 1 in D major ('Land of Hope and Glory') **12 September**
Romance for bassoon and orchestra* **23 August**
Symphony No. 1 in A flat major **29 July**
Duke Ellington (1899–1974)
It Don't Mean a Thing (if It Ain't Got that Swing) (arr. Harry Baker*) **9 August**
Bushra El-Turk (born 1982)
Mosaic* **21 August**

— F

Manuel de Falla (1876–1946)
Fantasia baetica (orch. Francisco Coll)* **19 July**
The Three-Cornered Hat – Suites Nos. 1 & 2* **19 July**
Louise Farrenc (1826–59)
Overture No. 2* **5 September**
Morton Feldman (1926–87)
Crippled Symmetry* **P@Gateshead**
Gerald Finzi (1901–56)
For St Cecilia* **17 July**
Göran (born 1974) and **Martin Fröst** (born 1970)
Nomadic Dances* **16 August**

— G

George Gershwin (1898–1937)
An American in Paris **17 July**
Piano Concerto in F major **13 August**
Rhapsody in Blue (orch. Grofé) **24 August**
Peter Graham (born 1958)
Force of Nature* **19 July**
Edward Gregson (born 1945)
Symphony in two movements* **19 July**
Sofia Gubaidulina (1931–2025)
Fairy-Tale Poem **P@Bristol**

— H

George Frideric Handel (1685–1759)
Theodora – 'From virtue springs' **21 July**
Charlotte Harding (born 1989)
The Orchestra: A Young Person's Guide (arr. Liam Taylor-West)* BBC commission **P@Bristol**
Joseph Haydn (1732–1809)
Mass in D minor, 'Nelson Mass' **9 August**
Symphony No. 44 in E minor, 'Trauer' **31 July**
Symphony No. 45 in F sharp minor, 'Farewell' **21 August**
Hans Werner Henze (1926–2012)
Erlkönig – orchestral fantasy* **9 September**
Gustav Holst (1874–1934)
A Moorside Suite **19 July**
The Planets – excerpts **25 July**
Imogen Holst (1907–84)
Suite for String Orchestra* **6 September**

Dani Howard (born 1993)
Concerto for Brass, 'SIGNAL'*
 BBC co-commission: world premiere
 2 August

— J

Leoš Janáček (1854–1928)
Sinfonietta **1 September**
Edmund Thornton Jenkins
 (1894–1926)
Dance Suite (reconstr. & arr. Tuffus
 Zimbabwe)* world premiere
 22 August
Betsy Jolas (born 1926)
Tales of a Summer Sea*
 UK premiere **21 July**

— K

Gabriel Kahane (born 1981)
Clarinet Concerto, 'If love will not
 swing wide the gates'* BBC
 co-commission: European premiere
 17 August
Vítězslava Kaprálová (1915–40)
Suita rustica* **1 September**
Oliver Knussen (1952–2018)
Flourish with Fireworks **3 August**
Erich Wolfgang Korngold (1897–1957)
Violin Concerto in D major **30 July**
György Kurtág (born 1926)
Kafka Fragments P@Bristol
Stele **22 July**

— L

Olivier Latry (born 1962)
Improvisation on B–A–C–H* **26 July**
Franz Liszt (1811–86)
Mephisto Waltz No. 1 **8 August**

— M

Gustav Mahler (1860–1911)
Das Lied von der Erde **21 August**
Rückert-Lieder **27 August**
Symphony No. 1 in D major
 1, 2 August
Symphony No. 4 in G major **27 August**
Symphony No. 6 in A minor **22 July**
Symphony No. 9 **11 September**
What the Wild Flowers Tell Me
 (arr. Britten) **9 September**
Wynton Marsalis (born 1961)
Concerto for Orchestra* BBC
 co-commission: UK premiere
 13 August
Felix Mendelssohn (1809–47)
Concerto for Violin, Piano and Strings
 in D minor* P@Sunderland
Violin Concerto in E minor **4 August**
Olivier Messiaen (1908–92)
L'Ascension – four symphonic
 meditations **23 July**
Meredith Monk (born 1942)
Panda Chant 2* **9 August**

Jessie Montgomery (born 1981)
These Righteous Paths* BBC
 co-commission: UK premiere **20 July**
Jerome Moross (1913–83)
The Big Country – prelude **24 August**
Wolfgang Amadeus Mozart
 (1756–91)
Aria 'Schon lacht der holde Frühling'*
 9 August
Aria 'Vorrei spiegarvi, oh Dio!'
 9 August
Horn Concerto No. 3 in E flat major
 23 August
Masonic Funeral Music **9 August**
Symphony No. 35 in D major, 'Haffner'
 23 August
Symphony No. 39 in E flat major
 P@Sunderland
Jacob Mühlrad (born 1991)
Helix* BBC commission: world premiere
 16 August
Thea Musgrave (born 1928)
Bassoon Concerto, 'Out of the
 Darkness'* BBC commission: world
 premiere **23 August**

— O

Gabriela Ortiz (born 1964)
Revolución diamantina* UK premiere
 12 August

— P

Hubert Parry (1848–1918)
Songs of Farewell – selection
 P@Gateshead
Jerusalem (orch. Elgar) **12 September**
Francis Poulenc (1899–1963)
Concerto in D minor for two pianos
 26 July
Sinfonietta* **26 July**
Florence Price (1887–1953)
Symphony No. 1 in E minor – Juba
 Dance (arr. Rhian Davies*)
 P@Bristol
Sergey Prokofiev (1891–1953)
Romeo and Juliet – excerpts
 29 August
Symphony No. 5 in B flat major
 30 July
Henry Purcell (1659–95)
Evening Hymn **21 July**
If love's a sweet passion* **21 July**
Strike the viol* **21 July**

— R

Sergey Rachmaninov (1873–1943)
Piano Concerto No. 3 in D minor
 1 September
Rhapsody on a Theme of Paganini
 3 August
Symphonic Dances P@Bristol
Symphony No. 2 in E minor **5 August**

Symphony No. 3 in A minor
 8 September
Radiohead
Pyramid Song (arr. Simon Hale*)
 9, 11 August
Maurice Ravel (1875–1937)
Alborada del gracioso **19 July**
Boléro **19 July**
Piano Concerto in G major **17 July**
La vallée des cloches (orch. Colin
 Matthews*) **5 August**
Steve Reich (born 1936)
Music for 18 Musicians P@Bristol
Tehillim * **2 September**
Ottorino Respighi (1879–1936)
Church Windows* **7 August**
Fountains of Rome **24 July**
Pines of Rome **24 July**
Roman Festivals **24 July**
Joaquín Rodrigo (1901–99)
Concierto de Aranjuez **19 July**
Concierto de Aranjuez – Adagio
 (arr. Kevin Bolton*) **19 July**
Gioachino Rossini (1792–1868)
Stabat mater **7 August**

— S

Kaija Saariaho (1952–2023)
Lumière et pesanteur* **27 August**
Franz Schubert (1797–1828)
Symphony No. 8 in B minor,
 'Unfinished' **9 September**
Robert Schumann (1810–56)
Genoveva – overture **7 September**
Symphony No. 2 in C major
 7 September
Symphony No. 4 in D minor
 (rev. version, 1851) **31 July**
Violin Concerto in D minor
 7 September
Alexander Scriabin (1872–1915)
Symphony No. 2 in C major **2 August**
Symphony No. 3 in C minor,
 'The Divine Poem' **3 September**
Caroline Shaw (born 1982)
Partita – Sarabande* **11 August**
Dmitry Shostakovich (1906–75)
Cello Concerto No. 1 in E flat major
 P@Bristol
Festive Overture P@Bristol
Symphony No. 10 in E minor
 18 August
Symphony No. 11 in G minor, 'The
 Year 1905' **3 August**
Jean Sibelius (1865–1957)
Symphony No. 2 in D major **28 July**
Violin Concerto in D minor **21 July**
Gwilym Simcock (born 1981)
Triple Concerto for Soprano
 Saxophone, Horn and Cello* BBC
 co-commission: world premiere
 6 September

Carmel Smickersgill (born 1996)
A Brick Thrown with Love* BBC
 co-commission: world premiere
 4 September
Josephine Stephenson (born 1990)
new work* BBC commission: world
 premiere **17 July**
William Grant Still (1895–1978)
Three Visions – No. 2: Summerland*
 24 August
Richard Strauss (1864–1949)
An Alpine Symphony **27 July**
Also sprach Zarathustra **21 July**
Ariadne auf Naxos **19 August**
Death and Transfiguration **23 July**
Four Last Songs **9 September**
Ein Heldenleben **26 August**
Der Rosenkavalier – suite (arr. attrib.
 A. Rodziński) **26 August**
Salome – final scene **26 August**
Igor Stravinsky (1882–1971)
Petrushka (1947 version) **17 August**
Symphonies of Wind Instruments
 (1947 version) **23 August**
Symphony in Three Movements
 10 August
Violin Concerto **29 August**
Karol Szymanowski (1882–1937)
Stabat mater **23 July**

— T

Dobrinka Tabakova (born 1980)
Orpheus' Comet* **30 July**
Joby Talbot (born 1971)
Path of Miracles P@Bristol
John Tavener (1944–2013)
Song for Athene P@Gateshead
Pyotr Tchaikovsky (1840–93)
Symphony No. 4 in F minor
 2 September
Violin Concerto in D major **2 August**
Kristine Tjøgersen (born 1982)
Between Trees* UK premiere **27 July**
Øyvind Torvund (born 1976)
Symphonic Poem No. 1, 'Forest
 Morning'* **29 August**
Joan Tower (born 1938)
Fanfare for the Uncommon Woman
 24 August
Traditional
Auld lang syne (arr. P. Campbell)
 12 September
The National Anthem (arr. Britten)
 12 September
Mark-Anthony Turnage (born 1960)
Festen Suite* BBC co-commission:
 UK premiere **28 July**

— V

Edgard Varèse (1883–1965)
Amériques **23 August**
Density 21.5* **8 September**

Index of Works

Ralph Vaughan Williams *(1872–1958)*
Fantasia on a Theme by Thomas Tallis
   4 September
Serenade to Music (arr. R. Douglas*)
   9, 11 August
Symphony No. 9 in E minor
   4 September
Giuseppe Verdi *(1813–1901)*
The Force of Destiny – overture
   24 July
Antonio Vivaldi *(1678–1741)*
The Four Seasons – excerpts
   (arr. Rhian Davies*) **P@Bristol**

— W

William Walton *(1902–83)*
Cello Concerto **24 July**
Symphony No. 2 **16 August**
Carl Maria von Weber *(1786–1826)*
Oberon* **6 August**
Anton Webern *(1883–1945)*
Passacaglia **16 August**
Judith Weir *(born 1954)*
Moon and Star **29 July**
Héloïse Werner *(born 1991)*
new work* *BBC commission: world premiere* **11 August**
Philip Wilby *(born 1949)*
Paganini Variations* **19 July**
John Williams *(born 1932)*
Harry Potter and the Philosopher's Stone – Hedwig's Theme
   (arr. Andrew Duncan) **19 July**
Star Wars – excerpts **25 July**
arr. Henry Wood *(1869–1944)*
Fantasia on British Sea-Songs
   12 September

— Z

Jan Dismas Zelenka *(1679–1745)*
Miserere in C minor* **9 August**
Hans Zimmer *(born 1957)*
Pirates of the Caribbean: Dead Man's Chest – Wheel of Fortune
   (arr. Stephen Roberts)* **19 July**
Bernd Alois Zimmermann *(1918–70)*
Märchen-Suite (Fairy-Tale Suite)*
   4 August

MISCELLANEOUS

BBC Introducing from The Glasshouse: Live at the Proms
   P@Gateshead
BBC Young Composer **30 August**
Bond and Beyond **25 August**
Enchanted: Alan Menken's Music for Disney **31 August**
First Night of the Proms 2026
   17 July
Horrible Science: The Big Bang Proms Experiment **25 July**
Last Night of the Proms 2026
   12 September
Miles Davis Centenary **20 August**
Prog Rock: A Fanfare for the Common Man **18 July**
Relaxed Prom **9 August, P@Bristol**
'Round Midnight **P@Bristol**
Ultimate Calm **27 August**
Under African Skies **5 August**
Words and Music **P@Mold**

BBC Proms

Controller, BBC Radio 3 and BBC Proms Sam Jackson
Director of Artistic Planning, BBC Proms Hannah Donat
Head of Arts and Classical Music TV Suzy Klein
Commissioning Editor, TV Stephen James-Yeoman
Commissioning Editor, Live Music, BBC Radio 3 Emma Bloxham
Head of Marketing and Publications Kate Finch
Business Sanoma Evans (Business Advisor), Rebecca Short, Tricia Twigg (Business Co-ordinators)
Learning Yasmin Hemmings (Senior Manager), Siân Bateman, Cat Cayley, Melanie Fryer, Laura Mitchell (Producers), Connie Badley, Dylan Barrett-Chambers, Deborah Fether (Assistant Producers), Charley Douglas (Business Co-ordinator)
Live Events and Planning Helen Heslop (Head of Live Events), Alys Jones (Creative Producer), Helen MacLeod, Charlotte Sandford, Marianne Tweedie, Sarah Woolhouse (Event Producers), Alison Dancer (Assistant Event Producer)
Marketing Emily Caket (Marketing Manager), Jennifer Hawthorn (Marketing Executive), Branwen Thistlewood (Marketing Co-ordinator)
Press and Communications George Chambers (Head of Communications, Classical Music), Jo Hawkins (Communications Manager), Freya Edgeworth (Publicist)
Commercial Rights & Business Affairs Emma Barrow, Sarah Bredl-Jones, Alina Colaco, Carol Davies, Geraint Heap, Wendy Neilson, Ashley Smith, Daniel Williams

Television Production Livewire Pictures Ltd

BBC Proms Publications

Publishing Manager Christine Webb
Editorial Manager Edward Bhesania
Sub-Editor Timmy Fisher
Publications Designer Reenie Basova
Junior Publications Designer Alex Stillwell
Publications Co-ordinator Julia Tsilman

Advertising Cabbells (020 3603 7930); cabbells.co.uk
Cover illustration Karan Singh/BBC Creative/BBC
Published by BBC Proms Publications, Room 4E, Broadcasting House, London W1A 1AA
Distributed by Bloomsbury Publishing, 50 Bedford Square, London WC1B 3DP

Printed by APS Group

APS Group holds ISO 14001 environmental management, FSC® and PEFC certifications. Printed using vegetable-based inks on FSC-certified paper. Formed in 1993 as a response to concerns over global deforestation, FSC (Forest Stewardship Council®) is an independent, non-governmental, not-for-profit organisation established to promote the responsible management of the world's forests. For more information, please visit www.fsc.org.

MIX
Paper | Supporting responsible forestry
FSC® C003270

 EcoAudio

In line with the BBC's sustainability strategy, the BBC Proms is actively working with partners and suppliers towards being a more sustainable festival.

ISBN 978-1-912114-23-8   © BBC 2026. All details correct at time of going to press.

Image credits for 'At a Glance' (pages 2–3)
Science Source/akg-images (Afterlife); De Morgan Foundation/Bridgeman Images (Ariadne); National Galleries of Scotland/Bridgeman Images (Oberon); Birsen Besler/Shutterstock (James Bond); anekoho/AdobeStock (Sagrada Família); Brad Pict/AdobeStock (Statue of Liberty); Hans Wild/Wikimedia Commons (Britten); Benjamin Ealovega (Mirga Grazinyte-Tyla); Danny Clinch (Dudamel); Wel Lai (Yuja Wang); James Hole (Yunchan Lim); Walt Disney Productions/Album/akg-images (Disney); Lion Television (Horrible Science)

Image credits for 'Mood Music' (pages 40–45)
Dani Howard
PRS for Music (Dani Howard); Science History Images/Alamy (Mercury); Unsplash+/Getty Images (the sea); jayfish/AdobeStock (signals)

Jessie Montgomery
Jiyang Chen (Jessie Montgomery); Everett Collection/Bridgeman Images (train porters); OMIA/AdobeStock (Sankofa symbol); Marlis Momber (Jessie Montgomery with her mother); NZ Collection/Alamy (steam locomotive); SR Productions/AdobeStock (Georgia)

Mark-Anthony Turnage
James Bellorini (Mark-Anthony Turnage); National Portrait Gallery (Bacon); Marc Brenner (Festen production); Album/Alamy (Festen still); Ian West/PA Images/Alamy (Olivier Award); Lara Cappelli (Turnage with Lee Hall)

Proms 2026 Calendar

Mon			**20 Jul** — **Beethoven's Ninth** 7pm • J. S. Bach, J. Montgomery, Beethoven Selaocoe, Hawkins, Wake-Edwards, Welton, Philharmonia Chorus, BBC PO/Noseda		**27 Jul** — **From the Alps to the Auvergne** 7pm • K. Tjøgersen, Canteloube, R. Strauss Alder, LPO/Gardner	
Tue			**21 Jul** — **Also sprach Zarathustra** 6pm • B. Jolas, Sibelius, *etc.*	Park, BBC PO/Storgårds	**Late Night Baroque** ☾ 10.15pm Dowland, Purcell, *etc.* Kilsby, JE/Dunford	**28 Jul** — **Sibelius's Second** 7pm • M-A. Turnage, Britten, Sibelius Johnston, BBC SO/Oramo	
Wed			**22 Jul** — **Mahler's 'Tragic' Sixth** 7pm • G. Kurtág, Mahler BBC SO/Oramo		**29 Jul** — **Elgar's First** 7pm • J. Weir, B. Dean, Elgar Booth, BBC Singers, BBC SSO/Wigglesworth	
Thu			**23 Jul** — **Afterlife: Visions of the Beyond** 7.30pm • L. Boulanger, Szymanowski, *etc.* Eriksmoen et al, LPC, BBC NCW & NOW/Bancroft		**30 Jul** — **Korngold's Violin Concerto** 7pm • D. Tabakova, Korngold, Prokofiev Baeva, BBC SSO/Lazarova	
			📍 **Middlesbrough** 7.30pm • RNS Presents ... RNS	📍 **Gateshead** 8pm • BBC Introd. Shakk		
Fri	**17 Jul**	**First Night of the Proms 2026** 7pm • Copland, Gershwin, Ravel, J. Stephenson, Finzi Lim, Atkins, BBC Singers, BBC SC, BBC SO/Stasevska	**24 Jul** — **John Wilson Conducts Respighi's 'Roman Trilogy'** 7.30pm • Verdi, Walton, Respighi Aasgaard, Sinfonia of London/Wilson		**31 Jul** — **Bruch's Violin Concerto** 7.30pm • Haydn, Bruch, Schumann Lozakovich, Deutsche Kammerphilharmonie Bremen/Wellber	
			📍 **Gateshead** 7pm • Feldman Gourd, Carlton, Sousa	📍 **Gateshead** 9pm • Nadine Shah RNS/Slorach		
Sat	**18 Jul**	**Prog Rock: A Fanfare for the Common Man** 7.30pm BBC CO/Ames	**25 Jul** — **Horrible Science: The Big Bang Proms Experiment** 2pm & 6pm • Borodin, G. Holst, J. Williams Caine et al, BBC NOW/Ní Bhroin		**1 Aug** — **Mahler's First by Heart** 7pm • Mahler Lewis, Aurora Orchestra/Collon	
			📍 **Gateshead** ☀ 4pm • Parry, *etc.* Gillam, BBC Singers et al/Jeannin	📍 **Sunderland** 7.30pm • Bacewicz, Mendelssohn, Mozart RNS/Włoszczowska		
Sun	**19 Jul**	**Black Dyke Band** ☀ 11am • J. Bingham, Berlioz, G. Holst, P. Graham, E. Gregson, J. Williams, Rodrigo, H. Zimmer, P. Wilby D. Childs, Black Dyke Band/N. Childs	**Boléro: Rhythms of Spain** 7pm • Ravel, Falla/F. Coll, Rodrigo, Falla Aguirre, Spanish National Orchestra/Afkham	**26 Jul** — **Olivier Latry Plays Bach** ☀ 11am • J. S. Bach Latry	**Poulenc and Adams** 7pm • Poulenc, J. Adams L. & A. Jussen, CBSO Chorus, Sydney Philharmonia Chorus, CBSO/Yamada	**2 Aug** — **Mahler's First by Heart (repeat)** ☀ 11am • Mahler Lewis, Aurora Orchestra/Collon	**Kavakos Plays Tchaikovsky** 7.30pm • D. Howard, Tchaikovsky, Scriabin Kavakos, BBC SO/Järvi